CW01629605

WAR
NIGHT
BERLIN

Other Books by the Same Author

Form, Space and Vision

Art and the Creative Consciousness

WAR NIGHT BERLIN

GRAHAM COLLIER

Published in 1993 by
The Self Publishing Association Ltd
Units 7/10, Hanley Workshops,
Hanley Road, Hanley Swan,
Worcs.

in conjunction with
Graham Collier

© Graham Collier 1993

This book is copyright. No part of it may be reproduced in any form without permission in writing from the publishers except by a reviewer who wishes to quote brief passages in connection with a review written for inclusion in a newspaper, magazine, or television broadcast.

British Library Cataloguing in Publication Data
A catalogue record for this book is available from the British Library

ISBN 1 85421 207 9

Designed and Produced by Images Design and Print Ltd
Printed and Bound in Great Britain by Hartnolls Ltd, Bodmin, Cornwall.

To the Aircrew of Bomber Command Royal Airforce 1939-1945

PREFACE

"There are no words with which I can do justice to the aircrew under my command. There is no parallel in warfare to such courage and determination in the face of danger over so prolonged a period . . . "

Sir Arthur Harris, Air Officer Commanding in Chief, Royal Air Force Bomber Commander.

Well, there you have it. Courage extraordinary. Expressed in the words of the boss himself. My old boss, although I was a hell of a way down the totem pole. Yet I suppose I saw more raw courage in action than ever came his way.

You're groaning already: not another book about the war – the "never has so much been owed by so many to so few," kind of thing? No, not that. That was Fighter Command: short, intense periods of adrenaline rush and danger. I'm talking about Bomber Command: six, seven, or eight hours of concentrated flying, waiting for the chop.

Seven men in a Lancaster. Three or four – could be five – nights a week. Each operational night beginning with the briefing in the late afternoon.

The night of 13 October 1942, started with such a briefing. And from the very beginning we knew – sensed may be a better word – that we were in trouble.

Chapter One
The Briefing

"The target tonight, gentlemen, is Berlin."

"Oh fuck!" The exclamation jerked out. Irrepressible. Somebody guffawed, then quickly developed a hacking cough, a sudden affliction. Chuckles were repressed, became wide grins – silent enough – and a few heads at the front turned to "locate the poet," as someone said afterwards. But those around him gave nothing away, deliberately looking straight ahead and keeping their eyes fixed on the Station Intelligence Officer who was opening the briefing.

Up on the platform the waxed ends of the Station Commander's moustache twitched gently.

Friday the Thirteenth, October 1942. 5 Group Bomber Command briefing with about a hundred and twelve aircrew present. A record ninety percent of the Squadron's Lancasters declared serviceable for the night's operation.

For us – myself and the crew – it would be our twenty-ninth mission over Germany and occupied Europe. After this, just one more to go to complete the magical number thirty. Then our tour would be complete. No more flying over Jerryland. Home-based, even ground jobs if one so desired. Almost there. Christ, how tightly we crossed our fingers and indulged our little personal rituals to influence destiny. Seven destinies. Irrevocably intertwined.

I think everyone present had been hoping against hope that the German Capital would not be chosen as the night's target. It was a long flight – seven or eight hours' round trip, depending on the condition of your aircraft for the return. Even at this stage of the war, when Bomber Command was in the process of building its strength with new machines of which the Lancaster was by far the best – and was developing more effective navigational and target-marking techniques, a trip to Berlin could result in a ten percent loss of the bomber force: say forty-eight planes and three hundred and thirty-six men on an average night.

So everybody sympathised with the sentiments behind the escape of the four letter word – and, no doubt, my bomb-aimer's indelicate outburst helped puncture the tension somewhat. For the last few months the Germans had developed elaborate defences to safeguard their Capital: at times the curtain of anti-aircraft shells seemed impenetrable; Luftwaffe pilots and ground defences collaborated more effectively, and some night-fighters had appeared equipped with a deadly new radar device.

The Prof. (the more or less affectionate title given to the S.I.O.) gave largely a repetition of his briefing four nights ago when Berlin was the target. The flyers listened restlessly. Yes, they knew about the high-flying German aircraft lighting up incoming streams of bombers with high-intensity flares dropped from above. And of what it was like on nights of thin stratus to be exposed as silhouettes when searchlights played on the cloudbase – targets on a screen – to the satisfaction of ground-gunners and fighter-pilots alike. Yes, they'd encountered the new Messerschmidt 110's and Junkers 88's – much faster and more manoeuvrable than previous marks; and seen the new radar aerials which sprouted like Christmas trees from the nose, allowing the pilot to home in on transmissions from a bomber's navigational aids. Who better than they knew that darkness was no longer a certain ally, that the bomber stream could be intercepted and infiltrated all the way to the target? Meaning that any one of us might have to sustain prolonged attacks while laden and flying a fixed course.

Berlin was certainly no picnic. Two squadron aircraft – fourteen men – were lost on the operation four nights back.

Myself, Duncan and Guterman were sitting together. Guterman – "Guters" for short – was frenetically scribbling on a notepad: not his usual practice at briefing sessions, but anything to keep his head down after Duncan's opening contribution to the meeting. There he was, wallowing in hysterical mirth, totally lost to what the Intelligence Officer had to say, scribbling away, shoulders heaving, staring blindly at the page. Watching him I felt my own stomach muscles tighten to suppress the urge of sympathetic laughter. The culprit, Flying Officer Jimmy Duncan, had just about given up. A short, pudgy-faced Cockney, he hardly looked the stuff of which heroes are supposed to be as, cheeks ballooning, he bent to sort out some problem with a pair of recalcitrant shoelaces. And I remembered when I was a choirboy – during a funeral service of all things – muffling a fit of the giggles during the eulogy and how cruelly the tummy muscles hurt.

Among our aircrews it was generally agreed that – after the acutely lonely and dangerous ride of the rear-gunner – the bomb-aimer had the worst of it. Taking the nose position, he lies prone in a perspex blister, sighting through a circular panel of optically perfect Triplex, nothing else between him and the ground. Where Duncan would be, somewhere over Berlin, down on his belly, out in front, guiding Titty B-O to the target for the last three eternal and vital miles of the run-in: the most precarious moments of any bombing mission. He must direct the pilot to fly steady and straight with total disregard for weather, bursting shells, or predatory night-fighters.

The mood in the room had become sombre when the Meteorological Officer began to describe weather conditions along the route. Outward-bound headwinds of twenty-five or so knots would slow the first long pull for altitude. But could be a help on the return. No cloud until over the Dutch coast; then the odd bank of thick cumulus up to about twelve thousand feet. Thin stratus over the target above seven thousand. And the possibility of severe ground mist over Lincolnshire after midnight. Worrisome: could cause landing problems and diversion to other bases. Ellis made a note of that. As flight-engineer he had to be a master of fuel-tank control, always regulating the flow from the wing-tanks to the four Rolls Royce Merlin engines, husbanding the gallons. You need petrol in reserve when diversions become necessary.

"Not much cloud cover," said Guterman to himself. "But no excessive turbulence, we hope!" Composure regained, he pushed his notepad over to me. Under the heading "Met Notes" he had written:

Oh to be a Wombat
Now that Winter's here
Batting through the Northern sky
To Valkyrie's woomby lair

Winds at 30
Cloud at 11
Misted airfields
After 11

White shrouded

The briefing was almost over. Or so it seemed. A few minutes for the Squadron Navigation Officer to advise on course-plotting, the usual good wishes from Group Captain Hawksworth, the Station Commander, and that would be it. Six foot three and a craggy boxer's face topped with straw-yellow hair, the C.O. was well known for his choleric temper, but he was a good pilot in his own right and had to be restrained by Group from flying too often on operations. Curiously enough, he was not particularly liked: some aircrew respected him, others thought him too "gung-ho" for their taste.

But instead of talking for a couple of minutes – the usual quick summing-up, etc. – he went on for fifteen. Apparently he felt we were in need of a pep talk in view of the losses we had been taking recently: eleven Lancasters in the last two weeks, all, it was surmised, the victims of Luftwaffe night-fighters whose newest radar turned night into day for them, overcoming our own jamming devices.

The Group Captain was describing the symbolic significance of Berlin to both sides, attempting to justify the moral aspects of area-bombing over a large metropolitan centre by talking about the "Nazi evil" and, "remember what they did to Coventry . . . " He concluded by telling us that we'd be almost the last squadron in. It should be all "lit up," he said. We'd have no problem in finding the target.

"What about the problem of them finding us," muttered Sergeant Guterman, surrounding his poem with a design of clouds.

"Ah, Squadron Leader Graham, you have a comment?" inquired the Station Commander, looking me straight in the eyes.

"Er, no, Sir. I think it was Sergeant Guterman here repeating one of the Met details out loud as he was writing it down."

"Very commendable," replied the Group Captain, the ends of his moustache on the go again.

So: watches were set.

Aircrews normally jostle out amiably from briefings – partly relaxed, partly resigned, wanting to get on with things, once an operation is officially "on". But on this occasion there was no steady move to the door to head out and perform pre-flight checks. Instead, cigarettes were lit and slow, luxurious breaths of smoke exhaled into the already heavy air. Men thinking within themselves. I'd not seen that before.

"Well," said somebody, "in at the last, are we. Good or bad, do you think?" He wasn't addressing anyone in particular – just staring into the distance through a rather well formed smoke-ring.

"Good and bad," I responded. "We'll be like moths around a bloody lamp. But everything on the ground may have gone for a *burton* by then anyway. No flak. And if we come in low . . . difficult for any fighters to get underneath us in the up-draughts from the fires. Not to worry, one way or the other."

Slowly, the room began to empty. Duncan, Guterman and I left "Ops" together. "God Almighty! What a bastard night to be bomb-aimer," exploded Duncan looking up at the sky. It was drizzling: cloud ceiling about two thousand feet; forward visibility no more than a quarter-mile. All-over gray. Depressing, one of those sea-frets that creep in from the Lincolnshire coast at the back-end of the year; sometimes moving off after a couple of hours but often drifting back – a real hazard for the after-midnight return. Losing visual contact forty feet above the ground is no joke. Pity – it had been such a clear nut-brown October day, dry and warm. Now the air was clammy and cold. Thoughts turned nostalgically to fires glowing in curtained rooms, tea and hot-buttered toast, and a book to last the night out.

"Well, there's one thing about this war," said Guters reflectively, "I'll never grumble in peacetime about being bored . . . or not having anything to do. I'll enjoy everything; particularly doing nothing. Funny how the thought of sitting at home on a wet Friday night with nowhere to go, and absolutely nothing to do, seems bloody marvellous."

And so we loafed down to the hangars – silent for the rest of the way – to wait for a truck and drive out to the aeroplane: the required and necessary visit before take-off, checking the daily inspection record with ground crew technicians and carrying out our own specialist checks while airframe and engine mechanics, electricians, armourers and instrument people were still around to be consulted.

A Bedford 15 cwt. came humming in off the perimeter track. A crowd of us tumbled over the tailboard and settled our backsides on the jerking metal floor. Duncan scraped out his battered old pipe. As usual, I closed my eyes and drifted.

A nudge in the ribs from Guterman. "What do you think of that?"

"Of what?"

For the second time that afternoon Guters pushed his notebook under my nose. In the dim light I could just make out:

Afterwards
Fair Lena
is never just
Afterwards
but Time Adrift.
Real before
never was.

"Mm; this girl's getting to you, Guters. She the one whose scent you picked up when you took the motorbike out for a spin, and found yourself heading willy-nilly for Nottingham? What did you say it was, a sort of 'intuitive telepathy, that suddenly set you haring off to the big city . . . and there she was in the pub, waiting'? Alright, mi lad, I believe you but there's many wouldn't. You're an incurable bloody romantic, Guters. I think you're going to need a bit of help with this one. She's obviously a powerful bit of stuff if I get the gist of what you're saying here." (I remember looking at him with one of those daft leers you put on when ribbing a pal about a girl.)

But he was unaware, deadly serious. "See, Johnny, you're missing the point. She's not your usual 'bit of stuff' – not like anybody you've ever met. I've tried to write about her in the Journal: not successfully. She doesn't translate. In the mind she's nerves and feelings, not words. When you're with her you feel you're a couple of thousand years somewhere else; even that you are someone else – known to her well enough but certainly not to yourself anymore. You just slip away into those fantastic green eyes . . . become pulled in by them: an optical massage – head to toe you feel your skin turning itself on. You know something pretty unusual's going on. And I tell you," here he lowered his voice and whispered conspiratorially, "she's gorgeous – her body I mean – like . . . " He suddenly stopped, voice tailing off.

"Well, thank goodness she's substantial in that department," said I, faint irony going nowhere. "So when are you going to introduce us? Unless of course you're afraid of the competition. Sounds as if you could be putting a hell of a temptation in my way. So go on, what's she look like?"

"Tell you what," replied our air-gunner, "I'll get the old Journal across to your room when I've finished my checks on the kite. That'll set you thinking, even though the writing's not adequate, can't convey the enchantment. Anyway, I was going to ask you to meet her next week."

The truck was now moving between aircraft dispersal points and ground crew on their way back to the hangars were climbing aboard. Titty B-O was the last stop before the Bedford turned to make the return journey. Duncan and Guterman went over the tailboard together and disappeared up the steps into the aeroplane. Sergeant Smith was already in the rear-turret, swinging it left to right on auxiliary power, guns sawing, giving his crucial defence post a testing pre-flight workout.

At this stage of the preparations I always took my time before going aboard. The sight of the Lancaster being readied for the night journey never failed to awe and impress. A swarm of mechanics and technicians were attending to her final needs, clambering all over her, moving silently in and out through the drizzle. In the front fuselage they were picked up by the cockpit lights, and when seen through the transparent nose became distorted in scale, a swarm of human tadpoles in the belly of Leviathan. Glassy snout high-angled in the air, front-turret turning under test with guns twitching like sensitive antennae, and bomb-doors open, exposing her capacious womb. Titty B-O straddled a trolley of unborn young bombs – ugly blind foetuses impatient to miscarry until dropped from the high skies. Seen against the glare of trestle-lamps she looked like some giant cosmic insect about to defend a clutch of young.

And I had to fly her. At this point – and it was always the same before every trip – I became nervous. No, afraid is closer to the truth. Legs suddenly less than firm, stomach sending out alarms, telling you you might not be here tomorrow. Tons of metal there, tons of explosives. All serving as a target. How to keep the thing airborne. The air so bloody flimsy. Myself suddenly frail confronting the death machine. Scared shitless.

But then there was always Flight Sergeant Skelton, senior N.C.O. in charge of the whole maintenance team, who regularly presented the aeroplane as invincible, and gave the impression that he regarded me in like manner – master mariner of the air, an ace among pilots. I don't suppose he'll ever know what an example of calm, matter-of-fact, "We'll fix 'em, Sir", confidence he imparted; how much I felt I had to live up to his expectations – how his assurance actually helped me get off the ground.

"Everything's checked, Sir. Form 700's all signed up. I got that new rigger to go over the hydraulics and find out where the oil leak was coming from. He's replaced a connector-union going to the mid-upper and it's as dry as a bone beneath there now. And" – he grinned as he went on – "nobody's interfered with Sergeant Guterman's notice, knowing as how he likes clocks around when he's in the air."

"Mm: good for you, Flight. Anything to keep Guters happy. You know how queasy he gets up there in the bubble. Must respect his wishes about not knowing the time, if it helps."

Dick Guterman really was a terrible flyer. Don't suppose he'd be much of a sailor either. Any slight turbulence and he was fighting nausea. And whenever it was necessary to take violent evasive action side-slipping, or diving for the security of cloud as when leaving Essen a couple of weeks earlier – poor old Guters just got to the Elsan bucket in time once we'd found a thick bank of protective cumulus and were flying straight and level again.

This had provoked Duncan, as usual, to be the funny man the next morning. "How do you get queasy in the turret, Guters? The mid-upper's the most stable place in the whole aeroplane. You'll have to take yourself in hand, you know. Or perhaps that's the trouble. Doing too much of it, old boy."

That afternoon Guterman appeared with a cardboard sign – finely lettered in his inimitable calligraphic script – which he suspended beneath the entrance to the turret. It read:

Sergeant Guterman, to his Friends:

No Clocks, Watches, or other

Mechanical Alarms

Near the Turret

PLEASE!

"Now what the hell's the meaning of that?" – from Duncan on his way forward through the fuselage. "Well," responded our worthy gunner looking down from his dome in a superior sort of way, "it's a reference to the fallacy of Time up here in outer space."

"My God, Guters! You mean you have phallic problems up there in that bloody thing? Good grief! For Pete's sake, try and keep your hands above the waist ready to grab those guns. Don't sit up there just holding your dick!"

"Don't worry, Dunc. Remember I'm pretty good on the old Brownings. Not everybody can shoot their own tail-fin off while the kite's going round in a ninety degree turn." (A reassuring reference to the night he'd shot away the central fixed stabilising fin while flying in one of the earlier Avro Manchesters. The gun mechanism interrupter-gear was at fault.)

"Good grief," Duncan continued, eyes wide in feigned horror, "no need to remind us of that fiasco. Good job they decided to get rid of the fin to the Lanc before you were tempted to have a go at that one."

A strange chap, Duncan. Funny as hell after a couple of pints; but then he would surprise you by moving quickly from the ridiculous to the sublime without batting an eyelid. One minute theorising about delaying ejaculation by pulling on a string looped around the scrotum to strangle the balls; the next holding forth on his favourite topic – Saint Francis of Assisi – explaining how contact with birds and animals are a possible way to a possible God. He was married with a six-month-old child, and had been a travelling salesman with a chocolate company before the war – a job that, if it had done nothing else, provided him with an inexhaustible repertoire of jokes. When he was on form he would have people in any bar doubled up, tottering out, gasping for air. But he was a devoted family man, talking always about his wife and child when we were alone as a group.

Flight Sergeant Skelton waited patiently that damp "Berlin" afternoon while I perused the serried rows of checks and the initials of the technicians who'd carried them out. When I was satisfied he signed himself, thus handing the aeroplane over to me as fully operational.

"Right: no potential snags you can think of, Chief?"

"No, everything's on top line, Sir."

"Don't forget to have the engine chaps wipe the cowlings clean. No finger marks for me to look at."

"No worry, Sir: they do it automatically now."

"You've told them why?"

"Yes, but really no need. The best of 'em reckon like us that the old kite'll perform well if she's shown a bit of care. Just like a woman, Sir."

Then my usual routine: up through the fuselage to the cockpit; sitting quietly in the pilot's seat surveying the array of instruments and toggle-switches, stretching right hand over the four engine throttles, feeling out the reach to the trim wheel. A ritual to be followed before every operation – a form of mental conditioning, repeated familiarisation with the controls so that one could fly blind if necessary. Lastly the electrical checks. All done. The aircraft was strangely quiet. I patted the half wheel of the control column. "Keep it up, old girl. Only two more to go." And then I remember wiping some grease from the roof of the canopy before returning to the tarmac.

The drizzle had stopped. Lingering mist dispersing rapidly. Flat, empty land to the horizon. Nothing intimate or protective. Airfields are incredibly bleak places. Provide little natural support when spirits are low. Now it had gone much colder and engine-mechanics waiting for the truck were blowing on their hands. Suddenly it was winter. Autumn had fled with lunch – sometime before the briefing while the going was good. Two ground-defence searchlight beams poked abruptly into the sky, nervously feeling their way like a lover's probing fingers; then just as quickly faded, closed down. I was surprised by the quick penetration of the cold – more an inside chill than out – sending the kind of shivers that tremble through the stomach when you're about to come down with something. The mid-upper turret was moving slowly from side to side through a hundred and eighty degrees, gun barrels elevating then lowering. So Guters was still up there, giving the new hydraulic connection a good going over. The light was fading rapidly: much too fast for autumnal October.

I watched Dick Guterman leave the fuselage and go hunting around among the trestles, finally returning with a small pair of stepladders. Opening them out alongside the fuselage door the mid-upper gunner climbed to the top step, level with the turret rim. Then, taking a handkerchief from his pocket, he spat on it and carefully wiped over the emblem painted just below his plastic dome.

Guterman's Wombat – always to be pronounced Woombat according to the artist.

Titty B-O's metamorphosis was complete. The remaining trestles were pulled clear. Festooning entrails of petrol pipelines had disappeared into the parent tanker. Bomb-doors were closed. She was transformed from an obese gargantuan insect to a sleek Amazonian bird of passage. Virgin. Power-leashed. A frightening paradox. Thirty beautiful tons of black death.

I should tell you about the wombat: Sergeant Guterman's insignia was about six months old, and, as a would be critic, I'm not sure I was particularly happy with it. I didn't think the drawing was up to Guterman's usual standard; also it had nothing in common with the aircraft's real *magnum opus*, Miss Titty Bang-On herself, the officially authorised mascot for the plane – official in that we'd all approved it. The wombat was an interloper, a private indulgence, too esoteric a talisman and, as such, would send confused signals to the Fates. After all, why bother with a wombat when you have the Earth Mother herself up front? But, as Duncan pointed out, there was a connection.

When the question came up about an emblem for the Lanc, all agreed that what was wanted on the nose of the aircraft was as formidable a nude as Guters could create: life-size, stretching from the front-turret to the beginning of the cockpit canopy. Naturally the artist had the benefit of everyone's opinion on the subject. Which made it a difficult job. For a painter of Guterman's class, modifying one's own vision in order to incorporate six other views took a bit of doing. Nevertheless, the result was a startling success. Miss Titty Bang-On, as she was ceremonially christened with a frothy head of beer, had everything. She possessed all that particular quality of feminine mystique which would allow her to function in the guardian angel league; she oozed the kind of overt eroticism that gave every member of the crew the necessary male confidence and satisfaction; and she looked every inch the Amazon, the ultimate female warrior, because everybody conceded that "hell hath no fury like a woman scorned". As Duncan delicately put it, she "had to be built like a brick shithouse."

A tall order. But Guters pulled it off. She was powerfully yet delicately curvaceous – a Botticelli-like Brunnhilde – with two enormously ripe breasts and nipples to match – nipples fashioned like shortened gun-muzzles from which twin streams of bullets erupted to pass out into space beyond the aircraft. She was painted in glowing magenta; a golden hue being used for the highlights, deep purple for the shadows. Six-inch Gothic capitals proclaimed her "Titty Bang-On". When finally unveiled she excited considerable interest; people from all over the aerodrome trekked out to see her. The ground crew were particularly proud. They initially gave her several coats of clear varnish, and from then on conscientiously cleaned her up after every flight.

But note: however well she worked invisibly, psychically, as a protectoress, it can be reported that there was at least one occasion when her guardian powers were actually witnessed. Flying Officer Duncan was quite prepared to swear that when he was manning the front-turret one night returning from Bremen, a German night-fighter came alongside to get a closer look; the pilot was so fascinated that he couldn't take his eyes off her – a respite which allowed us to slide away into an approaching bank of thick cumulus.

But no sooner had Guters completed the work – shoulder slapping all round and six free pints of beer for the artist in the pub that night – than early the following day he moved his platform to the rear fuselage, port side, and started to line in his Wombat beneath the mid-upper turret fairing. By midday the design was well advanced. Painted in red, on a circular ground of gold, Guterman's heraldic beast stood bear-like, sprouting two upward curving bat-wings. A large plaque surrounded by a decorative scroll formed the base of the design. In it was inscribed – in finely brushed Roman lower-case letters – what the artist described as "a little suitable poetry".

The Bat crept into the Crypt
Crapt . . . and Crept out again.

He said it seemed dead right for the bombing Wombat: a furtive kind of flitting around in the dark, dropping things here and there.

I turned up just before lunch. "Bloody hell, Guters; what the heck's that thing you're painting up there?"

"That, Johnny, is a Wombat, pronounced Woombat."

"A what?" I yelled from down below.

"A Wombat: comes after womb in the dictionary."

"Jesus, Guters, I know what a wombat is. But that thing looks like a flying grizzly or something."

"Well, it's not quite finished. It'll look more marsupial when I outline the pouch and put the whiskers in. And you know how well these little marsupes get around and see in the dark – like me in the mid-upper all night long, Sergeant Richard Woombat. Might as well have my coat-of-arms on the escutcheon up here.

Could help me out a lot. In days of old when knights were bold . . . and all that."

That was the moment when Duncan popped out through the fuselage door and joined me on the tarmac. "Bloody good job," he said, looking quizzically at the Wombat. "Pretty impressive, Guters. Looks as good as a Durer to me. More power to your elbow, I'd say. Funny you'd think up a wombat. Old Titty B-O up front and your bushy-tailed wombing bat back here. He probably wouldn't mind batting around a bit in her wombus, I bet."

I had to grin at this. "O.K., Guters, you can keep it if it's going to help your night vision. You and Durer, eh? My God . . . "

I have to tell you more about Dick Guterman. For alive or dead he is the principal player in this drama. He was a strong personality: had one of those minds that range easily over the whole spectrum of knowledge; and he was constantly discerning obscure relationships to make original observations about the nature of things, always seeking philosophical enlightenment. Boring? Not on your life. He was witty, cynical, droll . . . yet always significantly so, always lending force and edge to conversation. One's whole way of thinking became stimulated and influenced by his example. And he played a pretty important role in setting me on my way for the future by somehow introducing a genuine connoisseurship into my amateur interest in drawing and painting, into the function of aesthetics in general. He was also a truly brave man in finding ways to overcome his fear of flying, the physical reactions he suffered as a result, and his natural aversion to violence. We became close friends when sergeants together, a relationship which did not suffer when I was commissioned.

The wartime memories of Guters and the crew – the crazy and strange things we did together, the chameleon-like changes in personality which, once airborne, took over – remain immediate and graphic. They often supplant the tame goings-on of the present, occasioning sudden mental switches which sabotage reason and make nonsense of intelligence provided by contemporary calendar and clock. So much so that it's no longer possible to accept that current time is supposed to be IT . . . the cat's whiskers, the tangible living truth.

But to get back to Dick Guterman: rather than represent him myself I think it will be more effective to let him do the talking. Easy enough to accomplish by taking a passage from his Journal which has been in my possession since the afternoon of the Berlin operation I am now describing.

Before leaving on the Berlin flight four nights earlier Guters had written an account of how he spent the hours before take-off – a form of ritual preparation, of confronting and talking himself through his apprehensions. (It turned out to be a hell of a night: about ten percent of the bomber force lost – forty-eight planes, over three-hundred men. A toll taken by Luftwaffe night-fighters, anti-aircraft fire, and appalling mid-air collisions over the target.) What Guters wrote before flying that mission was strangely prophetic, seeming to foresee the mission we were now about to fly.

> A strong cup of tea first; must be made with condensed milk to give some body to the stuff and helped along with three heaped teaspoonfuls of sugar for energy. Impossible to eat before flying: nothing stays down on these long operational flights. Then the bath: always plenty of hot water in the Sergeant's Mess when a squadron's on operations – nothing like the luxury of a long, hot soak. Afterwards, into the flannel dressing-gown, to cool off on the bed in a flush of sweat. There's a sensuousness to this – every pore briefly aware of itself – a physical sensitivity which, paradoxically, work's to clear the mind – set it up to both accept and

weigh up the imminence of the evening's work dispassionately.

Always necessary to be a fatalist. Studying the Classics, even schoolboy stuff, drives this home. And once in a war no alternative philosophy shows itself to be worth a damn. Must accept the Greek idea that the playing out of each life inevitably takes place against the backdrop of an individual destiny, a destiny that must be accepted as one's fate or *moira*. Consequently, the hero's role is to take the Gods on; fly in the face of destiny and strive to win by the power of his own will. No flinching whatever they throw at you. Romantic? Certainly. That's the mould in which the man of the hour is cast.

But for some reason, the hot bath and flannel dressing-gowned, sweat-it-out ceremony are not doing the trick tonight. My head is filled with thoughts and images not conducive to a state of calm neutrality. I find it necessary to pace around, browse among the photographs and objects I've accumulated over the years and distributed all around this miserable little room – prized memorabilia: snapshots of me with Harry Snipe and Warwick Broadwell out on the Yorkshire moors with our bikes, clowning and gesticulating before the lens; and a collection of unusual shells, bones, bits of driftwood. Not forgetting my small collection of erotica: photos cut from papers and magazines – actresses, beauty queens, nudes from the nature monthly *Health and Efficiency*, together with postcards of Goya's "clothed" and "naked" Maja and Renoir's Bathers. A stimulating lot.

Finally, *the pièce de résistance*: one of those long, horizontal records grandly designated, "The School Photograph". Staring at all the old faces the room slips away, and I see myself standing at the back of the school hall during morning prayers – Snipe, Broadwell and Guterman, all three of us glassy-eyed as usual, giving nothing away to nearby staff as the headmaster droned on in his special "religious" voice.

"Time that devours all things – Ovid, you know," said Warwick out of the corner of his mouth.

"I remember," said I.

"So you're to be in on a big kill," Warwick continued, frizzy hair coming off his head all the way round at ninety degrees. Five-hundred bombers, eh? Half a million pounds of high explosives. Means justify the ends . . . is that what they said? Of course. Well you're the poor bastard means, Guters, the means for megalomaniacs and weak-knee'd politicians. Remember, Dick, whatever they say, when the time comes there has been – and can only ever be – one death in the entire universe:

"Yours.

"Remember how we used to argue about Alexander? . . . your hero he was, not mine. 'Visionary and leader,' you said: 'poet and soldier' . . . And I said he's just another celebrated killer – murdered more than one good friend personally and a few thousand others in conquest. All in the name of progress. Don't forget bringing Greek culture to the barbarians. But he called it homonoia *– a true brotherhood of man: a real Cause.*

"So, what do you think now, Dick – now that you're part of another great Cause, bringing bombs and promises of deliverance? Didn't have to be, did it? We could have stopped Hitler ten years ago if Europe had united and stood up to the sod. Politicians . . . To hell with 'em!

"And after the war? No more Causes? A likely story. Government and the Gross National Product need military Causes. Tell the man who died in 1916 that, after all, he was killed in a worthy Cause – the Great War, no less: the war to end all wars – so he's earned his place in history. He'll spit in your face.

"Afraid, Dick . . . afraid of the Inferno? What price Alexander now?"

I felt disembodied when Warwick had said his piece. Absently I picked up a spiral shell, traced the whorls with a finger, playing for time. I was not prepared for the sadness that swept in, the surge of nostalgia for the moors and dales of the north country; the overwhelming desire to cut and run for the boyish years of home, get out my old bike Hercules and disappear to the rock and the pool where I'd spent the most memorable hours of my life with the mysterious old shepherd.

Anyway . . . back to lie on the bed and turn on the radio. The brittle, polychromatic sound of Strauss' *The Hero's Life* rammed against the room's concrete walls – tightly stretched dissonances running the nerve-wracking gamut between contemplation and action. And moving disturbingly between the two dominant themes, came subtle chords of apprehension – ground-swells of musical alarm as the hero moved to the encounter.

Hardly the sort of music to send one drifting off to sleep. But I felt my eyes becoming heavy, starting to close. In an effort to combat the drowsiness I turned on my stomach and pushed hard against the mattress, hoping to achieve that paralysing combination of sensuous exhilaration and alarm that comes as the abdomen crushes some fragile life-cord, telescoping existence to the navel centre: a single sharp, poignant, point of being. But tonight the arousal made little difference. I drifted off to sleep. Was powerless to follow my own First Commandment "Thou shalt not sleep before the Night Mission". No way not to let myself go.

Numerous flickering lights out there in the darkness; the masthead lanterns of ships bobbing at anchor on a slight swell. Air warm to the face and sweet-smelling.

A beam from the land cuts through, shifts among a forest of masts and rigging, comes to rest on the slowly materialising form of a grand ship – a galley of Minoan design, high-sided with three banks of tars, and painted along the rails from prow to stern in the manner of the royal triremes.

And walking full in the beam, an archaically dressed but familiar figure leaves the middle-deck and steps ashore: a girl, gleaming in her gold-reflecting chiton, sways gracefully along the harbour wall to disappear into the night. But the sky is slowly brightening, paler horizon over the dark sea reflecting the first stirrings of the new sun.

I sit high on a small knoll above the port, enfolded in a high-backed chair of dense black wood. Intricate carving runs along the arms: tulips entwined with lilies writhing through the wood – damp wood, encrusted with tiny shells around which strands of seaweed are caught. My fingers come away from the arms wet and salty to the tongue.

The girl from the trireme has climbed to a point off on my right – a silhouette now running with long strides over the sloping headland. The rising sun catches her hair as it streams behind, turning it into an exotic bird.

"Lena . . . Lena . . . " I call, and then am after her, moving quickly without any sensation of touching the ground. Both of us take the stone wall ahead in stride, but then have to quickly check our pace when the ground falls off steeply to the sea. Here the air is no longer warm but crystal cool as of the north. And the brown sand of the bay where I now find myself is cold to the feet, hard-packed where it skirts the rock-strewn green water.

The girl stops at the edge of the sea and turns, sun behind her, face in shadow, hand raised against me, a barrier. Slowly she backs away until she stands with one foot on the first of a series of round, flat rocks which progress like a path of underwater stepping-stones out into the depths of the bay.

Still with her face towards me she moves progressively into deeper water until she lets herself down, floating on her back, hair trailing like some bright sea-creature's tentacles, short chiton tunic damp-tight to her body, And then the water turns to foam around her, propelling her out to sea at the head of a churning wake.

"Come . . . come on . . . stand on the stone, the first stone . . . " Her voice is lost in a rising wind.

Tentatively I move into the sea; reach the first stone in three feet of water, relishing the cleansing cold after the heat of the run. Then wonder for a moment where I left my clothes.

Slowly the stone rises to the surface, then begins to gather forward speed, a white bow-wave breaking from its rounded front, carrying me after her.

But she speeds ever faster ahead, all but enveloped by the sea. Coming out between the headlands we run through beds of anemone-like purple flowers which part to make way, and then link up behind to form complete circles of colour. Once through the sea-flowers she accelerates away in a spume of white water towards the distant horizon.

With that, I lose heart. At the same time my stone loses momentum and begins to sink. It is a slow descent, yet I find it impossible to strike out, float free from the stone to which I now feel rooted. As my head goes under I give up the struggle, lose the fight for air, take in the sea.

At once she appears before me, treading water, arms encircling my waist, pulling me in towards her; and the sea is shut out and I partake of her breath.

Yet the mind considers this an illusory recusitation and continues to anticipate dissolution, causing pain to gather as if from a blow to the chest, and bringing with it a sharp nostalgia for all that ever was in this life. Almost at the end I bring my eyes up and peruse the details of that exotically mysterious face. Her eyes are waiting, drawing me out beyond the water.

"Speak," I urge silently, "speak . . . "

At this an unnatural glow suffuses her, as if her countenance is the source of her own light. I see why she does not reply, why she is so radiant. The fixed lips of a mask cannot frame words, and a surface of silver-metal radiates an inhuman energy. The splendid, high cheek-boned symmetry of those features is a sculptor's creation; only the eyes within their metal cage are alive, calm and gentle, expressing the understanding and sympathy of guide and ally.

"You have been listening to Richard Strauss' The Hero's Life, played by the BBC Symphony Orchestra under its conductor Sir Adrian Boult. Tomorrow night at this time . . ."

I jerked upright on the bed, still half in and half out of the dream. Quickly switching off the BBC announcer, I found myself hypnotically repeating the last words I'd heard. "Tomorrow night at this time . . ." Where would I be tomorrow night at this time? No knowing. No knowing at all. And what was happening in the dream? No knowing. But she was there. That had to be a good omen. Yet I'd drowned. No, she'd saved me in the end. But the stone had sunk, gone down. The symbolism was obvious.

A depressing bloody dream: No? Circles of blue flowers continued to swim hazily before my eyes, and a silvered face came and went, making me long for the girl.

Almost time to go. I moved to stare bleakly across at the grainy old school photograph. Tomorrow night at this time . . . there's no knowing, is there, Warwick? So the answer to your question, old lad, is yes. Yes: I am afraid of the coming Inferno. Yes: as I have been every damn night from the beginning.

Fifteen minutes to go before I should join the others at the Flight Offices; grab parachute and harness, check oxygen mask and intercom function, then take the truck-ride out to Titty B-O.

A couple of things left to do. I remove Excalibur from its bed of cotton wool in the small cardboard box and rub it over with metal-polish applied to an old toothbrush. The bristles clean out the engraved letters, prevent a build-up of dried cleaner in the script. The final shine is imparted with a ragged old towel. Bought it five years ago in Blackpool when I was fifteen. The girl for whom it was intended had never turned up for our second date – another proposed bike ride into the country. God, I knew I'd been pretty inept on the first excursion but had planned to do better the next time – talk less about "life" and begin to get more the feel of it, so to speak. It was a cheap enough little gift: a chromium-plated, miniature dagger paper-knife on which I'd had a jeweller inscribe the name "Excalibur". For on the first date I'd got carried away talking about King Arthur; the little trinket was intended to make amends.

Now the chrome is faintly rust-pitted, the original flashy gleam dulled. But this hint of antiquity aids rather than diminishes the toy knife's efficacy. As a young lad, I'd always thought of Arthur's sword as a gift from the Underworld, and therefore charged with supernatural power. So, once named and inscribed, this cheap, holiday-town souvenir – with no girl there to be romanced by it – grew in symbolic value, taking on some of the historic invincibility of the original.

Never fly without it. Always keep it in the breast pocket of the tunic, beneath the leather flying-jacket. Feeling it there provides a sense of continuity: brings the boy's imagination up to date – turns the night journeys into quests against Darkness in all its forms, and provides a little Arthurian courage to this often very frightened junior knight.

> Finally, the ritual brushing of the teeth. The brush must be loaded with paste, just wet enough to produce a great foam in the mouth. Not be entirely rinsed out – should leave a coating which, when dry, gives a fresh, minty flavour to throat and mouth until we are well airborne. Then I bring the first stick of chewing-gum into service.
>
> Must stop writing, gather things together ready to go. Make the fateful move to the door. Check with Warwick, church organist and prodigy on the pipe-organ – Warwick who is somewhere out in the North Atlantic on convoy duty. A quick nod to old Harry Snipe, now dead, killed in the Battle of Britain. Flying a Hurricane.

To read Dick Guterman's Journal is a little like eavesdropping on a man in a confessional: one has a sense of invading the most private personal territory. An impression created by the depth of his reflections and by the intensity of expression. At times you have the feeling that if all this mental activity could *not* be expressed in words – written or spoken – then Guters' mind would self-destruct.

But let me retrace my steps here and return to when I left the aircraft at the dispersal point after making my final checks for the current Berlin operation. I'd decided to walk back across country rather than ride in the Bedford. It was just after four p.m. and I wanted the exercise. Setting out across the fields, skirting hedgerows and ditches, I found the newly cold air stimulating, a help in clearing out the cobwebs – tuning one up, so to speak, preparing reflexes for quick and precise responses. The sky was drying out as the humidity retreated, taking on that brittle clear afterglow which moves in when a damp and misty autumn afternoon turns unexpectedly into cold, early-winter evening. Visibility was improving by the minute: the distant roofs of the village and the sharp spire of the parish church stood out graphically in the thinning atmosphere. There was certainly no question now of the night's operation being "scrubbed" for reasons of bad weather.

The usual thought accompanied by the usual hollow sensation deep in the pelvis, pushed its way forward: would I be here tomorrow to see all the familiar sights; to be drinking in The Plough? The statistics of survival were not on our side – one in four gone every night; the more nights you fly the poorer the odds get. But we were almost through our tour of operations, twenty-eight trips to date, and I reminded myself for the umpteenth time that we did have a system. And it had served us well.

The method had been worked out at The Saracen's Head in Lincoln, a favourite haunt of 5 Group aircrew stationed around the city. Going on the premise that there were two basic hazards in flying by night over Germany – first, attack by night-fighter aircraft (especially if they came up from below and fired into the defenceless belly of the bomber); and second, the anti-aircraft barrage – it seemed logical to conclude that one should fly at a height (for as much of the mission as possible), where neither enemy fighters nor ground guns can get at you. The more we thought about it, the more relevant and reasonable this argument seemed. Heavy anti-aircraft fire was most effective when the shells were bursting between eight and twelve thousand feet, while an attacking night-fighter, seeking to come in behind and below, required a minimum fifteen hundred feet of airspace between the ground and us if he was to manoeuvre safely in our turbulent slipstream.

Flight Lieutenant Frank Ellis, our flight-engineer, had taken a beer-stained paper napkin from the counter and started to draw what appeared to be a simple graph. "Something like this," he had said, tracing over the up and down lines of his diagram with a pencil. "We fly at different heights at different parts of the trip. Look. First leg: leaving base, climb to five thousand feet until approaching the enemy coast – good for navigation, and a reasonable height for flying safely over the sea. Second leg: assuming we're not flying in pea soup, we come down to one thousand or just below to fly over occupied territory. We use large roller-maps of the terrain and fly visual – map read our way. If the weather's against it, low cloud for example, we fly no more than one thousand feet above the highest point around. On good nights at the very low levels where we can map-read, it's practically guaranteed that neither ack-ack or fighters can get to us. Then it's basically a flying problem for John. Even in poor conditions with minimum visual ground contact forcing us up a bit – and remember there's not much high ground on the approach to northern targets except the Ardennes – we'll still be pretty low. Not where they expect us to be. Third leg: climb to bombing height over target, five to six thousand, and drop the stuff. And on the last . . . down again to the lowest possible level and out beneath the defences. Once clear of the coast we can go home at any blinking height we want."

So this "lone-wolf", variable-height system was adopted. There's no doubt that such low-level stuff made it tricky for me: the pilot's in an unforgiving situation; no room for mistakes. The strategy calls for long concentrated periods of precision flying. Also, you know it goes against the grain – every nerve in the good pilot clamours for height. For space equals time – time in which to cope with the unexpected. On the other hand I had Ellis and Duncan to help as observers, reading the topography of the coastline, canal, rivers, roads and hills. And then there were the keen eyes of Sergeant Smith in the rear-turret: and he was a man who had a strong sixth-sense of what was out there well before he could see it. One negative aspect: flying in this way tended to increase fuel consumption, and without Ellis' uncanny ability to intuitively judge the petrol situation – as well as his skill in feeding from tank to tank for maximum economy – we would have run into trouble several times on the way home when diversions to more distant airfields were ordered.

Well, maybe that's the story of our survival. Anyway, after taking my cross-country walk I entered the Officer's Mess by the rear door and took the back stairs to my room. Unlike Guterman, I preferred not to spend the time immediately before a night flight closeted in the intimacy of my own quarters, surrounded by personal things. I knew well enough how debilitating that would be, given the introspective tendencies of my nature. So I washed hands and face quickly, collected silk gloves and scarf from a drawer, and went downstairs to my usual chair in the Mess anteroom where I could get some tea and cake.

Which is where my batman found me and handed over a brown-paper parcel securely tied with half-a-dozen pieces of string. Dick Guterman's Journal, delivered as promised.

A thick, leather-bound notebook with its title tooled in gold leaf on the front cover. I already knew the Journal was more than a simple diary of events. The author was always using me as a sounding board for the themes and ideas on which he reflected, and which then took form as a series of notes, essays, aphorisms, witticisms, poems . . . Yet I'd never seen the finished results – although several times of late he had said he was ready for me to read through the Journal and express an opinion. But that was as far as it went – the notebook itself never appeared. Now, with the sudden arrival on the scene of the recently discovered Lena, it seemed that Guterman's reserve in exposing his most personal thoughts and experiences was overcome. She obviously represented such a celebratory and powerful event in his life that he just had to let me in on developments. Or so I reasoned.

I ordered tea and a plate of sandwiches and settled comfortably in the chair. As I slowly turned the Journal's pages it became clear why Guterman had been reticent about handing the work over: the book was an uninhibited compendium of his most private and obsessive concerns. The writing was direct – no ambiguities or stylistic conceits to disguise the frank exposure of the author's esoteric world. Just about everything seemed grist for Dick Guterman's mill: highly personal thoughts on sexual preferences, "letters" to Thomas Aquinas, humorous notes to "self", pen-portraits of mutual friends, boyhood recollections, pages of pantheistic poetry, and essays by the dozen on music, historical inevitability, love, hate, lust, etc. I suppose the usual grab-bag of interests displayed by curious and able young men. But in reading the Journal it was obvious very quickly that a mature and wise mind was behind the writing - not simply that of a young intellectual. The insights displayed were original and illuminating, set one thinking, and were fluently expressed, displaying a genuine feeling for language. I suppose I was not really surprised. After all, everybody enjoyed listening to him - he was always provocative as hell. But I think it's always a bit of a bonus when a good talker becomes an even better writer. It was difficult to sum this Guterman up. But one driving force ran through everything, an urge best described as a need to, philosophically at least, reconcile paradox: to try and find the relationship between the extremes of human experience; see love and hate, happiness and misery, good and evil, life and death, as but sides of the same coin.

Six sandwiches polished off and I was still hungry. I beckoned the Mess waiter and ordered a second plate. "Ask them to cut the bread a little thicker," I remember saying, lighting my first pipe of the day, leaning back and looking at the ceiling.

No doubt - I said to myself - that for Guters writing is a disciplined form of catharsis: a way of returning from those mental labyrinths he's always getting himself into; not to mention the chance of relieving the pressure of feeling which swamps him from time to time: too much sympathy, empathy, for the life of the world - not unlike poor old Vincent van Gogh, but disciplined, under control, sublimated to mind. (The comparison jumped immediately to mind: I'd just finished reading an edition of van Gogh's letters to brother Theo.) Curious, I thought, that he writes practically nothing about the war or flying. Especially when you know how strongly he feels about the bombing of civilians; how miserably airsick he gets – every flight a trauma, even a simple daylight cross-country.

The new sandwiches arrived, together with a second mug of almost black tea. "Christ, Joe – that's a bit strong, isn't it? Put a little milk in it, there's a good lad."

Two sandwiches down and four to go. And then . . . there in the Journal was a whole page of dense script, headed by a title penned in the Gothic capitals and lower-case only Dick knew how to do. At last, the story of the girl. I began to read. Curious as hell.

> LENA AND THE SWAN . . . or, better, LEDA AND THE CYGNET
>
> Bit pretentious likening yourself to Jupiter the seducer, so no hubris here, Dick my lad. CYGNET – that's your standing, and a junior cygnet at that. But the Gods could not be offended when it comes to comparing Lena to the mythical and beautiful Leda, Queen of Sparta – LEDA – beautiful and mysterious enough to attract Zeus as lover in the shape of a swan; Lena mia of the same ilk – leaving one no room to manoeuvre, no way to dissemble. Must be true to yourself. Takes no time at all – Lena looking into your eyes – for the present to slip away; moving into a space with no boundaries, no points of reference, no familiar context of England, war, history. Odd to be taken over like that. A naturally mystical core to it because it transcends personal experience and values. Takes in spirit, heart,

head, and balls (no crudeness intended). Not easy to write about without sounding adolescent and sentimental.

Thinking now about those eastern Tantric priestesses whose job was to take the body through the ecstasy barrier, to reach the realm of the supernatural. Consider the benefits: freedom from fear of all kinds – death, of course, being number one; then release from ignorance, megalomania, ambition . . . And the big one – from fear itself. Something like that. She does something like that to you. With her you sense that you're home, free and clear.

How am I to explain the way we came together? Simple coincidence? Is that the only way to account for two people receiving similar images across time and space, directives that result in their meeting at the right time in the right place? Telepathy? That one would certainly be good for a few laughs from Dicky Dent. Wouldn't even mention it. There are some things in life that have a touch of the magical, the numinous, about them. But only to those who have been there.

When I went down to the farm to collect the bike last Sunday before Monday's Berlin operation, I had nothing in mind. Nowhere particular to go. No knowing how long I might be out. Not even thinking much about doing what I was doing. Just a desire to take a bit of a run into the wind, perhaps grab a quick pint somewhere. With a whole month's ration of petrol coupons untouched I felt as free as a bird. Six o'clock and I found myself heading down the Fosse Way on Hercules II, hat off, cobwebs blowing away in the slipstream, skin opening up in that stimulating way it does when bruised by cold rushing air.

The only thought in my head was of the ancient Romans who built roads like the Fosse Way – roads racing frenetically straight for the horizon, roads for the legions, quickest way from A to B, perfect for motorbikes with throttles open. Then, out of the blue, swimming around before my eyes like a mirage, a picture of the Saloon Bar at The Robin Hood in Nottingham – the same room where some of us had spent a couple of hours drinking that Saturday not too long ago. And with it an overwhelming and persisting urge to get myself there. That night. Right then.

Three or four miles on and I couldn't shake it. Neither rhyme nor reason to this, I told myself. But at the same time I knew I was on my way to Nottingham. To The Robin Hood. Anyway, I thought, rationalising the whole business, it's a good drive; a good blow. Have a pint of bitter. Come back under the moon. "Well, this is it," I said to Hercules II, giving him a pat on the tank – playing the game of course – "here's the omen we've been waiting for. Destiny calls. Maid Marion at The Robin Hood. Follow it up. Never turn away from signs and auguries. Isn't that what I've always said? It'll make a hole in the petrol ration, but what the hell . . . life rarely makes second calls."

There was nothing on the road. I roared through Newark. Wanted to get to Nottingham before dark. Blacked-out headlamp bloody useless. Felt a little mad, liberated from whatever – just like those Saturday mornings years ago when I pedalled the first Hercules up to the moors for the day.

Made the town of the notorious Sheriff by seven-thirty. The pub by seven forty-five. Which is where this affair with Lena started.

I write having but recently left her: the story recorded for myself while sight, feel, and scent are still pervading every perception; in order that I can always come back and refresh the memory of this first time. I know it is gong to be a struggle with the words to recount enough fact to give credibility, yet find poetic images to convey the essence of what went on between us. I must make sure that what I write will inspire memory – bring back the "wine and roses" of that evening – so that at times when life becomes down and out in the living, a hard pressed faith in its mystery and purpose may be restored.

Remember Alice? Walking through the Looking Glass from one world to another? The child in one thought it a perfectly reasonable and everyday thing to do. It's not easy to describe things like that – to render the mind's ability to engage more than one level of reality as if it were usual everyday practice. Which is what I must try and do here.

Seven forty-five is early by pub-time standards. But when I pushed through the door into the Saloon Bar of The Robin Hood there were quite a few customers around – thirty or more, propping up the bar, standing in small groups: Canadian Air Force types, some army, half a dozen or so civvies. I stopped at the corner of the bar to get my bearings, decide where I should best put myself to effectively survey the place. The girl was sitting in the far corner, eyes staring in my direction, welcoming, inviting, like those of an old friend. Christ, I thought, why am I not surprised? Oblivious to the din of conversation and the people present, looking to neither left nor right, I cut clean through the middle of the room towards her. No hesitation. I pushed straight through the drinkers, somehow avoiding spills and collisions: the old Woombat navigating spot-on in unfamiliar territory.

She stood to meet me.

"You're fifteen minutes late."

Now I'd nothing to say to that. It didn't make any sense at all. Yet I nodded, looked at my watch, and replied that I'd left the aerodrome too late to make it on time. I was struck by the quality of her voice: low and vibrant, musically resonant like that of a good contralto.

Taking off my greatcoat, I hung it over the back of a chair, waited for her to sit down. A musty fragrance like spiced sweat laced with honey emanated from her as she moved, blocking the pub odour of stale tobacco smoke and beery breath, setting us apart in a corner pocket of our own atmosphere. We sat looking at each other without speaking: an easy intimate silence – nothing awkward or embarrassing about it. At some point she smiled – an incredible gentleness to eyes and mouth – reached over the table and took my hand; gently ran her fingernails across the palm. *Finis* at that point to old Guterman. Split-second change. I was chosen: the object of favour, the one loved. I knew it. Instant confidence, self-esteem, cheer, blessedness . . . call it what you like. I had found Her. The olden daemons of inhibition and fear slipped quietly away and have not returned. Even now, alone, I am free – not overly worried of what might lie ahead. A marvellous light-heartedness.

There's always been the fear – no point in not facing it – the terror that turns you into an unthinking, paralysed bag of viscera. Could she have known that? It was only later that I told her it's not really a matter of fearing death itself, but of anticipating all the ways it can happen – in the air especially. There's no respite. It's not something you have to overcome just once. Continuously, you know that any night can precipitate the final moments. I told her that the only way to deal with this is to live purely, existentially – try to, anyway – recognise only the present moment, the hour, the day. But that for me, I can never *not* wander in the past and in the future, finding both as real as the present. And I talked to her of the visuals, of always sitting in the front row of a twenty-four hour cinema show – Lancasters, Halifaxes, Stirlings . . . exploding all over the place in great balls of orange fire; following them all the way down to the ground; no-one getting out, no way to the escape-hatches, no time for parachutes. Over and over again, one frame of film following another in slow motion, no matter where I am or what I'm doing. And wondering all the time what it'll be like.

Right! So describe her, Guterman . . . describe her: this is the place in the record to fix that face. Find the words, old son, while she's still as clear as day before your eyes.

The most mysterious of looks – an embodiment of the feminine to satisfy every man's private obsession. A surface-like cool, silvered marble. The form a perfect oval; broad forehead, elongated slanted green eyes riding on high thrusting cheek-bones, wide straight nose with flared nostrils splitting the features like the broad guard-strip of an archaic helmet, mouth rich and full and extended, curving exotically into the planes of the cheeks. The whole wrapped in a coppery fall of hair to the shoulders which, seen against the light from the wall-lamp behind, took on an incredible luminousity and burnished those wonderful cheek-bones with sculptural colour. If Caravaggio had walked in he'd have whipped her off to the studio then and there, and I doubt would ever have looked for another model, or indeed another mistress to share his bed.

The glories of her figure were not revealed until we stood up to leave, and she walked ahead between the tables into open space. Taller than I thought – perhaps five foot eight – slender ankles, full calves, thighs swelling into curvaceous buttocks, slim waist, broad shoulders, slightly swaying, erect walk, head high, hair a-swim in the air.

The Canadians whistled; the rest just gaped. I walked behind like King Dick.

As I write it's only five hours since I left her. I've become absolutely still in myself. As her lover I feel to be part of something much bigger than the world as I've known it: part of something going back a long way. In joining with her, the truth of things – the truth of what I am myself – becomes other than what I thought; the certainty of our ability to transcend our condition becomes indisputable.

First words to Lena: obvious enough – "Why did you say I was fifteen minutes late? How could . . . "

She cut me short. "Because I had a dream last night. In it I was looking for The Robin Hood. I was given directions to the street, saw the sign, and walked into this pub and sat at this table. Then you came in almost immediately. It was exactly seven-thirty by that clock on the wall over there. You sort of wandered over here as if you weren't sure just where you were going, then picked me out and came over. I can see your eyes now: bright, really bright blue and enormous, and so serious. I wanted to make you smile a bit. But I didn't get the chance. You leaned over the table and just stroked my cheek. 'I can't stay now,' you said, 'but I'll meet you here tomorrow at the same time.'

"I woke up immediately and wrote it all down – the name of the street and place; the time you said. Because I've never been here before, and you know how you forget dreams as soon as you wake up. All day I knew I had to come, silly as it seems. I was here at twenty-five past seven, waiting. Then you came in, fifteen minutes late."

I remember staring at her. She couldn't be making it up. How could she? I did turn up, after all.

When she finished telling me about the dream, that wonderfully sensuous mouth of hers curved in a faint smile, and the wide green eyes were frank and inviting, spiriting me off. That was when I first felt myself dissolving – becoming a weightless thing, slipping out of my old goosebumpy nervous skin and assuming a new and inexplicable authority. I sensed the change and knew it for what it was – the recovery of another and older self.

We had a drink. She took off her coat and leaned back against the wall, beneath the lamp, throat exposed. A simple, V-necked black dress emphasised the richness of her colouring, the startling contrast between skin and hair. She looked as good as Dietrich or Garbo. When she moved, stretching shoulders briefly against the chair-back, there was just a hint of full and shifting breasts. No control: I became hard as a rock; slid forward a little to hide the unexpected surges of the old scrotum. That was a remarkable thing for me: to be physically aroused and ready simply by looking at a girl.

We took our drink slowly, held hands over the table, and talked as easily and as intimately as if we'd known each other for years. By closing time there was little she didn't know about my life and the way I think and feel. Her eyes rarely left mine; were always sympathetic and encouraging. Yet I asked her few questions about herself – it never occurred to me to do so. I don't even have an address or a telephone number; I have no idea where she works – if she works – how old she is, or even her last name.

It didn't seem necessary. Can you imagine asking a miracle worker for biographical details while she's performing wonders? And, at the time, the intimacy was so complete that any such questions hovering around I immediately dismissed as interruptions that would break the spell.

"When do you fly again?" It was just before closing time and she was gripping my hand tightly. The question floored me; everything left my head and ran to the tips of my fingers where a last vestige of reality lay. I couldn't think for a moment: when was I to fly again? And why, a voice somewhere kept asking.

Finally – "Tomorrow, I think."

"You'll touch up the Wombat, like you said?"

"Yes: the wings need it – they've faded a bit. I'll firm them up in the morning."

And then she said something that I thought at the time was quite strange, yet nevertheless seemed completely relevant.

"Did you know that when you put the wings on you turned the Wombat into the winged-bear of Artio, the priestess who protects mariners?"

I had to confess that I was not aware of this particular myth; that I'd been thinking more of a "Pooh-bear-wanderer-of-the-night" sort of charm.

"Well, that's not bad either," she replied. "Pooh is a heroic little character . . . in the tradition of the bear-god cults. As we know, everyone needs a teddy bear."

I wonder what Johnny would say to that!

Outside the pub, the last of the Canadian whistles fading away, she turned, held out her arms and gave me a great big hug. "That's for the bear," she said; "this is for you," kissing me gently and lingeringly on the lips. Then she let her head fall on my shoulder; the musky scent streamed from the nape of her neck, and I would have wished time to stop.

We walked slowly away from The Robin Hood, my arm through hers, feeling the soft pressures of her body as we moved together in the dark. Happiness stuck somewhere in the throat: it hurt to swallow. I remember turning to look at her but the black-out was so intense her profile was lost. Yet the darkness and our silence seemed merely to intensify the mood we shared. I'd no idea where we were going. Then I realised that Hercules was still at the pub, so back we traipsed (I have no idea how we found the place again) – then set out once more. I wheeled the bike in the road while she held onto my right arm. When she asked me what time I had to be back at the airfield the next morning my voice almost gave out as I tried to reply.

I can't really estimate how long we walked. Difficult when you're treading on air; not even aware of the machine's heaviness. But we must have left the town behind for we were now on grass, between two tall hedgerows, and Hercules was suddenly dead-weight.

"Not far," she whispered, "only a few yards."

It was just possible to make out a tall slatted gate giving access to a dark spread of trees. Leaning the old motorcycle against the nearest tree I followed her closely as she twisted between the trunks, bending to avoid low branches, until we came to a door – old wood, unpainted. No need for a key; it opened on the latch.

"Hold on," she said, placing my arms round her waist, "the stairs are steep." I held her tightly, every move limb against limb, up the stairway, along a narrow landing, all in the dark, until we came to a curtained opening on the right. She released my hands slowly and moved ahead into the room, turning on a low light – a bronze urn-lamp by the bed which spread a diffused yellow glow through an old parchment shade. In front of the fireplace she bent to put a match to coal and kindling already set.

Fire going, she turned to face me, luxuriously stroking the back of her thighs in its warmth. I felt numb, inadequate, before her beauty; finding it difficult to comprehend what she should see in me. Yet at the same time I had no feelings of awkwardness or strangeness in her presence. "You must take those heavy shoes off. Here, sit in the armchair by the fire." Her hair fell around her face, a golden sheath sparking in the flames as she kneeled and pulled at my feet – first the boots, then off with the socks. Her hands cupped and warmed. I was ashamed of my feet's cold clamminess. Yet spontaneously – absolutely naturally – I leaned forward to stroke her hair. I never would have believed that I could be so easily and quickly at home with a woman. "Much too slow at coming forward, Guters," said Dick Dent the Squadron Casanova after a dance at the local hospital a couple of weeks ago. "You'll never get any oats that way. Women don't want to be placed on pedestals. You've got to grab 'em." Old Dent's gallant comments – "To help out," as he put it – seemed to belong to another life as she sat at my feet before the fire.

Turning sideways she rested her head against my knees, staring into the blaze. I was immediately overwhelmed with tenderness towards her, filled with emotion to the point of needing to babble incoherent "sweet nothings" in her ear by way of expression.

Where the hell have I been all my life to have missed living through something like that before? Sitting here in this miserable room on the aerodrome, writing about her – about us – I begin to think I must truly have been retarded all these years. Yet I'm not talking about the same thing that Dent's always going on about. Going to bed – "having a good screw, a real thrill", in the words of our resident expert – never seemed to me to be an end in itself.

Whatever was happening to us was something else: something that contained every aspect of the erotic; yet lifted us beyond, made every exchange from the glance to the word to the touch – even to the silence – a "trembling" matter: an agitation of spirit that flew in the face of God. Not the God of religion, you understand, but the God of life. No questions asked; no answers required.

We sat without movement until the fire began to die. At one point she laid her head back against my knees, eyes closed, the coppery spill of her hair caressing my skin. So this, I thought, is the true form of domesticity: the fragrance and touch of a woman before the hearth. A simple enough formula for fulfilment and peace.

I stayed as still as possible to avoid disturbing her, wanting nothing to change. For the first time I heard the ticking of an alarm clock somewhere in the background.

"It's set for six-thirty," she said. "Now you are warm we can go to bed. The bathroom's through there. And you can use my toothbrush. The water'll be warm by now – not hot – but warm enough. Get undressed here, by the fire."

She didn't wait for me to start: unbuttoned trousers and pulled them down over my feet. Underpants followed; then tunic, tie and shirt.

Lena ran her lips over my thigh . . . all the way to my mouth, then pulled me up from the chair, hands cupping between my legs. In the bathroom I brushed my teeth with her brush, washed myself down with her face-cloth. When I returned the fire was almost out; the bedside lamp masked with some diaphanous orange material which spread a low, warm light.

And there she lay. It was a sight I will never forget: the voluptuous perfection of her body burnished in the last gleams of firelight.

"I have to look at you," I remember saying, standing quite still by the bed, large bath-towel folded around my waist; firm notions of time and place rapidly sliding away.

"Now that you've looked at me," I eventually heard her remark, "you can take that towel off and come here. You will see me differently through your hands."

When I finally leaned over and ran the palm of my right hand slowly over her from ankle to shoulder, lingering for a moment atop the high nub of her breast, I ceased totally to exist independently as a person rationally, cerebrally, conscious. I became a lover, lost in her service, her instrument, guided by her passion which became my passion, a man enhanced and transformed by the woman. We lay on our sides, facing each other. The faint orange light patterned her body in a flow of dark recesses and luminous curved volumes. Our hands glided in and out, through and over; followed hypnotically by the eyes, hers so green and bright that it seemed they lit the way for both of us. When she raised herself and reached over to run fingernails across my abdomen, her breasts shivered, their weight moving one against the other in slow, trembling orbit. I watched, searching, obsessed with volume, eyes moving from their deep division to the jutting taper of each breast's peak, marvelling at the porcelain translucency of that final swell where blue veins ran to their confluence in rising nipples. And I saw the expectant trembling of her thighs; the pulse fluttering wildly in her neck.

When she finally slid onto me, gripping my pelvis between her thighs, I sank into a quicksand of rising and falling motion that obliterated all lingering traces of past experience.

If I write that such intense sexuality is a way to voyage to another country of the mind, to reach the stratosphere of feeling – a form of travel as extraordinary as anything in Jules Verne or H. G. Wells – am I simply burbling like some naïve adolescent? I can see the grin on old Dent's face, hear the familiar response, "For God's sake, Guters, fucking is fucking, that's all."

I'd make a mess of it if I tried to describe all the details of our love-making. I don't think language itself is up to it. But I should praise her skill and the wildness of her desire. Every time I thought we were satiated she would find some new means of arousal. I never knew we had so many erotic places.

When we fell asleep it was not for long. I awoke once to find her kneeling above me, swaying slowly from side to side low over my face, stroking me softly first with one breast then the other, abrasive nipple-points pricking eyes, forcing lips, while her free hand wandered to grasp and pull me into her again, until only the traces of her scent kept me linked to whatever, at that point, passed for our bodies.

I never heard the alarm-clock. When I came round she was shaking me by the shoulder, her dressing-gown loosely open, radiating warm musky air. A brush of a kiss across my forehead. There was a mug of tea on the bedside table.

"It's just ten past six, so you have plenty of time. Some good strong tea to start you off with." She sat next to me on the bed while I drank and ran her fingers through my hair. And when I finally put the mug down she moved forward and made a tent of her dressing-gown, pulling me down to her bosom. Her arms went round my shoulders and there was a fierceness about her holding. I felt very sad then – I can't explain it, small and vulnerable, like a kid again. We stayed like that for several minutes, every tick of the clock threatening.

"You must be going," she said finally, stroking the back of my neck. I pulled away with an indescribable sense of finality of real loss. I hardly remember dressing. In the bathroom I pulled the curtains open and looked out onto thick fog. Not a roof or tree to be seen.

Staring in the mirror when shaving, I was surprised to find no obvious change: no new look of maturity – firmer chin, wrinkles at the corners of the eye, calm piercing glance . . . all those details which denote the man of experience.

"Now you're ready." She was still in her dressing-gown, open to the ankles, barefoot. I could feel the warm air of the room ebbing away past me as I stood on the open landing. It was a bad moment – a feeling of panic that I might never see her again. I was not sure what to do. I had the wild impulse to ask for sanctuary: ask her to keep me there in her room until the end of the war. Legs and arms felt like lead. I seemed to have no power to move them. So I waited – a bag of nerves - trying to concentrate on fixing the sight of her in my mind.

She came forward out of the light and the warmth and stood facing me. Holding my head in her hands she pressed her lips against my forehead for several long seconds. She was stone cold. Hands and lips stone cold.

"You're freezing. Back into bed and get warm."

"Without you?"

"Yes."

"Impossible."

"This weekend – you'll be free this weekend – Sunday night?"

"Of course."

"I'll come here?"

"No: you'd never find your way alone. Let's meet in The Robin Hood at seven."

"Right."

"Now you must be off. And don't worry. I'm not going to lose you. Ever. As you'll find out."

It's odd how easily I remember every word. As I write I recall every inflection of her voice. I hear her clearly. See her standing there.

Hercules II was a bastard to start in the damp air. And the fog was so thick I couldn't see any house when I got to the gate and looked back. Engine ticking over, I turned the handlebars to the left on the grassy lane. I only knew I'd reached the road when the bike became easier to push and a metalled surface materialised beneath the wheels. Forward visibility was still practically zero – no question of getting into the saddle and driving off. Then the mist cleared abruptly. I was out of it – just like coming out of a cloud bank. I went round in circles at first trying to find a main road. Nobody around to ask. Really out in the Styx. Finally I came across a milk delivery man and was put right for the town. It seemed to be a heck of a way out. Can't imagine how we walked it last night.

Back here in the Mess in time for a late breakfast. Started to write about Leda and the Cygnet immediately afterwards here in my room – this ugly concrete cell which will have a hard time from now on to sell itself as "home", despite the books and these old miserable water-colours of mine. God, how bleak the bloody place is. But not for long. Only three trips left and we're out of here. Anyway, home is where she is. And she said she'll always be there. Remember that, Guterman, on the way to Berlin.

I feel much better having written this down. Words fix things in the mind, remove them from the flux of time, cause them to persist and endure. Help to guarantee the future.

Difficult to stop thinking how fantastic ordinary civilian life will be. If this was a normal day I'd have left her this morning to go to work, and already be looking forward to getting back for supper – in about six hours from now. Lena waiting. Peacetime: just imagine! Sleeping with her every night; starting a day with her presence in your senses, your pores . . . When the war's over, and I'm out of this lot, I'll never grumble about anything. Anything. Ah, Lena, Lena, Lena . . .

FINAL COMMENT: just thought of one reason why I automatically associated Lena with Leda: it's a matter of navigating in the dark, the old Woombat thing again. The beautiful Leda, wife of Tyndareus, King of Sparta, visited by Jupiter in the form of a swan, brought forth two eggs. From one issued the celebrated Helen; from the other the twins Castor and Pollux, renowned for their skill and bravery in battle. Ultimately transformed by Jupiter to become the two bright stars in the constellation Gemini, they have since served as the patron deities of seamen and voyagers – men searching the night sky just like myself as I swing the turret around in old Titty B-O. The winged Bear of Artio, no less.

I closed old Guters' Journal and poured myself another cup of tea, sipping the now lukewarm brew and staring reflectively into the middle distance. "Well, Dick my boy," I murmured into the teacup, "I'd say you've got yourself into something this time. Not sure what to make of it. Perhaps you dreamed the whole thing up – have you considered that?"

I drained the cup, spooned out the dregs of sugar and sank down in the chair. It was almost six o'clock. Fifteen more minutes before leaving for the hangars to prepare for the flight.

I must admit I was puzzled, unsure what to make of Guterman's story. Not that I doubted the veracity of the account in any way. Although I knew Dick's poetic turn of mind well enough, I also knew how objectively he responded to whatever was going on around him – how keen his perceptions were: a quality that made him an excellent air-gunner and had earned him the D.F.M. (Distinguished Flying Medal) and cost the enemy the loss of two night-fighters – one Ju88 and one MeIIo – on two consecutive operations.

"More tea, Sir?"

"No thanks, Joe. I'll be off in a couple of minutes. Take this last sandwich with me."

I put the Journal out of my mind, put my feet up on the coffee table and closed my eyes. It was going to be a long night – longer than the trip four nights ago on the Monday when Dick Guterman was writing about Lena. Berlin and back was at the limit of the Lancaster's range. And I didn't relish the prospect of arriving late over the target either: just too much visibility and too many fighters alerted, sitting around to catch latecomers, harry them on the return. But, as I've explained, we had our own system of getting in and out and it was particularly effective on operations involving large concentrations of aircraft. Not a method that would have been approved by the Station Commander: altogether too anarchic, and demanding better than average teamwork and flying skill. Yet we'd survived longer than most because of it. And, as a bonus, we had the services of a fine groundcrew: our airframe and engine mechanics were wizards at diagnosing and fixing problems. They kept Titty B-O on top line. "No, we're in good shape," I said aloud.

Mentally I ran over the route – one we all knew well – as near a straight line as you can get, barring detours to avoid the defences of major cities like Hamburg and Emden.

Yet I found it difficult to concentrate. Overshadowing my preoccupation with the approaching operation was Dick Guterman's account of his meeting with the girl Lena. She seemed too good to be true, more a wishful-thinking idea in the head than the real subject of an actual encounter. Even granting that old Guters – like a mountain peak constantly creating its own weather – invariably managed to function like a catalyst, attracting the oddest of people and going on to precipitate equally odd developments, there were aspects of this latest adventure about which I felt uneasy: the too easy assumption of mystical overtones; and I've always disliked the concept of predestination – makes it all too easy to sit back and wait for things to happen; rules out individual will and responsibility. And it's particularly negative if applied to the hazardous nature of wartime flying when you must aggressively attack every problem – impose your will on it until the last possible moment. So the more I thought about the circumstances of Dick's romance, the less comfortable I began to feel about it.

I'm groping for words here. Can't find the right ones. And I'm not a narrow-minded so-and-so when it comes to accepting the limitations of reason. But I felt there was something slightly sinister (psychotic?) about the whole affair: about the string of coincidences, the telepathy (if that indeed was what it was), the surreal implications.

Finally: just drop it, drop it, I said to myself. You're reading too much into the whole business.

But I would talk to Guters about it. The old boy must be feeling a bit strange himself after a night like that.

CHAPTER TWO
Take Off

Dusk was setting in as groups of aircrew members began to gather and walk down to their respective Flight Offices in the hangars to collect flying gear. Flying Officer Duncan, Flight Lieutenant Ellis and myself, caught up with Sergeant Guterman in the vicinity of Station Headquarters. He'd left the Sergeant's Mess in company with an old friend, Sergeant Dent – better known as Dicky or "Dirty" Dent – an older man, going on twenty-seven, and wireless-operator on Flying Officer Matthews' crew: a character always ready to raise everybody's spirits with ribald accounts of his love life, and anyone else's he happened to know about. Sergeant "Chalky" White, Matthew's rear-gunner, came up at that point and we all walked slowly past the front of S.H.Q., hands in pockets to present as unmilitary a bearing as possible – the prerogative of aircrew setting out on a night's mission.

"So where were you on Sunday night, Guters?" inquired Dent. "Saw you come in late on Monday morning. Just in time for breakfast."

"Nottingham," replied Dick guardedly.

"Nottingham!" echoed Dent in mock alarm. "You mean you went to the big city to see the girls all alone without asking me to show you around? Taking a bit of a risk, boyo!"

"He's right, Guters," chipped in Chalky White. "You need a few of us around when you go to that place. I must say you look a bit ropey. Don't you think so, Dent?"

"Worn out, I'd say," responded Dirty Dick the lady-killer. "What happened, Guters? Did Duncan pass on one of his cast-off nurses from the last Hospital Dance at Nottingham General?

"No, no: nothing like that." Guterman made an expansive theatrical gesture with his right arm. "I just went to meet a girl I know."

"You know a girl in Nottingham?" – somewhat incredulously from Dent. "How long have you known her? You've never mentioned it; never been very keen on coming to Nottingham with the rest of us either."

"Of course not," replied Dick Guterman. "Not much point in going to see a girl with a mob around, is there? Anyway I just got the urge to pop over and see her – we go back a long way, the two of us – so off I went."

"And stayed the night?"

"Of course."

"Where'd you meet her?"

"The Robin Hood."

"Good grief, Guters," interjected Sergeant White, "that's where all the enthusiastic amateurs hang out. Hope you gave the old dingle-dangle a good E.T. clean up afterwards. Much safer to find a real pro."

"Don't worry about it, Chalky. She only goes there to meet me. It's convenient, that's all. She's not one of their regulars." His tone was nonchalant; very man-of-the-world, I thought. Good old Guters; if only they knew!

"So what's she like?" inquired Dicky Dent, trying hard to sound relatively disinterested but obviously curious as hell.

"She's . . . well, you know those Botticelli drawings of Venus . . . ?"

"For God's sake, Guters, don't give us this high-art stuff – tell us what she's like in good common English: breasts, legs . . . you know . . . the things that count first. After that you can tell us about her eyes and lips . . . and then about her wonderful personality, true love and all that kind of thing."

Guterman grinned. "Jeeze, you're a flippin' philistine, Dent. Right, I'll tell you, just to make you jealous as hell, you old lech." He paused for a moment, then inspiration struck. "You know Marlene Dietrich?"

"Of course, you silly bugger, who doesn't!"

"Well, that's it. She's a dead ringer for Marlene Dietrich. In fact she's got better legs – longer and fuller in the thigh. And she's got much more on top: 'well developed,' one would say in civilised circles, Dicky boy. She's altogether more voluptuous, more . . . "

"Sexy?" volunteered Duncan, with a dramatically exaggerated leer pulling his mouth askew.

"Exactly," said Guterman. "Anyway, I'll tell you, lads, but it's not that easy to describe how she looks . . . "

"Not important," broke in Dent. "You don't look at the mantelpiece when you're poking the fire."

"Perhaps you don't, you old bastard," replied our air-gunner, "but some of us don't have our minds trapped in our pricks – true, Dunc?"

"Absolutely," said Duncan, "but maybe Dent's better off: remember what D.H. Lawrence said . . . "

"Oh Christ," moaned Dent, "now we're using literary references. Alright: what did D.H. Lawrence say?"

Duncan put an arm around Dent's shoulders. "He said that the problem with the English is that they have sex in the head, and that's not the place to have it."

"Well he's bloody well right, isn't he? I mean, that's my point."

"Of course it's your point, Dicky," chimed in Guterman, "that's what I've been saying all along. It'll be the death of you one of these days, though. For God's sake don't have a seizure when you're performing position 37 in that little M.G. of yours. We'd never get you out . . . stiff as a board, followed by rigor mortis all round . . . " He poked Dent in the ribs. "Don't forget that all important dictum: position in life is everything – which means that form must conform to space.

"Anyway, I was going to tell you what she looks like: she's got high slanting cheek-bones, green eyes, a wide and full mouth, nose straight as a die with nostrils slightly flared, a broad and, as they say, noble forehead, and copper-gold hair to her shoulders."

Chalky White let out a long, low whistle. "You must be making it up, Guters. That kind of woman just isn't around. And certainly not in Nottingham. Anyway, whatever . . . lucky you. Glad she's not your typical 'Robin Hood' type. Chances are you'd pick up a dose from most girls in that place. Not worth it, I'd say. The treatment's too bloody awful. Imagine that long umbrella thing down your tool – closed of course – before they open it up and pull it out to scrape . . . Think what that does to your John Thomas. I tell you, just the thought of it's enough to keep me from picking up a girl in that pub. Now, married women, for example, they're a different proposition: professional, clean as a whistle."

"Ah, you're a real pessimist, Chalky," said Duncan, breaking in, strong Cockney accent contrasting strangely with Sergeant White's sing-song, Welsh tone of voice. "You might turn Guters off just when he's got started. Take no notice of the miserable so and so, Guters, he's just jealous, that's all. It's not as if you're out every other night like Dent here, screwing any girl whose fool enough to get into his M.G. for a couple of minutes. And he's caught nothing yet: though he should have had the lot, from foot and mouth to petrification of the old root. It's not dropped off yet, Dent, has it?"

"No, still got it. A bit battle-scarred around the edges, but, apart from that, bigger and better than ever."

"Good for you, mate."

"Any idea whose first off tonight?" Guterman abruptly changed the subject. For some reason it suddenly seemed vital for him to know who'd be number one in the air.

"Yes, we are," Dent answered morosely. "You know old Matthews – he always likes to be first away. Once he gets into that driving seat you can't hold him back; he can't bloody well wait to get off. Never even bothers to give the engines a good rev up. Mag drops? He never looks at the booster gauges. He flies the kite like he drives his car – foot down to the boards as soon as he's out of the garage. Once the chocks are away, mate, we go round the perimeter track like a blasted greyhound. You just watch him swing that Lanc around onto the end of the runway: we never even slow down, boy, never mind stop with brakes on for a final run-up. He belts right on from the peri-track, puts on all the flippin' power and . . . God, do we snake down that tarmac! You think the old kite's going to fall to bits. He says it's safer that way – doesn't give the plugs a chance to oil up; says it gives you more lift if you yaw a bit on the runway – gets you into the air quick before anything can happen! It's a fact – we're just about airborne every time we veer off centre . . . before we even take off! God help us if ever we lose power before we get up.

"But once he's up there he's ruddy marvellous. He could fly that thing like a glider without any furkin engines. Yep: as long as we're up we're as safe as houses. The trouble is he's not so good at getting it down again. Have you seen him land? He flies in fast – one hundred and fifteen, one hundred and twenty-one knots right onto the runway, flaps and wheels down and dragging like hell. The kite's shaking like a bag of bones. Then he shuts everything off and just drops it. Says he doesn't like the idea of stalling on the approach!

"Well, I tell you: I don't look any more. I keep my eyes closed going up and coming down."

We walked along in silence after that tirade of dark humour: mixed responses all round, I suspect. Taking off with a full bomb-load is always a hairy business. I couldn't suppress a surreptitious grin. Dent's lugubrious account conjured up a funny picture: skinny, wild-eyed Matthews hell-bent in the cockpit while "Dirty" Dick, the great lover, was hunched up over the wireless table, eyes screwed shut. I bet my lot were thinking how glad they were that I was so fussy, running each engine independently at the dispersal point before taxying out, scrutinising booster gauges for any sign of power loss in the form of a magneto drop; then going through pre-flight checks with every crew-member. When it came to take-off I always lined up Titty B-O at runway dead-centre, held all four engines steady around Zero 600 st, then released the brakes. As a result, Titty B-O went down the runway flare path straight as an arrow. I preferred to keep her on the ground to the last minute – easier to abort if necessary; also gets you off the ground with maximum lift. The textbook way, I suppose.

I asked Guters if he'd like to go into Lincoln on Sunday: there was an organ recital in the cathedral.

"Sure: when's it over? I'm going to see her again on Sunday so I need time to collect the bike. I plan to be in Nottingham by seven at the latest."

"Well, it starts at two-thirty so we're bound to be back here by five for you to get spruced up. Should give you plenty of time to get to the big city on the bike. How are you for petrol?"

"Fine, thanks: I've only just started on the new coupons. By the way – had chance to read a bit of the Journal yet?"

"You mean about Leda, or rather, Lena?"

"Mm . . ."

"Yes, I read the whole story in the Mess. Well, to be honest, it does sound a bit far-fetched. I mean, did it really happen like that? On the spur of the moment – a sort of vision thing of the pub; and you driven out of your mind to get there? And did she really have that dream about the pub and the clock?"

"Everything happened exactly as you read it, Johnny. No fantasy; no poetic license. I went out for a simple drive on the motorbike; I wasn't out to try and pick anybody up, and Nottingham is the last spot I'd ever have wanted to go, anyway. You know me: I've never liked the place, and I'm not exactly swift at coming forward so far as the women are concerned. So we simply chanced on each other – a sort of organised chance, if you like: she had the dream and I got this sudden yen to head for the city."

"So how do you explain it?"

"I don't know: it either had to be sheer coincidence – and I don't know what the mathematical odds would be against that – or it was intended, set up by some kind of intelligence operating behind the scenes, some unconscious system kicking into gear. But I can tell you, it was as if we'd been together for years. Absolutely natural, everything flowed without thought or plan."

"And you said in the Journal that she volunteered no information about herself; nothing about knowing somebody on the Squadron perhaps – who'd talked about you . . . anything like that? Didn't you think it odd that she told you sweet fanny adams about herself – you know, the usual getting-to-know-each-other details?"

"No: as I said it never even occurred to me to ask."

"So you think she'll be there on Saturday in the pub? Do you think she's in this at the same kind of unearthly level you are?"

"Of course. Listen, Johnny" – Dick stopped suddenly in mid-stride and took my shoulder in his right hand, looking directly at me – "in a strange way I feel she's responsible for everything: that she's in charge of this, and the reason I'm so unself-conscious with her is that I know myself, an old part of myself, to be linked to her. I know it sounds naïve – an adolescent sort of wishful-thinking-romanticism with mystical overtones, for God's sake – but believe me, Johnny, from the moment I first saw her I knew she was no stranger."

He was absolutely sincere. Dick Guterman was the most accomplished and wisest man I had yet met at that stage in my life: incapable of deception, particularly self-deception. I accepted his explanation without prejudice.

"So when am I going to get a chance to meet her?"

"Sometime next week. We're on a 'stand down' this weekend. That'll give she and I some time together; then I can arrange it."

"Right," I said. Then, "Don't tell the others any of the details. Let them think she's an old friend, or just an ordinary pick-up."

"Exactly what I implied just now."

"What?"

"That I've known her a month or two but saw no reason to broadcast the fact with lechers like old Dent around."

"Good." I grinned.

"Up the Woombat," he said.

We had walked ahead of the others while talking and reached "B" Flight Locker Room in good time to get our gear together in leisurely fashion and in comparative peace and quiet. Silently we stuffed ourselves into flying-jackets and boots, collected the "Mae West" lifejackets, parachutes and harness, flying-helmets and oxygen equipment, before wandering outside to sit on the long bench by the locker-room door. For some minutes we sat without speaking, watching the myriad tail-lights of trucks buzzing busily around the perimeter track, servicing the scattered concrete aprons where the Squadron's Lancasters were dispersed.

Guterman broke the silence. "What did Dent say we are for take-off?"

"Second: Matthews is first."

"The weather seems good enough to go with our normal plan – at least on the way out?"

"Yes: Dunc's got the roller-maps. Coming back we could run into trouble at low-level." I pulled out the old "Sherlock Holmes" pipe I affected at that time and went through the slow ritual of stuffing it with tobacco, tapping down the springy shag, running a dirty old pipe cleaner through the mouthpiece, and using two matches to get it burning a fierce red. Second pipe of the day – one in the Mess before dinner, one at the hangars on operational nights. No conversation was possible until the thing was incandescent.

"It's going to be a rough night, Guters. God knows what the place'll be like when we get there. Hitting the city again . . . Well, I'm glad we've got an industrial target at Tempelhof: that's a legitimate one, at least. Not sure about the rest of it. Wouldn't want it to be my family living down there. You know the C.O. told us to remember London and Coventry . . . and I suppose he's right – but there's something sticks in the throat for me so far as this tit-for-tat philosophy's concerned, especially when women and kids are involved. I wanted to mention it when he'd finished talking but, God Almighty, I didn't have the nerve. It's what's called total war – 'saturation bombing' to destroy the will of the population. So when the new four thousand pound bomb arrived we called it the 'block-buster'. Logically enough: we've seen what it can do to a city block.

"But for the first time – when Hawksworth was briefing us this afternoon – I felt wrong being a part of it. Had a wild thought of dumping the stuff in the sea and flying round for a few hours until it was time to go home. And then the S.I.O. gave Matthews and me the gen about taking the secondary target at Tempelhof – so the problem was resolved. For the moment anyway." After this speech I drew hard on the pipe, brought it to the boil again and blew out clouds of smoke.

"Well, you know how I feel about saturation bombing." Sergeant Guterman stood up to stretch his legs, paced slowly up and down before the bench. "I suppose we could become a sort of limited conscientious objector crew who'd only do strictly military targets. How'd the others respond, d'you think?"

I grinned at that: "Well, speculating on your mutinous thoughts, Sergeant, I'd say there's two of us you'd have to watch. Don't forget that Ellis is a regular officer – career man; he'll always obey orders from the top without question. That's why he's so reliable and damn good. And Smith: I wouldn't be sure of Smithy. I think the war's very much a personal crusade for him. His father died a year after he was born – gassed in the trenches, somewhere on the Somme." I knocked the ash out of the pipe and slowly began to knead the bowl in the palm of my hand.

Guterman stopped his pacing. "Well, some crew should bloody well do it. Boy! Can't you see the headlines: 'Aircrew philosophers question morality of war effort'; or 'Cold-feet flyers opt for selective targets – women and children out'. *The Daily Mirror* would scream in six-inch caps, 'REMEMBER COVENTRY'. But you never know. It might start a movement. Manifesto: All conflicts to involve military personnel only. Wars to be fought in deserted regions. World-citizens of both sides pledge to accept the results and elect an International Tribunal to award prizes and penalties.

"An 'Ordinance' like that would allow the so-called leaders to practice their beloved power-politics without embroiling every Tom, Dick and Harry – not to mention Sally. It would gratify what chauvinistic emotions remain before we develop the sense to become truly a world society. And last but not least it would give the natural killers amongst us a chance to have a go; with luck, wipe each other out. Then we could get on with living our potential three-score years and ten, perhaps get some idea of who we are, and what we're supposed to make of it."

"Ah . . . what an idealist pipe-dream, Guters! Anyway, out to dispersal, my lad, on the next transport. Let's get cracking – Berlin and back. C'mon."

Whooo . . . ooo . . . oo . . . oo . . . oo . . . The crazy howling split the night – a piercing shriek rising to high crescendo before tailing off, hanging in the air, then starting all over again. The darkness was filled with running figures scattering towards the grass-mounded air-raid shelters as the ghoulish wailing gradually subsided in a few final wheezing breaths.

"C'mon, Guters, let's get a van. There's one just pulled in round the corner of the hangar. Pick your stuff up and let's get out of here. If it's a real raid and Jerry starts dropping stuff we're much better off out on the perimeter. And we'll be out at the kite and ready to go when the all-clear sounds. Dunc" – to the bomb-aimer who'd just joined us, trailing parachute and harness – "speed it up, mi boy: time we made the aeroplane." I commandeered the Bedford van just as the driver was about to head for shelter. "No lights" – to the Corporal behind the wheel – "head round the north side of the peri-track. Chances are they'll be coming in from the east or south if it's not a false alarm."

Guterman and Duncan clambered unceremoniously over the tailboard and sat in opposite corners, arms over the side, holding on. The airfield was deadly quiet, ridiculously peaceful in its blacked-out state of readiness for the threatened German attack. Duncan sat pensively, lost in thought as the van began its circumnavigation of the dispersal points.

"Got your stuff, Dunc?" inquired Guterman. Flying Officer Duncan took off his gloves and, undoing his flying-jacket, went systematically through his tunic pockets. He nodded: "Yes, they're all there: two of the wife; two of the kid. He's six months old soon."

"Better phone him up when we're back," said Guters. "Can he talk yet?"

Duncan grinned: "Talk? Are you serious? Of course he can, non-stop. I'm going to phone him after breakfast tomorrow if I can get through. The Jerries are really plastering London, you know, Guters. And the wife wouldn't let the kids be evacuated before the blitz started. But there were six killed in our street a couple of nights ago, so she's decided to leave; going to her sister's in Devon with 'em next Monday."

"You think this concentration on city targets is right for us then, Dunc – paying them back in their own coin? That's the only way to look at it, isn't it?"

The bomb-aimer didn't answer immediately. When he did respond the words came out very deliberately, slowly, as if barely escaping the thought. "I suppose so; we don't have much choice, do we? But I can tell you, there are families and kids down there just like my own, living ordinary lives, who had no more to do with starting this war than mine did. And I'm up there in front, looking right down on 'em: the one who decides when to let the bombs go. Sometimes I get the feeling that there's bound to be retribution – that we should not be bombing towns and civilians; that I'm putting my own lot in jeopardy. So I told the wife she'd got to leave London otherwise I'd pack the whole bloody thing up and come home and stay with 'em. And to hell with any court-martial."

The continuous high-pitched tone of the "all-clear" siren could just be heard above the hum of the Bedford's engine. The driver waited for the sound to completely die out then switched on his masked headlights. Almost immediately we left the perimeter and swung in around the starboard wing-tip of Lancaster F for Freddie, number L7516, otherwise known as Titty B-O.

The lady herself, reclining archly on the side of the fuselage between the front-turret and the cockpit windshield, looked ready for action, nipples thrusting illusionistically into space like the tips of two red-hot gun-barrels. The Wombat beneath the mid-upper turret was lost in shadow.

I was first up the ladder and into the aircraft, Guterman next. Duncan followed, still looking a shambles, equipment trailing. The smell of hydraulic oil was strong, the air cold and damp – after all, the old girl stood out in the weather most of her life. Dick Guterman climbed up into the mid-upper, clipped his flimsy little cradle of a seat into place, adjusted his helmet, checked the intercom plug. He sat high above everything, facing the rear of the aircraft, looking along the oval top of the fuselage right out between the twin rudders and over the transparent roof of Sergeant Smith's rear-turret. I can speak for him, knowing that once up there he began to feel strangely disembodied and his thoughts became anarchic, detaching themselves from the present and wandering back and forth over his life. He told me how memories came crowding in, sorted themselves out, became clear and detailed. Listening to him talk, I can tell you that Guterman, the man in the turret, was not consciously responsible. The man in the turret, the defensive eyes and sharp-shooting hands of our airborne citadel, functioned rationally, intelligently, and with deadly accuracy when he took the offensive. It was Guterman the humanist and thinker who, as the aborigines put it, went "walkabout" and conjured up those events of the past which gave him heart and nourished the values of his private world. It was a way to keep some hold on the centre when fear threatened to become mindless panic and the spirit to abdicate. For the assault was unremitting: acute air sickness, the shock of near-bursting shells threatening to blow us out of the sky, and the grim sight of burning cities.

I told him how lucky he was that such free-wheeling introspection clicking into play involuntarily, provided the means to transcend the deadly context of night operations and overshadow paralysing thoughts of self-preservation. Especially when it freed him to function almost nonchalantly, yet with such efficiency.

Forty-five minutes to go. All equipment checked and re-checked by every member of the crew. Flight Lieutenant Ellis and I working through every item on the cockpit checklist. Then it was time. Propeller gearing began to whine as engines turned over slowly, activated by the big starter-battery trolleys connected up under the engine nacelles by groundcrew mechanics. A cloud of exhaust smoke swept from the ports of each engine as it fired, briefly blanketing the mid-upper turret until the fumes dissipated, blown away as ignition eventually took over and airscrews revolved ever faster to bring all four power-plants, each of almost 1300 horsepower, to maximum revs for ground testing. I know old Guters never got used to it: wreathed in fumes, sitting atop the machine, a sort of *deus ex machina*, yet controlling none of the force that dinned the senses and set the airframe vibrating expectantly.

Sitting high, armour plate at my back, plying rudders, ailerons, elevators, I imagined our mid-upper gunner taking off his gloves, running his hands over the tubular metal seat struts, and finding them strangely smooth and shiny – not rough and damp, encrusted with shells and trailing seaweed like the chair in that dream of his I'd read about a couple of hours ago.

A great backfire from the starboard-inner, accompanied by a sheet of flame, had me reacting by running-up the engine strongly to check booster gauge and rev counter for sign of mag drop or power loss. Low scuttling figures ran beneath the mainplane and pulled the wheel-chocks clear. And then we were off, bouncing awkwardly on rough concrete, turning warily onto the narrow perimeter track, heading for the runway, using rudder, brakes and bursts of engine power to keep the aircraft dead centre. One wheel off on the soggy grass and all twenty-four Lancasters behind us would be held up, resulting in the loss of precious time and fuel while the offender was towed out of the way. Mandatory radio silence was observed at this time, so we assumed the air-raid warning must have been a false alarm: after all, the flare path lights were burning brightly, cutting the airfield cleanly down the centre and marking a prime target should any intruding German aircraft be around.

Flying Officer Matthews driving Lancaster D for Donald, old L7513 – number one off – was taxying ahead of us. Except that taxying was hardly the word for it: Matthews was haring along hell for leather, port and starboard wheels alternately about to leave concrete for grass, twin rudders twitching deliriously. In no time at all he was about to turn onto the north-east end of the runway. Watching his erratic progress I had a mental picture of "Dirty" Dent sitting at the wireless table, eyes tight shut, muttering, "He's at it again. Thinks he's in a bloody Grand Prix, he does . . . " And then, sure enough, without any pause for engine run-up or alignment of the aircraft, Matthews swung straight into take-off, throttles wide open. With the four Merlins at the full throbbing racket of their power, Matthews, Dent, White and the rest careened down the flare path, yawing first to the left then the right as Dent had described. The tail lifted prematurely for a moment at the halfway mark, and I thought Matthews was going to plough the nose in, car racing style. But the pilot corrected, took another two hundred yards of runway, and D for Donald lifted gracefully, settling nicely into a shallow climb angle. A reassuring sight.

De-de-de-de . . . de-de-de-de . . . de-de-de-de-de . . . The burst of gunfire seemed to explode in the cockpit, causing me to duck involuntarily.

"What the hell . . . " – from Ellis, as Titty B-O came to a halt, engines idling.

De-de-de-de-de-de . . . de-de-de . . . de-de-de-de-de . . . A second raking burst crackled the night apart. The flare path quickly shut down. Total darkness. Faintly, above the noise of our own engines we picked up the wail of distant sirens.

From my high perch I saw it all. Long lines of bright tracer bullets racing across the dark gray sky, cutting vivid red surgical incisions in the fabric of early evening. Flying Officer Matthews was no more than three hundred feet into his lumbering, bomb-laden climb when L7513 was stitched from end to end – from the bomb-aimer's front transparent nose-bulge to the rear-turret of the tail-gunner – by a thread of tracers straight as a die. When she hit the ground half a mile from the end of the flare path, the bombs went up – a stupendous orange flash that shook the ground and lit the sky as day.

I turned my head quickly, looking across Ellis out of the right window, towards the hangars, away from the exploding conflagration. But my eyes refused to focus normally: the wing-tips were blurred and marked the limits of what I could see. And the familiar roar of our own slipstream and exhaust was lost in the frightening sound of the series of air-cracking explosions coming from the direction of the Lincoln to Cranwell road.

Suddenly there was no reality to any of this anymore. I was living in a world of madmen. Somewhere along the line life had played us all false, creating values and goals that masqueraded as truth. I wanted to retch but there was nothing to bring up; to weep, but there were no tears to find. I was dry as a bone. Emotionally dessicated.

"God Almighty . . . " – an incredulous whisper on the intercom. Then, angrily, "A bloody Jerry intruder. And they'd given the all-clear. Stupid bastards."

Titty B-O was dark as a tomb: I had doused all cockpit and navigation lights.

"We're standing by," I told the crew. And then, as radio silence was abandoned, "The Control Tower says it's only one solitary Jerry and that fighters from Cranwell will be sweeping the area. We'll take off when they declare the region clear. I'm sorry: what a bloody mess-up. Why the hell did they ever give the all-clear?

Must have known the bastard was hanging around up there, waiting. Hell . . . if he wasn't dropping bombs or incendiaries he was obviously hanging around to have a go at one of us. Bloody incompetents. Damn! Nobody's got a fucking chance on take-off." I was surprised how hard and matter-of-fact my voice sounded.

The cockpit was flooded with light from the diffused brilliance of a nearby searchlight swinging upwards to probe the sky. I could hear the Station Commander on the R/T – "Get that searchlight on dispersal out at once. It's silhouetting the aircraft out there like sitting ducks. All operational crews – I'm waiting for positive word from Cranwell that we are free of enemy intruders. If this is not confirmed in five minutes all aircraft are to return to their dispersal points – pilots shut down engines and crews stand-by. All groundcrews are to return to, or remain at, their respective dispersal stations."

One by one all the searchlight beams around the aerodrome wasted away as power was cut. And although the new darkness represented increased physical security and protection should the Germans still be around, it was no help psychologically, serving only to intensify the effect of the explosive fire burning out there in the night.

We all sat quietly at our stations, every man alone with his thoughts. I told Sergeant Smith to leave the rear turret and come and wait at the restbed in the fuselage. But in the high cockpit I remained an unwilling witness to the distant conflagration. That lurking disbelief which momentarily suspends reality had to reluctantly give way. The sour edge of bile jerked in the throat. No chance. They'd had no chance at all. Safer at ten thousand feet with the hope of getting out on a parachute. Dent blindly muttering his last profanities as Matthews hurled them down the runway. No knowledge of the end.

Salt tears were sharp on the lips. I found it difficult to control a sudden heaving of the shoulders. And then a wave of revulsion at such waste, at such sudden violence done to the human person

– to our good friends – shaped itself rapidly into the need to wash one's hands of it – run, kill two birds with one stone: get away from the claustrophobic death-trap of this vibrating, oil-stinking, aluminium tube of an aeroplane, feel fresh air on the face, earth underfoot. Natural things. And give oneself a chance to live according to conscience – dictates of the heart. Cleanse myself from such slaughter. Slaughter I will be inflicting myself in three and a half hours from now. (Must it necessarily take evil to defeat evil?) Drop out of sight. Ten years on and nobody will remember. As nobody will remember Dent and Matthews. They're already just a typed statistic on some list somewhere. And what about those who loved them? Are they on anyone's list? Do they appear among the casualties? All that pain spreading from the point of death, ripples of sadness which never ebb to distant enough shores in the survivor's lifetime.

The Station Commander again: "We have three Beaufighters over the airfield at the moment. A fourth is pursuing an unidentified aircraft south-east at six thousand feet. As there appear to be no further intruders in the area we will proceed with the operation. The Beaufighters will circle it about one thousand feet and lose altitude, at their discretion, to escort each one of you on take-off. Good luck."

The flare path blazed into light. I heard my own voice – subdued and tight – speaking into the mouthpiece. "Listen: we're going for the best rate of climb the old kite'll give us. Be prepared for sudden manoeuvres. Gunners – you'd better have eyes in the back of your head the moment we start down the runway. If you see anything that looks like a Junkers 88 or an Me.110 – I don't care what the range is – fire off some rounds. Let the bastard know we know he's there. Discourage him from closing. But for God's sake don't belt off at any of our own fighters. You know what a Beaufighter looks like. Better get back, Smithy."

It was us next. I waited for the green light to appear at the Controller's caravan at the end of the runway. I remember that my arms felt disconnected, individual fingers wooden and uncoordinated. I couldn't get Dent's face to move from before my eyes. Dent – one of the unsung heroes of the petrol dump. Three weeks ago, just before midnight on a Sunday, a solitary German intruder had dropped a shower of incendiaries and a couple of high explosive bombs on the aerodrome fuel-storage tanks. Thousands of gallons of high-octane aviation petrol had roared in flames into the sky, explosion following explosion as one underground tank after the other went up. A dozen or so men working there had never been seen again. One tractor driver pulling a bowser in for filling was found running naked on a country road two miles away: he was quite mad and never recovered. Sergeant Dent, who was taking a short-cut across the fields on his way back to camp, was one of the first on the scene. He had run beneath the billowing flames and climbed into the cab of a burning three thousand gallon tanker, pulling the unconscious driver clear and running fifty yards with him over his shoulder. A few seconds later, the vehicle blew up. I'd noticed at the briefing that the relatively superficial burn-marks on Dent's cheek and forehead, while fading, were still blueishly obvious; angry-looking.

As his face hovered before me, I found myself trying to imagine and comprehend the moment of L7513's impact: contusion and flame against living flesh; the last split-second of consciousness in its full knowing.

The Green. We bumped slowly along over the concrete sets and swung into the turn and onto the end of the runway. The flare path stretched before, lighting the darkness to the world's edge. A short run-up on each engine, some jiggling of the tail for final alignment, and I opened the throttles, built up power against the brakes for a few moments before releasing them to send Titty B-O lumbering purposefully on her way.

Ellis held the throttles wide open – three thousand plus revs – supercharger manifold pressure fourteen pounds p.s.i. Her tail came up – held her down a little longer – pulled her into the air at speed. The flight-engineer selected undercarriage up – three hundred feet into the climb and flaps up – engine boost plus four.

Gun turrets turning through a near one hundred and eighty degrees – scanning left to right, right to left. No sign of other aircraft. Not even the Beaufighters.

At one thousand feet a long, banking turn to port – levelled out to commence the slow climb on a south-east course that would take us out over the coast.

Down below, on the starboard side, the glow of a large fire could still be seen.

Over the North Sea. The gunners had fired their test rounds. We'd climbed to five thousand feet. Synchronized the engines. Ellis had checked the aircraft black-out. It would soon be, "Enemy Coast Ahead" down the intercom.

CHAPTER THREE
The Flight: Guterman's Turret

Dick Guterman talked (and wrote) a lot about his turret. With his usual poetic turn of phrase he turned it into a microcosmic world of its own: the "orb" – in which, encapsulated, he rode or "swam" the night skies; somehow turning the terrible matter-of-factness of a modern bombing mission into the never-never-land of a mythological quest. Such was the Guterman way of creating an acceptable reality out of a painful and negative one.

A paradox that Dick – while being the most effective air-gunner on the Squadron – contrived to live an eccentric kind of airborne life in the mid-upper (witness his sign suspended beneath the turret entrance concerning Clocks, Watches or other Mechanical Alarums). His writings in the Journal confirm his need of fantasy. The account of his experiences in the turret during our previous mission to Berlin – the night after he had met Lena in Nottingham – makes strange reading. It reveals the presence of the two personalities he cultivated when flying: the "cat's eyes", on-the-ball gunner; and the prescient, free-wheeling savant and dreamer. It was obviously a way of keeping everything together – outer and inner – to the advantage of both. I'm sure that the way he described things on our last Berlin flight illustrates a typical night in our air-gunner's "turret life".

In the high mid-upper position Dick Guterman was indeed the eyes of the aircraft. He had saved us twice in the past from potentially deadly night-fighter attacks. And it was from him that we received warning of the first of the troubles that were to dog our present flight. Also, as events began to go against us, it was the mid-upper which became the focus of a developing drama. I can only surmise at what went on in Dick's "orb" of a turret – during the early stages of our present flights. But I can put together a reasonable account of events by presenting those parts of his Journal inspired by the last Berlin trip, over the same route, and under identical weather conditions; and by relating not only our official communications over the intercom, but also what I picked up through his "open" microphone.

Much of the time Guters suffered from the debilitating effects of airsickness, and blamed the cramped conditions of the turret for this. He was not a big man in the heavy sense of the word: but even a slim six-foot-one type had minimum head and leg room in the Lancaster mid-upper turret and found movement very restricted, particularly when wrapped in flying suit and parachute harness. Hunching over the gun-barrels, shoulders trying to fit themselves to the space, and continuously bringing eyes up and around to scan the sky, constituted a dizzying, disorientating exercise. For anything up to eight hours. While sitting on a narrow strap-up metal seat that no self-respecting parrot would tolerate as a perch without playing merry hell. The only guaranteed way to overcome nausea under such conditions is to keep perfectly still with eyes closed. But this is hardly to be recommended when lives depend upon a gunner's vigilance.

Mind over matter – that's how he managed it. On the only occasion when I was airsick, flying as second pilot one day, I was totally debilitated, weak as the proverbial kitten, incapable of functioning even halfway effectively.

> "Not a good night for the squeamish traveller – (wrote Guterman four nights earlier) – lots of low cloud turbulence at the outset over the Lincolnshire coast which intensified out over the North Sea, and was with us most of the way across the water. Too many troughs even for the Wombat. Be better off riding the swell below – a real night-swimmer."

The long sea route over the East Frisians islands was the route approved by myself and the navigator. It added well over one hundred and fifty miles to the total distance flown, but by flying at low altitudes – the basis of *our* private survival strategy anyway – and avoiding the heavy use of fuel in the long climbs for heights of seventeen thousand feet or so, it could be done; especially with a skilled flight-engineer monitoring fuel consumption. Also, the longer sea route was safer. If the miles flown over land – over enemy territory – could be reduced, then it lessened the amount of time the aircraft was a target for the German defences.

The first gleams of moonlight were playing over the cockpit canopy; would be causing blue rivulets to gleam along the turret's gun-barrels and impart a coppery luminosity to the hydraulic pipelines. Cloudbanks were dispersing, giving way to patchy cumulus hanging in the black space where stars were beginning to materialise, brittle clear. Falling away beneath, the air was blue-black, several tones lighter than that above, allowing the gunners in their respective perches to see through four thousand five hundred feet to the dull gleam of the sea.

We were flying straight and level. About two hundred miles out – weather less turbulent, visibility improving. By now I would think that the first stick of chewing-gum had done its work and Sergeant Guterman had decided that things were looking up: he said as much over the intercom and excused the pun. Said he expected to see the east coast of Ameland in the Friesians passing beneath him on the port side at any moment. Meanwhile he was turning the turret through its full range. No indication of any loss of hydraulic pressure: no leaks.

We were passing a little further north of Ameland than usual. Intelligence had hinted that flakships might be operating there; so flew directly over the next island in the chain with an absolutely unpronounceable name – which, from the air, seemed merely marsh and swamp. Now approaching the estuary of the Ems – Germanland straight ahead. I dropped the aircraft's nose slightly and Titty B-O began a gradual descent. The port of Emden at the mouth of its river is well protected, and this was usually the place I chose to start on the first really low-level passage of the night's operation – render us invisible to radar and unapproachable to both anti-aircraft guns and fighters alike.

Almost immediately it was necessary to make an abrupt change of course to south-south-east. Guns on the north-east shore of the estuary were beginning to bark: safer to make a short diversion and hug the south-west coastline above Groningen as quickly as possible.

The sudden turn and drop through space took the crew by surprise; there were some exclamations over the intercom, the loudest and most offensive coming from our flying wombat back there. No doubt he employed his favourite remedy of pulling on the crotch of his parachute harness with one hand while clutching a gun barrel with the other. He assured me that pressure around the scrotum always worked to help the body keep a sense of a fixed position in space; also that he felt it to be very important to help the aircraft's stability by sitting as still as possible, upright, leaning to neither right nor left in case he upset Titty-B O's aerodynamic efficiency. But then the so-called dictates of reason were readily abandoned up there in his bubble.

The bluish darkness was broken by prickings of red light streaming through space in long, converging lines: tracer bullets from something on the water beneath searching us out, but finding no target. Tracer streams seeking to pinpoint potential low-flying targets were a fairly common sight on operations. For some reason on this particular night the Ems estuary to our north-east was fairly riddled with criss-crossing lines of the stuff.

Twenty miles away on the right, Emden anti-aircraft was now decidedly curious. Flak clusters left the ground lazily, then accelerated like a stream of meteorites seemingly about to burst, only to pass well behind and explode – eruptions of orange and white flame – at the safe height of nine or ten thousand feet.

Nobody expected a heavy-bomber to be flying at the lower levels we occupied on the outward stage of the game.

Dick Guterman always experienced leg cramps in the turret. Difficult to move with the butts of twin Brownings pushing into the stomach and magazine boxes holding belts of ammunition tight against the feet. It was such a small circular greenhouse of a space, the mid upper. Two-thirds of the way down the spine of the Lancaster, about nine to ten feet round, the transparent dome rose some two and a half feet from its fuselage fairing. Seen from the outside, Guters was just eyes in a helmet, apparently sustained by an umbilical cord – a tube feeding the oxygen required for high altitude flying into a mouthpiece which also contained the intercommunication system microphone; the rest covered by flying-jacket and gloves all tied up by parachute harness straps like a brown-paper parcel.

"Bloody hell! . . . What the . . . " came over the intercom from the mid-upper as three resounding explosions threw the starboard wing down and under. Titty B-O lurched heavily, almost side-slipped out of the sky before I could counter with ailerons and full forward throttle to pull straight and level, prevent the stall I felt coming. An ack-ack salvo had fallen short of the general high-altitude barrage – the result of some error or malfunction on the ground that might have resulted in a lucky hit and detonated only a couple of hundred yards behind the tail.

"Pheeeew . . . " I sympathised with the involuntary release of breath which whistled through my earphones. For Dick Guterman, high in the turret dome, poised momentarily over three thousand feet of space, mind connected to the body only by the fluttering strings of stomach nerves, high explosive near-misses of the sort we had just encountered were devastating. The senses were wide open to their violence. And the inevitable evasive action could have you drowning in the night sky.

More activity on the intercom: Sergeant Smith calling through from the rear-turret, voice flat and steady, informing me that the near hit must have been a fluke – that the shells were once again bursting well behind them and several thousand feet higher up.

Guters came through to confirm Smithy's report; said that much more side-slipping through the sky like that and he'd be losing his lunch. But he was getting his sea-legs back; swinging the turret around and doing his eye exercises. Nothing to be seen in the sky – no other aircraft around.

My thoughts went back to the day after the last Essen trip when he presented me with a battered, old encyclopaedia. Opening it up, there it was, top of the page: *WOMB, noun – the belly or stomach; the uterus of a female . . . a dark or deep cavity that receives or contains.* "But no mention of floating, Johnny," he said: "of that liquid loss of weight you get up in the turret." And, underneath, on the same page: *WOMBAT, noun – any of a genus of burrowing marsupials resembling a small bear.* He was pleased as punch.

"What a combination, alchemy of words, WOMB and BAT: the womb-tomb-bat; the batting-tombing-woombat – woombing, batting, tombing, bombing."

"Bombing: you see, Johnny, how relevant the old Woombat is . . ."

The first intimation I had of trouble came when I noticed flickers of light dancing across the plexi-glass on the starboard side of the cockpit canopy. At the same moment Guters must have turned the turret a few degrees to his left to see what was going on. He reported that the exhaust flame-traps of the starboard-inner engine were spitting out red tongues of fire – long, thin flames pulling out into the slipstream and streaking across the top of the wingtanks before frizzling out at the mainplane's trailing edge. But what are you to make of a man who goes on to say that it was a cheery sight, provided a cosy corner of infinity?

"Reminds me of those winter nights by the fire reading about old Merlin and his magic," he went on. "Always felt there was a chance of discovering the secret of his power. What a man of knowledge he was. There was nothing like going off to bed to be tucked up with Merlin and the Black Arts. Nothing seemed impossible in those days. I remember the night they laid a fire in my bedroom when I was sick. Very snug it was. Very snug . . . "

"Hells bells, Guters, pack it up. Keep your eye on the starboard inner and those bloody flame-traps. What do they look like now?"

I could hear the whirring noise of the mid-upper as it took him round for a better look. "Well there's still a lot of exhaust flame, skipper, but it's more diffused, not such long streaks – still lighting us up like a Christmas tree though."

I made no immediate response. I had already instructed the flight-engineer to investigate from the canopy side-window. When Ellis responded his voice was distorted by static crackling through the system. "Right, Sir: flame-traps are still in position but a stud or two may have sheared and air could be getting into the manifold – feeding the exhaust a bit. I'll cut the revs back a fraction. Does it look any better now at your end, Guters?"

Silence for half a minute while Guters watched the flames shrink back to a more acceptable length. "Shorter and more erratic," he reported. "Just flaring a little towards the leading-edge then dying."

"Good: keep an eye on that engine then, there's a good lad. If the traps burn through we'll have to think again. Ellis'll check it from up here also. Alright? Not too hot for the Wombat?"

I could imagine our hot-shot sergeant grinning into the mouthpiece. I was always quipping about the Wombat. He gave me little credit for appreciating the power that small flying bear bestowed on the mid-upper and its occupant. For there he sat on high – after Smithy, the most important pair of eyes in the aircraft – solely responsible for checking a great swathe of upper air. I calculated we were between three and four thousand feet; we were slowly descending for our low-level entry into Germany over the

River Ems. The wide waters of the estuary beneath were starting to narrow.

At some point, with the turret returned to its central position, Guters – if running true to form – would put his head down for a quick change of scene and look obliquely down into the fuselage where he could just see the foot of the restbed. A few unbelievably ordinary things: a tea-mug, scarf, even a tube of toothpaste and a toothbrush might be littering the blanket. "Who the heck," he said on one occasion, "is going to clean their teeth en route to Berlin? But it was a travelling clock, precariously balanced, showing the time at ten-twenty p.m. that occasioned the following tirade in the Journal.

> Damn! Didn't they read my notice about clocks near the turret? I bet Duncan put the thing there deliberately. Now come on, Guterman . . . it's bloody stupid to be neurotic about time just because you find it mundane, restricting to the imagination, keeping you bogged down in trivia and routine. Just think how most people would be lost without the clock: yes, it is ten-thirty a.m. and you are still here; check in later to confirm you're still with us. Time for tea-break, ladies and gents, time for a pee – time to go home, listen to the news, go to the pub, go to bed, make love . . . time to get up, make breakfast . . . TIME, GENTLEMEN, PLEASE!
>
> Living like that leaves the mind at half-cock. Besides, time in intensity has nothing to do with time in duration. Remember that night over Essen? Nothing guaranteed or reliable about time then. Dropping four thousand feet like a ton-weight until the skipper regained elevator control and pulled out at about one thousand, beetling away over the rooftops lurching like a drunk. Falling down the sky like that

> the clock gives up. Ye Gods . . . the incredible age of memory: other years, other places, other Gutermans. All in two minutes. More dimensions than the clock can measure. You certainly can't put all your eggs in the "here and now" basket.
>
> Statement by Professor Guterman: Clock-time and being are not synchronised – life's not just a series of linear splutterings of chronological events. More like a multi-dimensional fuse box, a great knot of wires feeding in from every direction and shooting off many active sparks simultaneously. More lives than the proverbial cat.

I was scanning ahead. Not too happy about the sky advent of extensive areas of ground mist which were obscuring forward vision, clinging low to the sea; responsible for new, bumpy air. I took a leaf out of Guterman's book, started on a stick of chewing-gum to counter the acrid taste in my mouth and the slight discomfort that threatened, and unexpectedly had a quick and vivid recollection of the morning when Duncan defended the flying bat – or bear, if one preferred Lena's mythic interpretation – in the face of my sarcasm. (God, was it only six nights ago that the Lena phenomenon occured?) "The fallacy of time again," I said aloud into the dead intercom. Silently to myself – "You listening, Dunc, you phallic philanderer!"

Yet I should have known the Wombat would meet with the bomb-aimer's approval. Duncan believed in charms; knew how the rituals worked. Before every operational flight he placed two photographs of his wife in his left tunic breastpocket; two of the child in the right. In addition, the carefully folded menu of their first honeymoon dinner at the Skindies Hotel, Maidenhead, was wrapped in protective brown paper and slipped into one sidepocket – while a small sand dollar gathered from some beach on their one and only summer holiday in 1939, went into the other. Our bomb-aimer could no more fly without these talismans in place than he could by running around and flapping his arms about. And you should see the performance of putting these magical things into the respective pockets. It had the intensity of a priest raising a chalice for consecration.

I flipped on the intercom: "What do the flame traps on that engine look like now, Guters?"

"Just a minute, skipper," – swinging the turret round for a better view. "Well, the exhaust's still flaming – but it's not as bad. More a flicker; nowhere near the leading edge."

"Good. Keep an eye on it."

There was an early passage in Guteman's Journal about flame traps referring to their ineffectiveness on the Avro Manchester, the Lanc's precursor.

> What a bloody death-trap that aeroplane was (he wrote). They should never have rushed those great Vulture engines off the drawing boards – only two per aeroplane – driving enormous propellers – very under-powered – limited ceiling. Vultures full of bugs when we got 'em. Only one reliability factor: they could be relied upon to give trouble. When exhaust manifold studs sheared – and they did it all the time – fire spewed out as if from a flame-thrower. Had to shut the engine down immediately. Any engine problems with a Manchester and the outlook would be grim. Have to abort the mission. And then try and get back. Many good friends lost attempting to do just that. Impossible to keep the thing in the air on one engine . . . Wait a minute: what about old Herring – Squadron Leader "Kipper" Herring – brought a Manchester back all the way from Berlin with one engine out; airscrew nicely

feathered. Nobody else ever managed anything like that, even in daylight.

Saw him land it. Seemed to be hovering over the end of the runway for hours – an exhausted moth attracted to the flare path lights. No one knew how he did it. Not even him. We were bloody lucky the Squadron was converting to Lancs when we arrived. Only did two daylight cross-country's and one night "op" in a Manchester. Wonder how Rolls Royce came to call them "Vultures"? There's a hell of a lot in a name. Look at the Merlin for example: named after the old wizard? Must be. They usually perform beautifully. The Vultures were rotten from the start.

It's all a matter of Fate, my boy. Six months earlier and we'd have had to fly with the Vultures.

I instructed Guterman to look at the starboard-inner again, Merlin or no Merlin. "Let it know it's being watched," I said. It was behaving itself: at least so long as I kept the revs down.

It was unlikely that the present spill over of flame would be visible from the ground. But I was not so sure as to how exposed we now were from above where the greater danger lay.

Both sides of the estuary were now discernible. We were favouring the east-most, quieter bank. Would swing due south to head down the river proper in three or four minutes. I told all three gunners to keep their eyes peeled for fire from light-calibre ground defence positions; give their turrets a good workout. Asked the mid-upper to particularly check the "taboo track" interruptor gear which prevented the trips from being depressed to fire the guns when the rudders were in the way . . . otherwise we'd have some very skimpy steering devices left out there. Calculated we were now about three hundred and twenty miles from Berlin.

It had been a lucky night so far: apart from the near-miss by the Emden batteries. Both the weather and the coastal defences had been kind to us. The ground mist was dispersing – looked likely that we could continue low-level until climbing to bombing height. But I noticed that the moon was getting stronger by the minute, and only flimsy cirrus was drifting about at around twenty thousand feet. No cover for us in the higher altitudes.

The transparent night sky always inspired our Wombat gunner: this was his response in the Journal to the night of 9 October.

> God Almighty! – Up there, Guterman: north and west. Aren't those the six stars of the Southern Cross coming out? See the jam the Milky Way's in? Can you imagine stars and planets having light-years of space to manoeuvre in that lot? Now you know what Pascal was getting at: "It – the Universe – is an infinite sphere whose centre is everywhere, its circumference nowhere."
>
> Difficult to see much significance in human affairs. Even death: "We shall die alone." Pascal again.
>
> Isn't it absurd, me sitting high in my capsule – a fraction of an inch off the ground so far as the stars are concerned, while the Jerries take pot-shots. What a game – what a cosmically insignificant little lot we are, screwing our lives up in the great political power-plays of national expansion, ego, ambition . . . yet every man Jack to die alone in the end. Why rush it, the stupid bastards. "We must glorify war, the only hygiene in the world," said the first Italian fascists in the Futurist Manifesto. You've got to admit the human race is absurd. "The soul gets into its underpants; the mind

washes its feet in the bathtub." Pascal again, I think? Must be.

Horoscope page in last Sunday's paper: "*The Stars and You. Virgo: Can't avoid the familiar duties, but be ready for surprises. A time when the tides of fate are running strongly.*" Funny you should immediately think of Leander – Leo-Andrew, manly lion. If that had been his horoscope would he have set out one more time to swim the Hellespont – at night (like me, after all) – flailing against that fast moving black water, that current from the sea of Marmora as treacherous as any turbulence you find on the night flight? Would he have seen it as a warning that the statistics pile up against one? One night too many? But he was spurred on by the prize at the end of the journey: the beautiful Hero, once virgin priestess of Aphrodite. Leander knew the chances but he went, nevertheless. What do you think happened to him on that last night? Halfway across he picked up the flame in Hero's tower window, and homed in on the European side of the straits. Then, perhaps, the stars withdrew. Or a sea-fret misted the night sky, obscuring both flame and star. And then a rising swell – turbulence; too far out to turn back. No options but to continue. A classical case of meeting one's fate – what the Greeks would call the fulfilment of his *moira*. Remember when you had to learn Keats? "Sinking bewildered mid the dreary sea/ 'Tis young Leander toiling to his death . . . /O horrid dream! see how his body dips/ Dead heavy . . . " You'd think that the Gods would ensure that his body landed well away, not right beneath her tower. Not them. You've got to feel for Hero when she saw his body below: it's almost impossible to imagine that kind of despair. Hopefully it was so intense she was dead already before she struck the rocks. Two night journeys then? Together at the end? Of course. How else are you to live with life.

And for me and the priestess Lena – the same philosophy? The same.

"Everything alright back there, Guters?"

"Yes, skipper" – turning his head to look at the troublesome starboard-inner – "no change."

We were descending gradually, heading for the river at about three thousand feet, the estuary about to be left behind. Suddenly it seemed extraordinarily peaceful out, with just that slight murkiness to the air which afforded protection from higher flying German night-fighters. The Gods were being kind. But I was well aware one should never take them for granted – "They help those who help themselves," my father had drilled into me. Better do some eye exercises. Perception gets dulled with constant peering into distant space. The usual quick switching of focus: first on the instruments, then out to the port-inner engine nacelle. Do this, back and forth, until the eyes can focus almost instantaneously on each with every shift from one to the other. The exercise strengthens the eye's rectus muscle for making quick change of focal length; always after every practice session I found myself able to clearly differentiate between space and object, however rapidly I turned my head in the sky search. "Cat's eyes Graham," they used to call me – cynically, you understand – in the Mess. Must admit I was something of a fanatic in practising the routine.

"What a spread of stars piling up: sky's getting really jammed" – this was Dick Guterman muttering loudly to himself. As usual he'd left his microphone active: not a good practice. Neither blandishments nor threats had cured him of it.

Behind us, higher in the sky, somewhere in the vicinity of Emden, disintegrating puffs of bursting shells floated silently in the lower sky at about eight thousand feet. Definitely not the height for someone to be going through the coastal defences. Should be much lower down or much higher up. I wondered if it was a Lancaster, one of ours . . .

Time to go down a quick right turn, nose in a shallow dive, and we semi-side-slipped towards the River Ems. A sudden manoeuvre for the weak stomach, but some instinct told me to get to hell out of there. At the same time, I kept us weaving tightly from side to side should any unexpected ground opposition in the form of light anti-aircraft fire be encountered.

"Gunners, keep your eyes in the upper air. We've seen Jerry night-fighters around here before."

Well, Dick was right about one thing: chewing gum helped. Gave the jaw something to do; helped maintain perceptions and limbs at the ready. Saliva began to run again, fresh juice mixing with the dry spittle on the tongue and cutting the sharp bile building in mythroat.

Titty B-O levelled out above the river at just over fifteen hundred feet. The familiar pattern: in over the Ems estuary; low level down the river for about forty miles, turn left to cross the River Wesser just south of Bremen and head east across Luneburg Heath – more or less hedge-hopping if weather permits; visual contact with the ground as long as it's possible, using large-scale roller maps of the terrain. In this way we confuse and neutralise the dangerous defence belt of radar, night-fighters, and anti-aircraft guns of the Kammhuber Line; as well as avoid major cities and their defensive rings. Then, somewhere approaching Oranienburg – about thirty to forty miles north-west of Berlin – we should start the climb to our relatively low-level bombing height.

I sometimes wondered if we were doing the right thing: the system carried its own risks and dangers, particularly when in the target area. And – whatever the "higher-ups" might think – we were still around. Even coming in over the target at a relatively low altitude – between four and five thousand feet – pays off: leaves the main defence activity to go on above us at anything above fifteen thousand feet; it's also more accurate in terms of hitting the target. We'd all agreed to it despite the danger of bombs falling from above and a possible lucky hit from high-altitude-intended anti-aircraft fire. And there was always the advantage of getting in and getting out fast – a lone raider, clear of all that fighter and bomber congestion in the upper air. No: no doubt about it. It's a crafty scheme. I asked Ellis to check the starboard-inner, our recalcitrant engine. He reported no change – flame traps holding up.

I tried to stop thinking about the fact that this was mission twenty-nine – next to our last op. We were the only crew left out of those who joined the Squadron with us fresh from O.T.U. Too many crews "buy it" in the first half-dozen trips. And here we were . . . heading for the big city again . . . but I knew the strain was telling. I was finding it harder and harder to keep awake as the night progressed – especially over the longer hauls. Low level is not everybody's cup of tea. You have to know just where you are at all times, and have a mental picture of the terrain in your head. Can never afford to be caught out by high ground. So we stayed clear of the Ardennes and I knew the height of every hill and hillock everywhere else. At least, just about. Also, any pilot on this lark had to watch constantly to avoid a natural tendency to fly "in" to the ground . . . even though it seemed he was maintaining a constantly horizontal course above it; it was especially a problem when flying low over large bodies of water. Anyway, we were all very good at it. Even on murky nights! Three pairs of eyes working together: Duncan, flat on his belly in the bomb-aimer's front bubble reading the roller maps fitted on their "toilet roll"-type handles; Ellis monitoring the altimeter – not too accurate an instrument at lower levels – by maintaining constant visual contact with the ground; and Yours Truly trying to fly like an auto-pilot. Got to be a natural at sensing any change in the aeroplane's nose up or down attitude, and in making split-second changes in course.

"Guters . . . Smithy . . . " – my voice was crackling away on the intercom – "we'll follow the usual drill across to the Elbe then climb to about four thousand south and west of Oranienburg to head south to Tempelhof – that should keep us away from the route of the main stream. Smithy – keep a sharp eye for anyone creeping up beneath us: the fighters know by now we're blind and vulnerable underneath. Guters, keep those bat's eyes peeled. The moon won't be as obscured on the last leg. Watch out above. And Tubby – be ready for anything on the ground that's not too surprised to have a go at strafing us. You can scare the hell out of 'em from the front turret. How's the mid-upper functioning, Guters?"

"Fine: been swinging it round a bit – pretty dry."

"Good. And the starboard-inner?"

"The same: still flaming a little from the traps, but much less visible from up here."

The intercom went dead; the incessant roar of the four Merlins took over the cockpit again. At one thousand feet the ground looked all too sinister in the pale light of a moon that seemed soured – greened rather than silvered. The Ems twisted sinuously on its course flanked by dreary marsh-ridden banks. Empty, mournful country.

The lower air over the dark-gray ribbon of river became increasingly bumpy as we flew south, filled with "potholes" as Guterman called the down-drafts which could cause us to drop twenty feet at a time without warning – leaving the stomach behind until the aircraft rose to meet it on the upward surge. I was always aware of the problems presented by an over sensitive stomach. How Dick Guterman kept his eyes in the upper sky, searching left and right for the tell-tale black spot showing up in the ambiguity of space – the first sight he would have of a hostile enemy fighter – I'll never know.

We were encountering turbulence again – whipping the tail about – rudder pedals juddering wildly beneath my feet. It was getting very cold in the cockpit – beginning to feel it sooner than usual. Then I remembered the promise of winter in the air of Lincolnshire that afternoon – the climate of a peacetime world that had suggested fire-lit cottages, tea and toast; a time when aeroplanes were just an esoteric means of transportation, nothing much to do with the man in the street.

Made a quick swing to port as the river changed course. Banking at forty degrees. The Ems tilted crazily beneath, and then, with one last tadpole wiggle, we were away, the water left behind as we headed east for Luneburg.

Flying straight and level now at about nine hundred feet, the scrub-grass and marsh of the dreary river world was gradually giving way to lush green farmland dotted with neat white farmhouses and their high-peaked barns. Not much chance of anybody getting at us from down there unless some German farmer tried a pot-shot with a hunting rifle. Countryside all the way to Oranienburg. A few small towns like Schneverdingen on the edge of Luneburg Heath – where we'd seen someone go down a week ago, and flown well to the south of it since to ensure being out of range of the Hamburg batteries. Flat as a pancake generally except for the rise to the plateau of Luneburg Heath – a change in altitude to which Titty B-O responded faithfully.

This was a good section of the course for our man in the mid-upper: with luck would be straight and level all the way across the Heath. I had to smile as I thought of Lena, copper hair against white body, green eyes and silver mask . . . while there old Guters sat in his plastic orb nippled only with muzzles.

The clouds above were moving higher in the sky and breaking into small clusters, allowing the thin light of the young moon to illuminate their airspace more effectively: throwing the forms of landscape and buildings beneath them into high relief. Many a German farmer must have been hurled violently from his sleep as the roar of Titty B-O's engines breached the night's drowsy silence, only to wonder what had passed as the blast faded, lost in the rushing wind of slipstream. Interesting country: gave the gunners a chance to ease their eyes from searching space and look down on the details of ground life. Small stunted trees of unusual shape limbed out into the sparse air, grasping at marauding airborne strangers like ourselves. And the open doors of barns afforded momentary, yet telescopically sharp, glimpses of harrows and hoes, tall scythes, sacks of grain, carts, and the snub noses of tractors.

Open pasture now quickly turning to forest: low, round-topped trees mushrooming in clusters between the retreating farmhouses. Time to bring the aircraft round a couple of points south-east to keep well away from Bremen and Hamburg off on the port side.

Beneath us was the last farm in open country – most likely where Guters spotted the bicycle four night's ago: a machine dropped on its side isolated in a pocket-handkerchief of space between the steeply roofed house and high garden walls.

It would seem – from what he wrote in the Journal – that the bike had acted as a catalyst to release a rush of feelings: nostalgia and memories that raced to mind bringing with them a great singing truth – the knowledge that his own trusty Hercules, his boyhood 3-speed cycle, still at home in the garage, had once transported him to the very centre of things: to the great anvil rock where, overlooking the magic pool deep in the moors, he had been privy to extraordinary revelations. Yet despite the quick pleasure and immense satisfaction this recollection obviously afforded him, the reader can tell that the tears lay not far away. For at that moment he sensed that the early promise of a life close to the heart of the world, a life capable of taking him on an ever increasing penetration of his own mental complexity, suddenly seemed unlikely to be realised as we rushed frantically towards the inferno that lay ahead.

And although he no doubt turned his eyes vigilantly back to the sky, his mind clearly took refuge in conjuring up Hercules, the rock, and the pool.

> Remember the day you got old Hercules – that Friday afternoon – the day after the tenth birthday? Hadn't been able to sleep for a week waiting. The first and last "grown-up" bicycle you ever had: adult eighteen" frame which meant – because you weren't tall enough – that wooden blocks had to be fitted to the pedals to let your feet make contact. Remember thinking that their presence was unbefitting a true adventurer; so you decided to grow like hell in the next three months in order that the bloody things could be taken off?
>
> That first weekend with Hercules. First true freedom. First sense of your own independent existence – you with yourself going your own absolutely exclusive way. Saturday morning oiling everything – chain, chromium knuckle-joints of the brake rods, hub-bearings . . . everything that moved. Four huge jam sandwiches in the saddlebag and four pennies in the pocket for gingerbeer on the road.
>
> A fine day, a new bike, empty moorland waiting . . . God, a life opened up!
>
> It didn't take long to learn the trick of getting up the long hills. Never anticipate reaching the top – or wonder how long it's taking or bother to look at the scenery. Just stand on the peddles, glue eyes to the road

beneath the front wheel, lean forward over the handlebars and pedal in rhythm to the beat in the ears. Two miles later and there you were – first test passed – Hercules and rider triumphant – fifty miles of empty moor and valley spread out beneath.

"Oh boy . . . " you yelled out, whizzing down the first slope, wind against the eyes, moaning in the ears. Past the huge rocks that looked like Easter Island sculptures catching the first strong sunlight after winter. Presences, real presences – watching Hercules-Guterman heroically violate the taboos of their archaic world. Or so it seemed on that innocent day.

Five short miles to the place where the wall was broken down – a place to be curious about once it was glimpsed during an outing in the old man's new car. No job at all to lift the trusty steed over the gap and hide it among the close-growing young firs.

Strange that you knew which way to go – which sheep trail to choose through the wood of moorland oak – and can still recall the thrill of anticipation in setting off. A quarter of a mile and the track left the trees behind. High craggy cliffs on either side. Another hundred yards and then . . .

"Jee-sus," as Duncan would say . . . the sheer drop to the ravine where the pool lay darkly in its basin of white limestone. Left the mouth dry, and the hairs on the back of the neck standing up for themselves. The black stream sidling in from the north, slithering with silent force when compressed between those enormous mushroom-like boulders, then racing and spreading over the shallow rock shelf to mingle with the deep water of the pool itself.

There were adders down there, sunning themselves on flat stones: lazy snakes – never bothered to move when they were pelted with pebbles.

Frightened and fascinated: you knew this was no ordinary river pool. You'd have to be a geologist to account for its dramatic appearance – the rock walls standing thirty feet above the surface of the water and widening like the belly of a great bottle to give the impression of a water-filled oval amphitheatre, seventy yards across and one hundred yards long. And a brooding age-old stillness everywhere, holding one thousand ghostly resonances. Definitely not a pool. A lake or mere. Waiting. For you as it turned out.

Standing high over the water on the right-hand side was a huge rock. It projected from the near vertical cliff in the form of a great anvil. Scared and intimidated; yet you knew you had to scale it. Claim it. But not at once. First you must present yourself and be accepted. So you sat and waited, a kind of an acolyte, until the fear eased, and alliance to the elemental power of the place was gained.

Remember what happened to time: the Rip Van Winkle effect? At some point you set off. There was only one way to get up – from behind where the anvil was connected to the limestone face by a narrow saddle of turf and rock.

Up and over on the belly – that was the only way to do it without looking down. Then you sit upright and shuffle forward on your backside until you're straddling the pointed front, gripping it tightly between the thighs, perched high above the water.

You'd never heard such silence. Oh yes, you can hear silence like that: Nature compressing the vibrations of millions of lonely years.

So there you were, all of ten years and two days old, perched precariously between land, water and sky – sniffing the cosmos, you might say, on that turret of a rock.

Then – the following weekend – you took formal possession of the rock-throne, and thereby of the lake, by burying that old and much prized wooden pencil-box beneath the great anvil stone. After Hercules it was the most important thing you owned, with three secret compartments opened by pressing hidden springs. In each was a talisman to work its sympathetic magic with the naiad of the lake. You went in the top section – just your head cut from one of those scroll-like school photographs; in the second space lay the skeleton of that small frog you'd tried to keep alive in a shoe box after your father had partly run it over in the driveway; and in the lower and most inaccessible part lay the *pièce de résistance* – funny to think about it now – the great fertility offering . . . the rubber contraceptive filched from the old man's dressing-table drawer and laid out to its full six magnificent ritual inches. Slightly used.

Always that odd lighting effect on the lake, remember?

It only got direct sunlight for a couple of hours in the middle of the day. The rest of the time the white cliffs absorbed all the light from the sky, reflecting a pale lunar-like gleam over things in the ravine, making a constantly changing pattern of shadows. Very black water. Always.

The weekend of the pencil-box ritual: you sat astride the anvil and knew that for countless years the rock and lake had been waiting patiently for you to come. It was then that you decided to exercise great magic and command the Spirit of the Mere. What a nerve! That half-whisper, half-shout, down to the water: 'I am here, the great magician Guterman, in the name of Merlin and all Angels . . . '

Then she came – streaming green lake-grass hair, rushing upwards in an arrow of white foam, blue-green breasts just breaking the surface, then turned at breakneck speed and was gone – a flash of marble perfection plunging to the depths, the same Lady of the Lake who delivered the great sword Excalibur to Arthur. What a face! Just a split-second glimpse but . . . eyes closed as if in a trance, flared nose and wide mouth, sharp-edged, geometrically precise. And gleaming.

Phosphorescent.

But why on earth did you have to lug that huge stone onto the anvil and heave it into the water? Bloody silly thing to do. One heck of a boom from the lake. Deep, deep water. And then that blast of cold mist that suddenly enveloped the anvil. Freezing. Dangerous. Good job you swore a solemn oath never to violate the Underworld like that again.

You warmed up immediately.

Great feeling of contentment after that – lying stretched out, sucking an aniseed ball – you couldn't think of anywhere you'd ever rather be. A real sense of being in on something mysterious. Important for a disciple of Merlin.

There were days straddling that rock when you weren't sure who was who or which was which. The minute you got over the saddle and were ensconced on that spur of a throne, came the ritual lines:

I sit on You
But is that true
Is it not I
Sat on by You?

Always the sense of dual identity there: the meeting of two selves; two worlds. You could never tell anybody about the arrival of the old man. Altogether too private. Think about him when you're perched on the back of old Titty B-O heading for that trap of a city, Berlin. You'll be able to see him as clear as day.

It was a heck of a shock when the old man turned up. He only came once – that last Saturday of the summer holidays. Hercules was six months old. And school was due to start on the Monday. Harry Snipe had been away all summer – you were looking forward to seeing him again at the beginning of the week.

Lying flaked out on the anvil – remember how hot that summer was? – when, out of the blue . . .

"So tha's coom agayen, lad!"

It scared the hell out of you: you sat up like a jack-in-the-box. He was sitting on that patch of level grass, just above and to the right. Some old shepherd, you thought, with his heavy Yorkshire accent, wandered over from off the moors. Except for that unusual leather smock with its whorl design of inlaid metal – not like anything local farmers ever wore. Oval-thin and deep-lined leathery face; strong nose and tall forehead; close-cropped, steel-wool hair. But once you caught his eye the other details were forgotten. However old the rest of him, the eyes were brilliantly alive: bright, electric blue, shoving out volts of energy. Impossible to turn away.

"So tha's on thi new machine agayen then?" And before any chance of a reply, "Well, I wonder what th'old Saxons'll think o' it." No chance to get your wits together and ask him what the heck the Saxons had to do with it.

"Tha knows where tha's put thi machine, lad – reet there in th'open space between the wall and trees? Well yon was t'Saxon burial ground for these parts. Aye, and a few Danes found themselves laid up in there too. There was a fair skirmish up on t'moors here one night. Some stragglers from Guthrun's new army comin' through from t'coast. Cut down to a man they were. Uthric – he was t'local Saxon chief and a Christian – gave 'em decent burial. Consecrated ground, it was. But when t'Norman barons moved up this way and built t'new abbey church in t'valley they consecrated another spot and this 'ere was abandoned. In fact, they dug up a few o' th'old chiefs and reburied 'em in th'abbey grounds over yonder. Caused a lot o' trouble around 'ere, that did, I can tell thee. We was allus uneasy with William o' Normandy's lot."

Now that bit of information was an eye-opener. Bit of a shaker. You thought you knew every old church and monastery round about – and the nearest abbey ruin was Rievaulx, fifteen miles to the west.

"Tha wouldn'a know it, lad" – without you yourself saying a word – "there's noan a trace of it left. T'were abandoned after t'Black Death – no monks left by 1350 –

and t'stones were all taken by farmers for walling-in when t'sheep came later." Now that was the first time his eyes let you go: when he looked out down the ravine towards the distant heather-clad slopes.

"Aye," he continued reflectively, "there's no shortage of spirits abroad on these moors, lad." Silence then. Neither of you spoke. Then you asked him if the mere had been there in Saxon times.

"Aye . . . reet from t'beginning. It's allus been 'ere. And this stone – where tha's sitting now – was t'old Druid altar for these parts. Long before t'Romans came all trees atop this valley were oaks; went deep in t'forest in those days. Aye: this lake was lost in t'middle of a reet grand oak forest. That's why t'Druid priests made it a sacred spot." That was when he suddenly seemed scary – just for a moment or so. He turned, holding you again with those sparking hypnotic eyes, a crinkly grin all over his face, and chuckled a dry, raspy, penetrating sound.

"Eee . . . I don't know if they'd like the idea o' thee sitting up there on their altar, lad." He waited – remember? – grinning at the look on your face. Then, "But don't worry – 'appen they'd rather have thee 'ere than anyone else. Reet where tha's perched now was where they offered t'Rite o' Transmigration o' Souls. Every winter solstice it was. Still t'custom when t'Romans came and put a stop to it. Under Trebonius, they were: about ten thousand o' em. Toughest lot they ever brought north. But they didn't like this place. Camped over yonder, just where those young firs are atop the cliff. Used to get all their water downstream. Never came down 'ere. Said the lake's haunted, and 'appen it is. It's a strange one alright, this 'un. After a big rain it heaves and sounds off alarming like.

They've never found bottom. Tha can go down for miles in this limestone, tha knows. Well, it was Trebonius' legionnaires who built t'road back there – tha knows it – runs straight as a die across moors, reet up north – although it's nobbut a track now."

There was a sadness in his voice – a quality you'd not detected before. Then he looked away, head turned upwards and to one side, very still, seemingly carved like the rock itself, as if to catch the sound of something. And a mist came from the water – a noon-heat sort of vapour, reaching almost to the point of the anvil. You remember thinking you were midway between two worlds: Hades lapping our feet, the blue sky of Orpheus above our heads? It took a few moments to adjust one's ear to the sound: air murmuring to itself, music yet not music, no tonality nor cadence, simply a monotone humming that appealed as music appeals. It had a strange soporific effect, wrapping you up in cotton wool and floating you straight off the rock. You had to hold on tight: the graze marks on your thighs were red for days.

"Come on, enough's enough . . . " – or something like that – you yelled out to the water, and turned to look at the old man. It was with a huge sense of disappointment that you saw he'd gone – gone without even saying goodbye.

The strangest thing about the whole business – and no less so at this point, years later – was the sudden awareness that the air was clear as a bell, no trace of mist. But more . . . the cool of evening had set in. In fact you were shivering, thin summer shirt inadequate now that the sun was not somewhere overhead – where it should have been – but low on the horizon over the moors.

Eight o'clock by the wristwatch. You just made the road with Hercules before it got dark in the wood. In the house by nine-thirty.

Half a life ago. The stuff of which dreams are made of? Of course. But real stuff, real dreams. And has anything changed, Guters? What is there particularly real about being in a bomber, every other night, a few hundred feet off the ground, heading for a firestorm?"

I made the next change in course, banking Titty B-O sharply to port. The ground tilted dizzyingly, forcing eyes back on the search. A flat land of fields and hedges beneath, and a minute later, two rivers running almost parallel, a mile or so apart – the Aller and the Leine. We had turned on a more north-easterly bearing, gained a little altitude, giving Hanover and its airfields a wide berth. Our height according to the altimeter was around twelve hundred feet. Still low enough to be considered hedge-hopping, particularly as we were approaching the higher ground of Luneburg Heath.

Guterman reported he was bringing the turret back dead-centre after checking on our flame-happy engine. Flying fast at this relatively low height he'd see the twin rudders and elevators twitching like victims of a nervous tic as I constantly corrected to maintain direction and height. Not much room for error in such restricted airspace. And riding the thrashing tail it was the rear-gunner who took the worst of it. In comparison to the rear-turret, the mid-upper was relatively stable; Guters had often said he could never have functioned like Smithy in that last turret-segment of the fuselage, hanging out over space, seeing nothing of the aeroplane that supported him; sealed off by the armour plated dopes at his back. It was a most God-awful position to ride. (Guterman had tried it one afternoon on a cross-country test flight and been sick as a dog.) Also a terrible sense of isolation. Stuck there absolutely alone – the first target of fighters coming in from behind; often trapped in emergencies, unable to open the doors and get back in the fuselage to grab a parachute and bail out. And one of the most responsible jobs in the aircraft.

The rear-turret possessed the strongest defensive armament of the aeroplane: four Browning machine-guns as opposed to the mid-upper's two. But in addition to the skill and nerve required to shoot coolly at fast moving attackers, every pilot depended on the rear-gunner for accurate and unimpassioned information about the position of incoming fighters and instructions as how to evade them. Also, "Tail-end Charlie" as the gunner was sometimes called, had to report on the accuracy of flak bursts, as well as provide navigational assistance by keeping his guns trained on a flare-float in order to calculate drift.

Sergeant Guterman said he always offered up a little prayer for Sergeant Smith riding the rear end – bloody thankful that he himself wasn't out there. Noakes, our navigator, confirmed that the small town way over to the left was Schneverdingen; the heavy anti-aircraft barrage to the north coming up from Hamburg.

I decided to go up a few hundred feet – play safe with higher ground now beneath us. And tell the gunners what was going on, what to expect.

"Guters, Smithy . . . Tubby: going up to two thousand over the Heath. Visibility doesn't look good ahead: variable low cloud. So we'll leave ourselves a little more room. When we cross the Elbe we'll turn sou' sou' east towards Oranienburg. Go round it on the west side and start climbing to bombing height. Due south, then come in to the target from the west. Avoid as much of the city as possible. Don't forget – we're the late arrivals tonight. But be ready for the solitary fighter who's looking around for people like us out of the mainstream.

I watched the countryside retreat, roads unravelling between the doll-like houses as if pulled from a bobbing ball of string. At two thousand feet the land was almost gone as we entered the lower reaches of dark nimbus moisture that swept around the aeroplane like stretched-thin strands of cotton wool.

A soft rain streaked the canopy. "Ah, woombat stuff at last," I imagined Dick muttering to himself happily. "A watery womb – that liquid floating which no dictionary mentions. The universe reduced to an aerodonetic capsule inhabited by me, Guterman, captive to a transparent orb, the perfect breast. Take a letter:

> To Hieronymus Bosch: c/o The Garden of Delights, The Prado, Madrid.
>
> Dear Hieronymus:
>
> You were absolutely right. Up the Orb!"

Just his style.

I came through on the intercom again: "Don't know how long this'll last. It's good for us – we still have just enough visual with the ground and we're pretty well protected from above. Let's hope it stays this way and doesn't clamp down as a real 'pea-souper'."

But just the opposite was the case. Over the Elbe the drizzle faded out and the last flimsy wisps of pale cloud caressed the cockpit canopy as they emerged into a sky silvered with stars and pale moonlight. A mosaic of water-globules fell slowly down the windscreen, glistening and sparkling like tiny jewels. The atmosphere now clear as a bell – limitless space – not the same sky which only a few moments before had wrapped us comfortably in a blanket of moist security. It seemed to me that even the racket of the four whirring propellors intensified once they were released from the muffling damp.

It was well that the meteorological forecast of continuous light cloud at ten or twelve thousand feet en route to the target was a miscalculation. There were some large patches of cumulus just above us around six and seven thousand feet, but no continuous cover at higher altitudes. And only one hundred and sixty miles to Berlin – between forty and forty-five minutes' flying time.

Clusters of searchlight beams were probing the sky around Hamburg, and new shell bursts from the Wolfsburg batteries to the south-east were lighting things up at the unusually low height of about six thousand. I throttled the engines back a rev or so now that we were at altitude, once more flying straight and level.

It was on a routine swing of the turret that Guterman reported he'd spotted the distinctive silhouette of another Lancaster off to our left, and above us, flying into the scattered cumulus. Caught briefly in a gleam of cloud-reflected moonlight, it suddenly became the focus of a growing concentration of smoke puffs emanating from the Wolfsburg area. Shell bursts were just a bit too close for our own comfort – though it was unlikely that the ground-gunners could adjust trajectory quickly enough to catch Titty B-O at such a surprisingly low altitude. As usual, the close proximity of the ground provided a certain sense of security from anti-aircraft fire. In this business there were only two laws of survival – either fly very high or very low: the in-between stuff was for the birds, actually and metaphorically.

So what the hell possessed the crew of the other Lanc to be going through the defences at seven thousand?

Sergeant Guterman twisted in his turret and looked again to the ten o'clock position in the sky where the other plane had appeared. He said there was no sign of it. I was just about to turn away and breathe a heavy sigh of relief when it happened.

The other solitary plane was higher in the sky, but the searchlight had her – first the cluster of white probes, marking, holding; then the blue master-beam pinning her like some giant butterfly, turning, twisting, plunging. There was no escape. It was over very quickly. Not much more than ten seconds after the blue beam's grip. As near as damn it a direct hit.

The Lancaster fell: a flaming orange ball trailing a plume of dense black smoke. Automatically we began to count – one, two, three, four . . . waiting for a flowering of white parachutes that never came. And lived the terror of the blazing tumble all the way down to the moment the doomed aircraft hit the ground in a shearing sheet of flame and exploding bomb-load. A numbing sorrow – a bleak, lead-weight paralysing sorrow; tears of compassion barely surpressed. The sudden and violent obliteration of seven lives induced a great despair. One minute they were there – loving, fearing, laughing, hoping . . . hoping to get through to at least one more weekend, as did we ourselves – the next not much chance of putting together one fingernail from the lot of them. What a hideous waste; an outrage against body and spirit.

Weariness and pain pulled me down over the control column. I wanted to close my eyes and sleep. See and feel nothing more.

At that moment a shell burst in the sky behind and above us and rocked the aircraft violently; the tail dropped sickeningly in a freak down-draught, pulling for a stall. Sergeant Smith reported in to say that the glare was blinding – but deceptively so as the explosion was several hundred yards behind us; obviously one more accidental round from some gun-barrel below incorrectly elevated – and one that ordinarily would have been totally wasted; yet as we happened to be there, flying our planned low-level route, it could have resulted in a fluke hit. We'd never run into aberrant fire like this before.

My response was to apply power, bring the nose safely down and drop a few hundred feet in a shallow dive. Smithy's voice in the earphones advised that the ground was quiet – nothing more was coming at us; we were definitely on target.

The sudden demand for power had again upset the equilibrium of the starboard-inner engine. Flame spilled freely from the exhausts. Guterman yelled a warning into the intercom. Ellis and I responded immediately. Cut back the throttle. Re-synchronised. A few anxious moments before the tongues of fire reluctantly retreated. There was turbulent air at this level. Dick was going to need more chewing-gum. I pulled the stick back and climbed as gently as possible to recover lost height. Air temperature in the aeroplane had fallen. Wished I could get up and stamp around a bit; instead I slapped my thighs, hunched and "de-hunched" the shoulders in an attempt to improve circulation and warm up.

The outside air was now taking on the brittle clarity of a freeze. Already contrails were forming, condensed streams of water vapour tracking out behind into the far distance. Very visible. Perfect "lead-in's" for enemy fighters. And minute particles of ice now glistened over the upper surfaces of the aircraft. "Damn," I heard Guterman say, "icing at this height? What the heck's it going to be like higher up over the target?"

Icing up: a pilot's nightmare. Ice on the leading-edge of the mainplane, or over any of the control surfaces, creates terrible handling problems. The Lancaster was wired to transmit de-icing heat along the whole front length of the wing: but the system was unreliable and often incapable of dealing with prolonged and severe spells of cold. Perhaps, I thought, that was why the other Lancaster stayed lower down – yet not low enough – because its de-icing equipment was not working at higher altitudes. The Met man at briefing had made no mention of freezing conditions. Which could indicate that the unexpectedly severe atmospheric condition was relatively local. But how could the others have known that . . .

I concentrated my attention on the instrument panel; told the gunners to keep their turrets turning. There was nothing out there. But in my mind's eye I still saw them falling, heard the awful babble of trapped voices, incoherent, swamped with fear. The cockpit was becoming colder. I was finding it difficult to control the shivering, inside or out. It reached every extremity. I worked on the eye exercises again but found concentration difficult.

A passage from Guterman's Journal comes to mind:

> "To gain relief from the infinity of space it's necessary from time to time to drop your head and peer into the confined and relatively secure limits of the fuselage. There, beneath you, are the ammunition belts feeding the rear turret undulating soundlessly on their elevated runways – long, shiny snakes made up of hundreds of shimmering 303-type vertebrae-rounds.
>
> Always absolutely deserted in there – yet strangely domesticated by the suspended clock and toothbrush. The clock-face still showing the same time. Makes you wonder if something drastic has happened. Suppose they'd all baled out and it was my destiny to fly on alone, *ex gravitas*, the Flying Dutchman of the skies. Or perhaps nose-and-tail sections had separated, shed their occupants, then joined up again like parts of a night worm, leaving me alone in the mid-upper orb to carry out the most important mission of all – the solitary Leander night-swim, the ultimate quest to discover if there are any shores beyond – in the dark, as every good Woombat knows, facing those after-midnight sea-frets which attempt to swamp the spirit, as well as drown the body."

It was at this stage of the flight that Guterman's trouble with the turret started. I will do my best to describe what it must have been like for him as he found himself squeezing the master-grips with a strength born of desperation. Nothing happened for several seconds, then the turret moved jerkily a few inches one way or the other before stopping completely, dead as a doornail. He no doubt followed standard procedure and waited a few moments for hydraulic pressure to build. There would be enough moonlight reflecting from the front astrodome to allow him to check out the pipelines for signs of leaks. Meanwhile, Sergeant Smith was reporting a clear sky at the rear. Must have relieved Guters to see the rear-turret turning, know that Smithy was fully operational – that at least four of the six machine guns protecting our tail would give a good account of themselves.

For the first time on any night operation, I didn't feel to be in charge of things. My mind was easily side-tracked – images of Matthews, Chalky White, Dent . . . and other lost faces intruding. Told myself I must stop trying to imagine what it must have been like in the stricken aeroplane – only four hundred feet up. At least five or six seconds of full consciousness if not killed outright by the tracers. Dent's voice going round and round in my head . . . "Not important: you don't look at the mantelpiece when you're poking the fire." I would miss Dent. But Dent was reduced to any number of very small pieces. With the rest of L7513's crew.

Guters, desperately squeezing the master-grips to return the turret-dead amidships, was having no luck. No movement. The damned thing was stuck, facing sideways, about twenty degrees left. Lay off the grips, he would tell himself. Give pressure time to build. Maybe it's an airlock in the system that'll dissipate if you're patient. He would have waited a couple of minutes. Squeezed again. The turret remained immobile. More time, he'd argue. He knew that some of these jams are temporary. Try the grips separately – first the right, then the left. No good: the turret failed to budge. Last resort: a series of short, violent, jabbing squeezes on the grips. No go. And then there'd come the sickly odour of hydraulic fluid, edging the teeth, queasing already liquid guts. Despite the turret cold, sweat would be damp beneath his eyes, pricking as garlic will after a highly spiced dish. He'd release the grips and bend low to search the copper pipelines entering the turret from the fuselage. He'd find, running shamelessly, a line clearly fractured somewhere.

When he pulled up to report to me, the Junkers 88 was there: flying a parallel course about half a mile away with a couple of thousand feet more altitude. The odd assortment of aerials sprouting from its nose was clearly visible. I could imagine his anger – anger and frustration together. He knew how effective these planes were – how they could vector in from two miles and close accurately to within two hundred yards; whatever the weather. Also, the newer Junkers had cannon, rendering our own fire-power – simple .303 bullets - ineffective if not futile. Yet we did have a chance with six machine-guns firing together – he and Smithy working in unison could put up a hell of an offensive stream of lead.

But what was the German up to, flying so passively along up there? He must have seen us. At that distance Titty B-O was as visible as a double-decker bus. Guters would be pressing the grips instinctively to line the enemy fighter up. A useless reflex now. "Christ all bloody mighty . . . " I heard him swear quietly – "just my lousy luck." Without turret mobility he could hardly hope to follow a moving target through the gun-sights. He called up to report; at the same time Sergeant Smith came in to say he'd spotted the Junkers.

"No chance with the turret, Guters?"

"Fractured pipeline, skipper. Oil everywhere. I can work the guns up and down in this one vertical position, but haven't got any lateral arc of fire."

Smith broke in before I could respond, suggesting that we slide off gently on the port side – slip out of radar range in case we'd not yet been seen . . . lose a few hundred feet to where it would be difficult for the fighter to get beneath, or sit in slipstream. The sky slid past as the starboard wing rose and we fell slowly down and away.

The fighter was no longer in parallel flight when we levelled out at eight hundred feet. He had climbed to about three thousand and was directly behind us, high above our tail. All Dick Guterman could do was to elevate the Brownings to maximum height in order to follow him down with fire if he came in to attack at the right angle – one that brought him within the narrow vertical slit of sky the mid-upper's guns still controlled.

After a minute or so Guters reported there was no change in the fighter's position. It might be that the German hadn't seen them after all. But I was going to take no chances. Decided to shave off a few more feet of altitude and risk the poorer visibility at the mistier levels nearer the ground. Immediately Guters came on to say that the shape of the Junkers was changing. The antennae plastered all over the nose had lost their semi-profile definition and merged into a new, foreshortened configuration.

"Sir . . . he's seen us. Coming down behind – one o'clock – head on – at about twenty-five hundred feet."

"Right, Guters. If he veers anywhere near your jammed side just fire the guns off to show you're functional. Smithy, you fire in that vertical, see-saw pattern you talked about . . . before he gets in range. His position seems dead right for it. Might discourage the so-and-so if he's not too experienced."

Smithy told me later that the 88 was coming in at a steep angle – the slimmest target for the rear-gunner. But the speed of his dive caused him to yaw badly as he kept correcting to keep us in his sights. I reckoned we had about five hundred feet of vertical airspace to play with in terms of taking evasive action. Steep bank to port, full left rudder, fall sideways for three hundred feet, wrestle aileron controls to starboard, a climbing torn to the right, opposite aileron and diving again . . . The much faster fighter had to constantly throttle back and adjust his speed as he tried to follow our manoeuvres. I lost him for a minute, but then the German got the hang of it and tucked himself in behind, high enough to avoid the turbulence of our slipstream, and just too far out for the guns of the rear-turret to be effective. He began to follow the Lanc's manoeuvres – quick learner. Getting the timing just right.

Dick's rage and chagrin must have been impossible to contain – especially if at any point the enemy moved briefly into the narrow vertical path open to fire from the mid-upper's guns. He vented his feelings by following my instructions and releasing bursts of fire, even though the Junkers was keeping a safe distance. He could at least warn the Jerry off. Sergeant Smith in the rear-turret was holding his position dead-centre, all four gun-barrels – twice the mid-upper's fire power – moving slowly up and down to the limit of their vertical elevation. As yet Smithy had not fired: he was waiting for the moment when the German might misjudge the distance a fraction, come a little too close, and give the rear-turret's four Brownings a chance to score a hit as well as send out a warning.

We flew through the first flimsy streaks of ground-locked vapour, but it offered little cover. Easily dissipated by the propellers it was puffed away like flimsy kettle steam.

I decided enough was enough – threw the four engine controls wide open, at the same time skewing the aircraft into tight starboard turn. Flames from the starboard-inner shot into the slipstream, and the ground – very close at this point – came up with a rush. Without throttling back I held Titty B-O in the tightest possible turn, completed a full circle, and flattened out at about one hundred feet. The suddenness of the movement shook everybody up before they realised what I was up to – the nature of the chance I was taking. For seeing us lose altitude, with one engine apparently on fire, the German pilot may well think Titty B-O was finished, and break off the engagement – hang around to observe a conflagration that would not occur, and realise too late that he had lost his chance.

Back on course and streaking a bare hundred feet above the land, I eased the revs on the starboard-inner engine. For what must have seemed to Guters the umpteenth time that night the flames shrank back into the exhaust ports. He looked out beyond the tail and reported that the upper sky was empty. No sign of the enemy fighter. The abrupt explosive hammerings of the four rear Brownings, clamouring through the steady beat of the engines, would have taken him completely by surprise. Their vibrations passed up and through the mid-upper, and along the whole fuselage.

"Damn, damn, damn . . . " over and over the words came cross the intercom, through clenched teeth, as Guters saw what the rear-gunner saw, knowing there was no way he could move his turret mechanically, hoping for some miracle of sheer will-power. And then the racket of the machine-guns in the tail was overwhelmed by the heavy, air-displacing thumps of exploding cannon shells: a sullen series of single, growling detonations that rocked the air.

The Junkers was coming at us from where it was not supposed to be, from where, theoretically, it couldn't be – from ground level – boring in at ninety degrees on the port side – avoiding the slipstream of our four Merlins. There was nothing Dick Guterman could do to help. His guns faced starboard. Could not be brought to bear on the enemy.

It must all have been very sudden. The flash of the shell-burst searing the eyes, flaring in behind them, hot to the bone. Light swelling and glowing. Air everywhere expanded. A fraction of a second later, high between the ribs, a crushing incandescent pressure obliterating all sensation.

Chapter Four
After the Attack

I had to frantically work the trim-wheel to keep the nose down and counteract an unbalancing drag at the tail-end while Ellis checked engine and fuel-tank gauges for tell-tale signs of damage to these vital areas. From the cockpit window the flight-engineer could see no visible sign of mechanical trouble resulting from the attack, no spewing oil or fire, no holes riddling the mainplane. Nothing seemed to be missing. For Titty B-O had juddered and hesitated alarmingly before lurching erratically forward again as the cannon-shells from the Junkers were exploding. We had obviously been hit. And had no airspace to play with: the ground was uncomfortably close – certainly no more than a couple of hundred feet beneath us.

Yet all control surfaces were responding. Apart from the maverick starboard-inner, engines were performing normally. But she was handling sluggishly – like a waterlogged boat that was slow to answer the helm – tail-heavy, dragging in the sky.

"Tubby" – to Entwhistle, the wireless operator, who occupied the front turret when we were over enemy territory – "better get back down the fuselage and see what the damage is. It feels to be somewhere aft of the centre-section. Smith . . . how are things down there? Where's the Junkers gone?" The rear-gunner's voice came through distinctly. "Well, he missed me, Sir. But he hit something. I felt the whack alright. It's a bumpy ride at the moment. I got him in one engine just as he began to shoot. Most of his shells went beneath us. His port engine caught fire and he dropped away quickly, heading west, about one hundred feet up,

I'd say. He was firing cannon, skipper. Bloody menace, that stuff. Where did he hit us?"

"I don't know, but she's dragging a lot at your end. I'm trying to compensate with trim. Tubby's checking. Good job, Smithy. That spray technique of yours is difficult to avoid. He took a chance coming up from ground level like that. But Guters' turret's stuck. Can't get him to respond on the intercom. Your hydraulics O.K?"

"Yes: turret's working perfectly, but there's a hell of a draught back here coming from somewhere."

"Sir . . . " Sergeant Entwhistle's voice broke in.

"Yes, Tubby; what's it look like?"

The wireless operator's voice was strained and taut. "It's a mess, Sir – a real mess. There's a big hole about three feet across in the fuselage, top and bottom. The shell seems to have come in low down on the fuselage side just about at floor level – and been deflected upwards to come out at the top. It hit just behind the mid-upper – hell of a steep angle. It . . . it's blown most of the turret out."

For a moment I could not respond. Then came the question: "What about Guterman?" A long pause before the wireless-operator replied. "He's caught in there, Johnny. Stringers and fuselage-skin are all jammed together. You can't even see inside. I'll need a light. There's no way to get at him from down here. And there's so much bloody wind noise there's no way he can hear me shout."

"Right, Tubby" – I suppose my voice sounded unnaturally business-like – "stay with him. Ellis is coming down to take a look. Hang on tight round that hole . . . I'm going to see if we can get some climb out of the old kite. She's got the power; elevators are good. We'll decide what to do after Ellis' report."

Flight Lieutenant Ellis left the cockpit, collected the emergency torch from its clip, and headed off down the fuselage. An ex-sergeant mechanic – both airframe and engine – there was little about the Lancaster he didn't know. When he dropped down from the mainspar and saw the damage I heard his involuntary whistle as he plugged in his intercom. Then, "Bloody hell," softly, as he played the torch beam on the remains of the turret and around the holes top and bottom of the fuselage. He described how the eccentric deflection of the cannon shell after it pierced the floor of the fuselage had most likely prevented it from exploding in or near the bomb-bay; and also caused it to miss the push-pull rudder and elevator control rods which ran low down along the fuselage sides. Yet it was that very same angle of deflection which had resulted in so much damage to the mid-upper.

The turret was mangled. Ellis told me later how he dropped to his knees, crawled round the cavity in the floor and, looking upwards, directed the torch into the tangle of metal. Gradually his eyes began to separate the bits and pieces. Sergeant Guterman had been blown up and back: one shoulder was jammed tightly against the butt of a displaced gun which tilted him to the right like a horseman caught by an opponent's lance; while the other Browning had been blown from its mounting and pierced the thick flying-jacket in the vicinity of the ribs on the left side. Between the two of them he was gripped like an unresisting rag doll. From the waist down nothing could be seen: large jagged pieces of Alclad fuselage-skin and twisted girder-like stringers, festooned with broken angle-brackets and bits of the turret's frame, blocked the space. Twisting awkwardly to try and position the beam directly on the air-gunner's face, Ellis saw that nothing was left of the transparent turret-dome. Only the rear fairing remained to provide some protection from the slipstream, and to support Guterman's head which was thrust hard back against it. To all intents and purposes the turret, and about nine square feet of the surrounding fuselage, had become a gaping hole through which the flight-engineer could see the sky.

Only after a struggle to position the heavy flashlight in the wreckage where it could shine directly up to Dick Guterman, was

Ellis able to fully perceive the bizarre effect created by the turret's disintegration. In the force of the explosion one gleaming piece of duraluminium had been pushed upwards to curve, like the visor of a knight's helmet, around his colleague's forehead and over his eyes. It gleamed like armour in the light of the torch. In stark contrast the exposed left cheek below it was burned black. The rest of the face seemed to be untouched – save that a thin trickle of blood, running from the left corner of the mouth, had congealed and gave the appearance of an ugly gash. But at least the bleeding had stopped. At one point Ellis thought he saw a slight flutter of respiration in the front of the throat, but he could not be sure, and increasing turbulence as Titty B-O climbed convinced him he should get back to the cockpit.

He finally extricated himself from the tangle of metal into which he had pushed further than he realised, scrambled back up the fuselage and stood alongside the restbed, thinking hard.

"Shall I get the fire-axe and first-aid box?" I heard Tubby Entwhistle shout over the increased racket of engines and wind in the fuselage.

"No: we can't get him out of that lot. We'd do more harm than good. Better get forward. The skipper'll want you in the front-turret from now on, I'd think. I'll tell him what the situation is."

Entwhistle apparently took the flashlight from Ellis' hand. "Right: you go on up. I'll follow in a minute. Something to do first." Ellis saw him snake his way back to what remained of the mid-upper and, straddling the hole in the floor, crouch to illuminate the base of the turret. Two large pieces of twisted duraluminium obstructed physical entry. Jamming the torch between two deformed lengths of the turret's skeletal frame, he exerted as much pressure as he could muster against the larger of the duraluminium pieces until it was finally bent backwards about forty-five degrees. There was no wreckage immediately behind to block entry. He employed the same tactics against the second sheet, but this was tightly caught and yielded only a few inches. Nevertheless, he was able to force a gap large enough to take a shoulder and an arm.

When he brought the torch to bear he told me he could see Dick Guterman's right arm dangling loosely between two broken stringers.

Fighting the rush of night air invading the aircraft, and leaning backwards and upwards while holding on to what remained of the turret rim with his left hand, must have been a difficult position to maintain, but he managed to get one arm into the space, force the thick leather of his flying-jacket between the sharp-edged pieces of metal to penetrate what Duncan had jokingly once called "the womby wombat's wank-pit."

Sergeant Entwhistle later said he felt it was vital to try and communicate in some way with Guters – let him know that someone was there. Slowly, unable to see how far he'd reached, he explored the space as extensively as limited arm movement would allow. When he found Dick's right hand he held on as long as he could, squeezing gently, until cramp compelled him to withdraw.

On his return to the wireless-table he plugged in the intercom and told me that as he took the air-gunner's hand he felt Guters respond with a faint grip of his own.

We were slowly pulling up to four thousand feet. Low cloud obscuring ground visibility. Heavy anti-aircraft fire high in the sky directly ahead at a distance of fifteen to twenty miles.

"Noakes . . . " – I called to the navigator – "we've been flying pretty well sou' sou' east, averaging about two hundred knots, even allowing for all that evasive screwing around back there . . . and the cannon-shell damage. So that should be Oranienburg ahead – where the flak's coming from. Yes?"

"No, I don't think so, Sir. We've dropped down further south than that according to my reckoning and a minute ago when I was spotting in the astrodome, we ran out of this wispy stuff for a couple of seconds and I saw Brandenburg off on the right with that skinny, U-shaped lake at the end of it, so those must be the Potsdam batteries ahead. Can't mistake that lake. Got to be Potsdam. How are things in the rear? I heard Tubby when he plugged in on the intercom. Guters: is he . . . "

"Just a sec . . . Ellis is back."

The flight-engineer stood in the aisle next to the old co-pilot's seat, reached over and connected to the intercom socket. At twenty-six, the oldest member of the crew, he was also the most reserved: tall, heavily moustached, with regular features; he looked the archetypal Guard's officer. Cool as a cucumber, it usually took six pints of draught bitter to get him going. Now his mouth was drawn a tight line and his shoulders were stooped.

"Well," he started, "it's a damn great hole but I don't think the control rods are touched. The shell's taken a few stringers out around the turret, but luckily passed between the bulkhead formers. It hasn't weakened the airframe so far as I can see. But the hole's very near the centre of lift at the tail – can't tell how the aeroplane'll respond if we run into any trouble and lose power; the Lanc's tail-heavy by nature anyway. Be a matter of trim and stick and what engine resources we have. You may have to watch out for a stall if we lose airspeed. It might help if we got Smithy out of the back to lighten things up."

"No: he's the only eyes and defence we've got back there. What are the chances of getting Guters out? Can we lower him from the turret and get him into the fuselage and onto the restbed?"

"Not a hope. That thing's so mangled it'll take torches to cut through to him. You can't even get up in there to do any lifting. We've just got to get him home."

"I don't know," Frank Ellis said quietly, "I don't know. He's unconscious and badly hurt. He's got no oxygen so we have to stay around five to six thousand. He's going to suffer from exposure and probably freeze to death. There's not much we can bloody well do."

I found myself playing for time. I fiddled with the trim wheel, adjusting to counter a momentary tail-heaviness. Called up the rear-gunner: "A bumpy ride back there, Smithy?"

"A bit choppy. But it's bloody cold. And there's a hell of a lot of ack-ack starting up behind us – around Brandenburg – a real barrage. Wouldn't like to go back through that lot. We must have disturbed them. They're bringing the range down – detonating around five thousand."

"What's the fuel situation, Frank?"

Ellis scanned the gauges and adjusted the feed from port and starboard wing-tanks. "For some reason – it might be the starboard-inner – we're drawing more from starboard than port. I'll try and equalise it. It's alright, but going to be tight unless we get rid of the bomb-load soon, and can keep a straight course back home."

I made the decision I was to regret all my life. When Noakes had given our true position I'd immediately turned two degrees south in order to skirt the Potsdam guns which were blazing away ahead. Now, with the intensity of that flak behind us, I decided the best way home was via the target. I briefed the crew.

"We're two degrees further south than I thought. The fuselage damage is bad – we have to get rid of the bomb-load and lighten up. When we go round Potsdam in a couple of minutes we're on the way home – shortest way to go north again. We'll be coming over Tempelhof from the south so we might as well jettison the bombs as near the target as we can get – from about five thousand. Once clear we'll drop down again and shoot out north and west. The aeroplane's still very flyable: we're already on the right heading and should be back at low-level in about ten minutes. It's the quickest and surest way to get us and Guters out of here. And we shouldn't have to take any violent evasive action – there won't be much ground defence left as we'll be last into the target area. If we turn round and go back the way we came . . . that's where all the activity is. Behind us. So the southern suburbs of Berlin are probably the safest place to be. It's not possible to get Dick out of the turret: it's pretty well shot up. We've got to lighten the aircraft and get home as soon as possible. I think this is the best way to do it. Stay on the intercom. Turning north on the home leg any minute . . . right, Noakes?"

"Spot on, Sir. One minute. We're just leaving the lake and river behind. Then fourteen miles to Daimler-Benz – say four minutes to the marshalling yards."

Duncan, who had partly emerged from his front perspex observation bubble beneath the rudder-pedals to go to Guterman's assistance, reluctantly scrambled back to lie prone in the bomb-aimer's position and began to check his airspeed indicator and altimeter. It was his job to take us the last few miles to the Tempelhof railway yards at a height that – given our present situation – allowed little room for manoeuvre or error; I understood his fear for Dick Guterman; knew he was thinking to himself it was better to get the job over as soon as possible for old Guters' sake – get the target in sight first time, make one perfect run and get to hell out of it, bombs gone. For a moment I wondered why not drop the bombs now – anywhere, on anything: lighten the aircraft up immediately and to hell with Tempelhof. Seemed just common bloody sense. What the heck did I want – another bloody medal?

Ellis was back in his seat pouring over the gauges. Noakes was at his little table behind my seat plotting positions and setting the shortest course home, working with bearings supplied by Entwhistle. I told the wireless-operator to cut out "Gee", the radar-grid reference device: it was too helpful to enemy night-fighters, sending signals which enabled them to "home in" on us with great accuracy. Indicated ground speed over the southern approaches to our target was one hundred and ninety miles per hour. On the ground, surprised gun crews hurriedly lowered their sights – the great majority of attacking bombers were coming in high from the north – and called for searchlights to rake at lower altitudes. But by the time they'd adjusted for the range, we were through; the wall of steel which went up in our wake fell fully half a mile short.

In the aircraft there was no time to dwell on our troubles. Every task called for intense concentration. Only Duncan, flat on his belly in his tiny greenhouse, had to face the outside world head on, eyes wide to the easy likelihood of disaster as he searched the way, the map of the southern environs of Tempelhof etched in his mind. While in the rear fuselage the night wailed like a warning siren through the holes.

"Messerschmitts . . . four Messerschmitts straight ahead – three, four miles – our height – climbing for altitude." Flying Officer Duncan spoke softly, in a matter-of-fact tone of voice. Already glare from ground fires was reflecting into the lower sky, creating a dull crimson backdrop against which the fast-moving small planes appeared as black silhouettes.

"Probably reinforcements making for the city to engage the last of the main bomber force," I responded. To Tubby Entwhistle who was now in the front turret – "Keep a sharp eye up front, Tubby. Chances are there'll be enough to keep them occupied higher up. Damn . . . " – as Titty B-O's nose came up sharply and I had to work the elevators hard to level her out. Hopefully she'd be more at ease with the bombs gone. But it would be difficult holding her in the heat updrafts over the target. There was a lot of fire down there. Not even possible to see the target-marker flares. Might be a bonus for Guters: at five thousand feet the air should be quite warm. What a damn crass thing to think.

"Frank" – to the flight-engineer – "call out height and airspeed every thirty seconds until Duncan starts to direct us for the run in. Bomb-doors should be open in a couple of minutes at most."

Flying into an unpleasant, orange-curdled sky – a phenomenon reported by all the aircraft coming late to Berlin that night – for by midnight the city was a sea of flame. Below, an already wide assembly of railway lines was growing steadily more extensive as the mainlines from Nurnberg, Leipzig, and Dresden came together in the Tempelhof suburbs. We were almost there – following the central tracks around the long north-west turn in to where they entered the marshalling yards that served the Daimler-Benz facility. The roofs and chimneys of greater Berlin's southern extremities stretched away on either side – the usual dreary close-packed industrial clutter, but now seen dramatically against a distant backdrop of flame growing steadily more intense as we got nearer to the city itself.

The latest trim-setting was holding us steady, permitting rudder, elevator and aileron function to compensate effectively for the loss of stability in the rear fuselage. It seemed strangely peaceful in the aeroplane for a few seconds – an illusion that we were silently and surrealistically gliding along as in a dream: no engine roar, bursting shells or intruding searchlights. I hoped it would stay that way for Dick Guterman's sake. I'd built up a mental image of the wrecked turret from Ellis' description – a picture that kept intruding, and on which I concentrated, in the irrational hope that by so doing Dick might be subliminally aware that he was not alone in his extremity.

The dream-like spell was quickly shattered. Down on the port side, about half a mile to the west, an unexpected barrage – salvo after salvo that turned the sky at about eight thousand feet above and ahead of us into a heaving morass. Groups of guns were firing in series, erecting barriers of simultaneously detonating shells; any one of these could have knocked us out of the sky on their way up had the gunners not mistakenly assumed that we were seeking height for a bombing run over Berlin itself, and so set their range in anticipation of our ultimate altitude and position. At least this seemed the only likely way to explain the tactics of the German batteries. But the miscalculation, if it was such, presented Titty B-O with three thousand feet of insulating upper airspace to dampen the explosive charge of each round. Even so, the air around us was disturbed sufficiently to create plenty of wing wobble which she handled well, although causing her to roll like a ship caught in a beam-on swell. And then, disaster almost. One particularly violent down-draft thrust the starboard wing down and under. For a moment it seemed the plane would be tossed on its back.

"Christ . . . " as we went over, right-hand lurching for the throttles. But Ellis was ahead of me, ramming all four levers to the gate as I pushed the stick forward to maintain airspeed and effective aileron control. Even-keel again, regained without serious loss of height, and before the wing had dropped much beyond forty degrees from the horizontal. As Titty B-O threatened to slide out of the sky I seemed to catch sight of the mid-upper turret, wide open to the night, Dick Guterman inert and unable to hang on, kept in place only by a biting harness of tangled metal.

No respite from the guns and the turbulent air they created. Quite deliberately I dropped Titty B-O one thousand feet: air somewhat calmer: more space between us and the shell-bursts – more difficult for the ground batteries to bring the range down quickly and effectively.

"Altitude forty-one hundred; groundspeed two hundred and twenty." Ellis' flat voice broke in, difficult to hear even in the headphones because of the roar outside. Again I was reaching for the trim-wheel, leaving me less firmly in charge of the jolting control column than I would have liked. Even at this lower altitude the turbulence of the barrage was as bad as any I could remember – and that without a partially disabled aircraft. And at the back of my mind was the growing conviction that I'd made a serious error of judgement: that I should have ditched the bomb-load immediately after the Junker attack and turned for home as soon as Noakes had identified the lake at Brandenburg. The damage we'd sustained and the unknown fate of Guterman were more than sufficient reason for aborting the mission. I couldn't think what the hell had possessed me to continue. I should have avoided Berlin altogether. I had thought that coming in from the south – with the main bomber stream approaching from the north – would ensure an easy approach; kill two birds with one stone – get rid of the bombs and be on the way home at the same time.

"Stupid, stupid bastard," I whispered to himself.

As I was muttering, the cockpit was lit by a series of excoriating flashes that obliterated all physical features of the flight-deck. We were open to one incandescent sky-world, each man a grotesque shadow floating momentarily in white-hot light, only to be lost in impenetrable darkness, senses suspended, as the flare-up died. The salvo that followed was even closer. The aeroplane lurched, seemed to stop in mid-flight, then drop into a vacuum.

"Sssh . . . " – just a sibilant escape of breath from a voice on the intercom as the Lanc hung painfully, propellers thrashing. Defying laws of normal human reaction time Ellis had all four throttles momentarily through the supercharger gate. The half-second he gained saved our lives. The almost instantaneous boost of emergency power provided the forward acceleration necessary to avert the stall.

"Four thousand feet: one hundred and eighty airspeed indicated." The flight-engineer reeled off altitude and speed as if we were casually going round on practise "circuits and bumps" back at the aerodrome.

How many of us heard Duncan's hissed, "Shyste . . . shyste almighty . . . " as he lay in the forward position, visually open to both sky and ground, I don't know. He alone saw the guns flash down below, then awaited the arrival of the shells, while at the same time having to keep his mind on the job of "reading" the terrain and directing the progress of the bombing run. By now the ground batteries must have concluded that this particular attacker did not intend to climb to normal bombing height, and were lowering their sights to put up an increasingly accurate screen of exploding shells. Shock-waves swept the aircraft. No alternative but to weave left-right, left-right . . . then full power – pray for the starboard-inner – nose slightly down to minimise the stall-inducing drag in the rear. The altimeter needle slowly unwound.

"Thirty-nine hundred feet; airspeed one hundred and eighty . . . " from Ellis.

Duncan told me later that this was when he closed his eyes, and that when he opened them a fraction of a second later he faced a changed landscape. For now the ground below was totally wasted by bombardment – more thoroughly than he'd ever before witnessed. Obviously many bombers of the secondary force had preceded us here and, for once, all found their target. The vast web of railway lines had disappeared in a moonscape of craters. No anti-aircraft guns in this wasteland. Trailing wraiths of smoke floated over the nose and canopy while the cockpit itself glowed red, on and off, as we passed over a series of ground fires which flared skyward with every new explosion – delayed action land mines doing their deadly work. Duncan lay stretched out, eyes pressed to the transparent sighting panel, seeking to identify our precise target area in the devastated no-man's land below. The up-drifting smoke pyres made his task more difficult, obscuring ground details, as he searched his way through the yards.

"Dunc: holding level flight for the run. Smithy . . . I doubt anything down there'll get to us, but keep your eyes open for fighters higher up."

"Righto, skipper – there's a lot of activity around twenty thousand feet: still some of ours over the city – ten miles away, I'd say – but I'll watch to see if any fighters peel off in our direction."

Our rear-gunner's normally phlegmatic voice held a note of elation. Smithy had carried with him an implacable hatred for all things German as long as he could remember – no doubt from the day on which he'd been old enough to comprehend the nature of his father's death on the Somme. And now – on this, the first occasion any of us had seen first-hand the result of such integrated bombing – he must have felt a certain satisfaction at being one of the participants. "About time . . . " I heard him mutter before he went off the air.

"Altitude four thousand . . . Airspeed one hundred and seventy." Ellis read off the new figures; adjusted throttles for better engine synchronisation. This close in the destruction meted out to the marshalling yards really hit home. No doubt now that though Tempelhof was not the principal target, whole squadrons had been involved – and that for once the success rate of finding their way accurately to the designated target was phenomenal. There were no signs of "fringe" bombing due to poor navigation or lack of resolve. Here and there, some distance left and right from the tracks themselves, were buildings with the walls still standing to simply define an empty shell: leading our bomb-aimer to wonder if our particular target would indeed still be standing. It seemed impossible that anything save some great natural disaster could have caused such desolation. Surely nothing on the ground would live through it. Ahead of us, at about ten thousand feet, a lone aircraft of the earlier squadrons released its bombs sending shockwaves through the forward terrain.

Duncan was experiencing real difficulties in sighting: neither clear visibility nor a steady run-in were on his side. Also, as he told me later – speaking his mind directly – thoughts of Dick Guterman were very much on his mind: frustration and anger that Guters was having to suffer this ordeal – abandoned and unprotected – when our prime consideration should have been to get him home with maximum safekeeping.

But then he put the thought out of his mind. He knew well enough that at this point we all depended on him to direct the aircraft safely to the moment of bomb release. A mile or so ahead, where twin tracks left the main Berlin lines, he caught a glimpse of what he was looking for: the clustering of water-towers servicing the Daimler-Benz workshops and storage facilities.

"We're spot on, skipper. Hold . . . hold . . . a touch to the left, good . . . steady at that . . . "

"Altitude four thousand, airspeed one hundred and sixty," intoned Ellis. Duncan surveyed his own altimeter and air speed indicator, checked the ground speed; reviewed our heading on the gyro-compass repeater. "A fraction more left, Skipper . . . steady . . . hold it there."

Suddenly we were caught in a powerful up-draught, and soared like a glider for twenty or thirty feet, then dropped, airscrews whirring uselessly until they gripped the air and carried Titty B-O forward again. I eased the throttles up a notch – stability insurance for when the bomb-doors opened.

"Fuel's going to be tight" – Ellis warned, reading the gauges – "save the power if we can."

Cockpit momentarily wreathed in thin cloud; we rose and fell in dream-like fashion. Even the engines sounded muted, overcome by the gasping and troubled night.

"Open bomb-doors." Peering forward, Duncan estimated the target to lie fifty seconds dead ahead. At that moment, as the belly of our machine became exposed, what must have been a giant petrol-dump went up. A roaring "whoosh" obliterated the sound of the engines and a split-second later a column of displaced air picked up the aeroplane like a ball caught on a waterspout. Ellis pushed throttles forward for power. With both hands on the control-column I fought elevators and ailerons to keep the mainplane horizontal. Miraculously we dropped back on course –

everything as it should be – as if we were on wires. *Mirabile dictu*. The great sheds of Daimler-Benz lay directly ahead. Still intact.

"Level, skipper, level . . . hold, hold. Right a touch . . . little more. Hold her there . . . throttle back a notch. Good. Dead right. Perfect . . . steady . . . steady. . . " His voice drifted into silence for the last tense seconds of the run. Then, squinting through the bomb-sight, his thumb came down on the electric bomb-release button – on "Mickey Mouse", ironically called. As the four thousand pounder and its surrounding cluster of thousand pounder bombs dropped to earth Titty B-O lifted skywards like a giant whale breaching from the weight of the sea.

Slowly the bomb-doors began to close, sealed off the uterine cavity, eliminating the extra drag, and sent us soaring into the night. Always the same when bombs were gone: an incredible sense of weightless relief – a need, felt by both men and machine, to recover the spirit of virgin flight: a cleansing, an exhilaration, expiation: a return to life on equal terms . . . if all that makes any sense.

"Dead on, Johnny. We straddled the lot." Duncan's voice was flat, lacking the Cockney lilt and usual exuberance that followed his announcement, "Bombs gone." But in the rear-turret the usually laconic Sergeant Smith was ecstatic. "We got 'em, Sir . . . Right down the middle. Every shed's going up. Hell of a mess. Won't be any engines or bearings out of there for a while!"

Chapter Five
The Way Home

I pulled Titty B-O round on the homeward west-nor-west heading at four thousand feet. Only then – as if a door into a compartment of the mind had opened – did the full impact of Dick Guterman's fate strike home; only then did the urgency of it take over; dominate every decision and action I was to take. I have never been able to satisfactorily explain my resolve to proceed to Templehof after the Junkers' attack. Or to forget it. Duncan taxed me about it once, years later at a reunion; but dropped the subject when he saw the confusion and difficulty I experienced in responding.

The northern extremities of Berlin lay below us, lost in fire and smoke. Once completely clear of the city it would be due west all the way – save for a slight northerly swing round Hanover to avoid the Luftwaffe presence. That would take us across the narrowest part of the Zuider Zee, over the North Sea towards East Anglia, well positioned to land at Woodbridge in Suffolk – the 'drome set up to receive damaged aircraft like our own. It was the shortest route over land – where most of the dangers lay. Given the fuel situation, the state of the aeroplane and possible fog over eastern England, Lincoln and home base were out. A slight bonus – landing away would save about half an hour's flying. In another couple of minutes we would descend to our customary low altitude both to avoid detection and minimise the possibility of encountering freezing conditions.

Or so I reasoned as I re-trimmed the aircraft – finding new balance settings of stabilisers and tabs now Titty B-O was free of the bomb-load. "Noakes" – on the intercom to the navigator – "keep us some twenty miles north of Brandenburg, Hanover, and Osnabruck – that's crucial. Then out over Holland via the Zuider Zee and Alkmaar. Most direct. Fewer ground defences."

Duncan squeezed his way up into the cockpit and stood alongside Ellis, absently watching the flight-engineer make fuel calculations on his knee-pad. He observed our heading on the gyro-compass; and seemed surprised at our course. He shook his head sharply like a dog dispelling some temporary irritation in order to restore a clear view of the world, then leaned over in front of Ellis. I had to raise my right helmet earphone to hear what he was shouting. "You won't need me for a while – Entwhistle's in the front turret – I'll go and check on things at the back. We've been thrown around a bit. Dick's position could have changed. Might be able to get to him. I'll plug in down there and let you know." I nodded. His job was done. And the front turret was manned. Only nearer home would it be necessary for Tubby to leave the gunner's front-position and start transmitting an S.O.S. to Base.

What went on after Duncan left the cockpit is a story in itself. I only heard it from his own lips a week after our return when I visited him in hospital. He received the Distinguished Flying Cross for his gallant attempt to reach Dick Guterman. He was obviously bemused as he stood alongside Ellis in the cockpit, a condition which he told me took some time to overcome, and of which he was first aware as he stepped down over the main-spar and a sudden dizziness caused him to shut his eyes, hold on to the rim of the bulkhead and lower himself to sit on the step. He put his head down and waited for the feeling of faintness to pass. Tired . . . tired: it seemed to him we'd been flying for days; thought that if we could make two hundred knots with the kite in that condition . . . we could be home before two in the morning – under ideal conditions, that is, he reminded himself. He crossed his fingers, patted the side of the fuselage affectionately and got to his feet. The torch was in its clip – where Tubby Entwhistle had replaced it on his return from the damaged turret.

It was dark in the centre-section, and even with the aid of the flashlight Duncan's eyes took time to adjust. But his ears had already picked up the strange whistling moan that sounded above the steady beat of the engines. Still somewhat weak at the knees he moved on carefully towards the rear. The light picked out the gaping hole in the floor as he came to the ammunition boxes which fed the mid-upper. He edged around the breach sideways, back hard up against the fuselage stringers. Only when he had circled the hole's jagged edge was he in a position to look up at the turret and see the full extent of the damage.

Open to the night – above and below – Duncan felt a moment of panic. If anything were to give way at this point he was on the wrong side of the hole! Immediately the illogicality of the thought brought a wry grin: "The front half of the bloody thing's not much use without the rear-end, is it, you stupid bastard?" he said aloud. Bracing shoulders against one of the oval formers he continued talking to himself. "God: what a mess. Why the hell did we go on to Berlin? You wouldn't think the kite'd stay in the air. Johnny should have come down here and looked at it for himself. Well, hope you get us home, old girl."

The words dried up. With all the deliberation he could muster he brought the torch beam up to where the cannon shell had exited the aeroplane. He could see a damn sight more sky than he liked between the twisted struts and bits of duraluminium – space through which the night air hissed and rushed greedily to glut the gap. Going down on one knee Duncan slid apprehensively beneath the base of the turret. In this position the airflow took on a different note as it came funnelling through the fuselage – a whistling sound like mountain wind up-drafting through high rock chimneys; changing to a roar where it encountered the slipstream above. Fleeting strands of cloud-filtered moonlight gave a grisaille-like effect to the torn metallic surfaces, graying and silvering them, creating grotesque patterns in illusory low-relief which confused the eye more effectively than any deliberate attempt at camouflage.

He told me that his first thought was how lucky we'd been: that if the frame of the turret had not absorbed the shell's impact we might all be goners: tail-end amputated . . . no time for anyone to get out.

Thank God for calm air, he thought, at least we were now flying straight and level – the aircraft steady except for a slight shimmying in the tail. It gave him a chance to see if he could get through to the old Wombat. Straightening up, back jammed tightly against the starboard fuselage wall, Duncan grasped the turret's bottom rim with his left hand and began to work away with his right to enlarge the opening fashioned by Entwhistle. Bit by bit he was able to break off or bend away the obstructing pieces of duraluminium skin and twisted ribs, until he could get head and shoulders directly under the turret-base and push up into the turret itself. He was not prepared for what he saw.

Duncan, more frequently than any other member of the crew, had joined Guterman and myself on our forays to pub and cinema, as well as to the odd organ recital in the Cathedral. In fact Guters – something of a prodigy on the piano himself – had not only persuaded Duncan to attend a Sunday afternoon piano recital at the Usher Hall, but had also chivvied him into visiting the local art school one night to "sample the native talent" – by which he meant the models used in the life-drawing class in which both he and I were enrolled. A hilarious evening was had by all.

Dick Guterman had many friends – was universally liked for his wit and total ingenuousness. But Duncan and myself were closest to him. So when Jimmy Duncan was finally able to look up through the debris and see in the sulphurous moonlight the grim plight of his friend, a profound wave of sadness swept over him. He could not look away – as if the visual link itself carried a communication, became a vital charge capable of positively influencing the ebb and flow of life. "C'mon, Guters" – pushing his face into a grin – "we're on the way back. Remember what you said in The Saracen's Head last week: 'It's never over 'til it's over.' Don't forget it, old lad."

He told me that this physical closeness to our good friend brought drifting memories of Guterman's past – mind-images hovering before the pallid and blood-streaked ghost in the turret. Floating vignettes of Dick "rising to the occasion": snippets from those shows of eccentric brilliance which, from time to time, broke out and eclipsed the quieter, more reflective man.

There was that surprising evening in the Sergeants' Mess . . . when he sat down before the battered old upright piano and, without a scrap of music, played Chopin sonatas – extemporising in jazz-like fashion when the mood took him, swaying slightly on the stool, eyes closed, lips pursed as if he was whistling to himself. Non-stop until the bar closed at midnight; a couple of hundred drinking aircrew appreciatively quiet – not that Guters seemed aware of them once started. Three pints of beer on the piano lid – all that was required to get him going and release any one of a number of lurking Gutermans. Wild applause as the pianist takes his bow, the twisted grin in place, nervously smoothing hair back off the forehead, yet displaying just the right element of reserve and dignity that, as the artist himself put it . . . "signifies the distance separating the virtuoso from the hack amateur". The virtuoso was more than a little drunk; yet Duncan was always surprised by the remarkably convincing authority Guters acquired with the right amount of alcohol under the belt. He could be wobbling at the knees, yet speech would be precise, mind sharp and aggressive, demeanour dignified, impressive.

Then along came Guters the funny man: at the bar in The Saracen's Head with Dicky Dent, the Squadron strategist in seduction, who made a formal presentation of a purple packet of Durex contraceptives to Dick who was then five pints down. It was

Chalky White's birthday – old Matthews his skipper buying the drinks.

Dent chose the occasion to make a short but apt little speech. "Here you are, Guters: for when the time comes and you can do the real thing. To keep you safe. Until then" – raising his glass – "here's to the fallibility of time in the mid-upper!"

Cheers all round. Old Guters nonchalantly accepted the packet, face giving nothing away, while thanking one and all for their consideration and support. He pointed out that as the date on the packet – after which use was not recommended – happened to be the coming Sunday, "Dirty" Dent, doubting his own stamina to perform twice in the same week, had sensibly recognised the one man always capable of rising to the occasion at the drop of a hat, or rather at the drop of a skirt, and therefore able to make full use of such a gift before the approaching deadline. Again, cheers all round the bar. Very droll was Guters; always a jump ahead in verbal sword-play. The packet sloshed around on the bar-counter all night as beer glasses were filled and drained.

Duncan had a graphic picture of the first of us screeching off home in Dent's two-seater M.G. driven by Matthews – Guters sitting atop Duncan's shoulders doing his wombat navigation act. "The night-active marsupial," he announced, "seeing superbly in the dark to get you all home in one piece despite the inaptitude of the bloody driver."

"What do you mean?" yelled Dent. "He's a damn sight better with the car than with the Lanc."

Image succeeded image: the art school affair now . . . the never-to-be-forgotten art school scene. Guters the maestro on stage. Four quick beers each for the three of them, then down the hill and into the art class. "Professor Duncan – Associate of the Royal Academy – just visiting," Guters had informed the aged drawing teacher, giving him a gentle slap on the back which had him coughing and spluttering all the way to the front of the class. Duncan remembered making a few half-hearted attempts to draw, but spent most of the time studying the model – measuring her up with his pencil, one eye closed in the manner of artists – attracted by the well-built, somewhat chunky lady in her early forties who he said exuded that look of disappointed and frustrated sensuality that makes so many matrons appealing.

Duncan was impressed with Guters' obvious mastery: taking out a small water-colour box and brush from his tunic pocket, the maestro was somehow putting the nude together on the paper with blobs of watery stain – of subtly varying tones – without drawing a line as such. Up came our venerable instructor, head permanently on the shake, rimless little spectacles shivering on the end of his nose, obviously disconcerted by "Renoir" Guterman's fluid technique. "Er, Sergeant . . . er, may I suggest a little er . . . correction here . . . " – pulling out a pencil – "a little too much emphasis, er . . . distortion . . . across the upper thoracic region. Let me er . . . "

That was it. Guters, on his feet, whipped the pencil from our little teacher's hand, jabbed it neatly into the top pocket of the man's suit. Cleared his throat . . . and before the astonished educator could get any words out himself, launched into an exposition of female thoracic anatomy. Making drawings in the air, brush flowing freely in the creation of invisible examples, Guters set out to prove his point that in women with a well developed and heavy bosom, the clavicle is structurally important as an anchor for the mammary gland.

Duncan told me that even then, wedged in the turret, he had to smile at the recollection. But that was only the first part of the demonstration. On to the model. A hand beneath the breast in question, jiggling it up and down, while instructing the astonished class to observe the relationship between the breast's fluid volumes and the thrust of the clavicle above it. The woman just standing, a silly and uncomprehending half-grin on her face as the Master concluded his exposition by giving her a wink and a jaunty thumbs-up sign. Then walking back to join us looking pontifically serious. The two of us convulsed in our seats. The class of housewives and older men explosively quiet – a silent hysteria that held only until the art master, voice thin and uncertain, responded. "Er . . . well . . . thank you, Sergeant . . . "

General collapse into gasps and stutters of frustrated mirth. The ruffled little instructor announced a ten minute break and retreated to the staff-room with as much dignity as possible.

And so the images went cartwheeling around in Duncan's head until he realised that his hands were bleeding from contact with the sharp edges of tangled metal. The sight brought him back to the present, to the harsh realities of the situation. Somebody had to get up there to Guters. See if it wasn't possible to do something about protection from wind and cold. Duncan looked at his watch – he'd lost complete track of time after starting the bombing run. Saw that forty-five minutes had elapsed since Ellis made his damage report on the turret; and in the meantime they'd been badly thrown around and nobody had reassessed Guterman's situation.

Obviously, bare hands could do no more: the obstructions that remained – girder-like stringers and struts – would need heavy duty metal cutters to effectively separate them. If Guters was to be reached it was not going to be directly through the turret. When the waning moon disappeared into cloud, Duncan could no longer see sky through the turret-space. For the moment Dick Guterman was lost to the outside night. Slowly and carefully Duncan extricated himself from the wreckage; made another search of the damaged area – top and bottom with the flashlight beam. And in doing so realised that there was a way to get to his friend. A plan began to develop which, he thought, had a reasonable chance of working.

Pale moonlight once again filtered into the fuselage. On his knees, twisting precariously, Duncan made a final survey of the turret scene. The light might have been playing tricks, but it seemed to him that the air-gunner had been thrust higher in the metallic ruins than when Ellis had first reported on the situation. Head exposed to the slipstream, flying helmet gone, hair streaming forwards as if electrified, it appeared that only the steel lances of the guns held him in place. The pale film of light imparted a strange sense of peace to the face, disturbed only by the dried run of blood at the corner of the mouth.

Duncan stood by the restbed cleaning up the cuts on his hands with an iodine solution, working out the details of his scheme. The more he thought about it, the more he knew it could be done. He plugged in and called me up on the intercom. "Johnny . . . there's no chance of getting to Guters by going up through the turret – have to cut a way clear with heavy equipment for that. And it looks as if he's been pushed upwards by all that turbulence on the run-in. He's very exposed. Got to give him some protection from the slipstream otherwise the odds aren't good."

"Well . . . " I must admit my response was hesitant. I was wondering just how much we could diminish the slipstream by cutting airspeed and still fly safely low-level with the drag problem created by the hole back there. "Listen, Dunc: we're at about two thousand now north-east of Celle. Once we've cleared the Hanover perimeter I'll drop to fifteen hundred and try reducing power a little. But we're short on fuel – can't play around and can't afford to loiter either."

"As long as we're not using oxygen a few hundred feet aren't going to make much difference." Duncan spoke slowly, giving equal emphasis to each word. "We've got to cover him up somehow – as soon as possible give him protection from the wind. And the only way to do it is from the outside. If somebody gives me a leg up, and holds on to my feet, I can get out of the fuselage hole in front of the turret. It can be done – I've surveyed it. There's enough skin ripped away to let me get through between the stringers which are intact and hold onto them for support.

You can get up there through the lower bit of turret we've cleared. Send Ellis down, Johnny, to give me a leg up and hold onto my ankles. If I can get a couple of blankets wedged behind Guters, and rig up some sort of covering over his head, it could make all the difference."

God, I was dubious – sceptical would be a better word. "How can you handle anything out there, especially blankets – they'll blow right out of your hands. And how're you going to hang on to anything while you're holding them?"

"I'll make a roll of the blankets down here; stuff it under my flying jacket. I can grip the stringers with my knees, and if Ellis holds on tight and you cut the rate of knots to somewhere round one hundred and forty to one hundred and fifty for a couple of minutes, I think I can lean out and drop the whole package behind his head."

I sweated on that one. Finally I agreed. Told him to wait for the cloud cover ahead. To waste no time experimenting if it didn't prove feasible. That I wanted to get downstairs and away, pretty damn quickly for all our sakes.

Contemplating the action that Duncan felt compelled to take now reinforced the belief that I had made the wrong decision to continue to the bombing run. It was not a matter of distance or time – our return route was direct, as the crow flies – but of the violence to which the aeroplane, and therefore Dick, had been subjected. Why hadn't I jettisoned the bomb load immediately after the Junkers' attack? And why had I made the naïve assumption that we could nip in and out of Tempelhof straight and level, as if on a simple Sunday afternoon cross-country junket? The Potsdam batteries were notoriously dangerous. Their attack had completely undermined my plan of making a steady and uneventful bombing-run and getting the hell out. I suppose I could not have imagined the intensity or the extent of the turbulent "weather" set off by a raid which had been so concentrated. None of us had been in anything like that before.

Even so, I should not have gone on to the target. It was a bloody stupid decision, based on the poorest of judgement. A temporary derangement. Must have been.

Ellis gave the instruments a final check before going down to the restbed. First, he and Duncan folded a couple of heavy brown blankets in such a way that one end of the coverlet formed a relatively thick pad, leaving enough length to pull out and spread forward for extended protection. Duncan's plan was to push the padded end down behind Guterman's shoulders where it would be held by his weight, and then bring the remaining length over his head and tie each end to one of the gun-barrels. He made two holes in the forward corners of the pad through which he knotted long pieces of thick string taken from the "bits and pieces" box Ellis always brought aboard. As an afterthought he bored two more holes at the padded end also, thus enabling him to prevent the head-rest part from opening up by looping string round its two sausage-like extremities and tying strong knots.

The moon-obscuring cloud was still limiting visibility while this was going on: a thick, mucous-like vapour which slithered over the cockpit canopy as if to encase Titty B-O, seal her off from the sky proper, transform her into some kind of chrysalis, pull her down and under. Standing beneath the turret Ellis found it difficult to envisage how Duncan was to climb up and perform in such threatening pea soup. For even though the aeroplane was flying noticeably slower, slipstream would still be over one hundred and fifty miles per hour.

Ellis was thinking that when Duncan pulled clear of the fuselage interior and faced the force of a wind that could pluck him from the fuselage back like a fly, some hold more secure than a grip around the ankles was going to be essential. Not only would such a poor anchor provide very little stability where it was most required – at the centre of gravity around waist and pelvis – but it would severely hamper leg movement and therefore Duncan's ability to feel for his balance. His feet must be free to constantly adjust stance and position like a mountain climber. What was needed was a lifeline of some sort round the waist.

Ellis signalled Duncan to wait and went to collect his parachute from by the mainspar. A couple of minutes later he had ripped the pack unceremoniously open and had the restbed covered with yards of the once meticulously folded silk. It was the tie-lines he was after – the tough cords connecting the parachute canopy to the body harness – four of which, totalling in length about twenty-five feet, he cut loose. Duncan protested this destruction of Ellis' chute to no avail. His colleague simply went ahead extracting the tie-lines, and finished the job by tying the four of them together, end to end, using the immovable bend knots employed by sailors. He had his lifeline.

Wasting no time on explanations – the purpose was self-evident anyway – he secured Duncan to the line by tying him first around the waist before bringing a loop tightly round the top of each leg, in the groin, to make a strong crotch harness. The other end of the line he fastened carefully around his own waist. This done, he indicated how he would brace himself against the intact bulkhead to the rear of the turret, where he could both monitor Duncan's progress and play out the line as required. "I'm going to keep the line taut all the time," Ellis shouted, "give me more anchor control." Duncan unclipped his oxygen mask, tightened his flying-helmet, and slipped as much of the blanket-pad down the top half of his flying-jacket as far as it would go.

When I later questioned him about the feasability of squeezing himself, pad and all, up through the space, he said it never occurred to him that he couldn't do it – said that all it took was a lift around the thighs from Ellis and his shoulders were through, feet already groping for the flight-engineer's shoulders. Feet in place he was able to bring elbows up and hoist himself through the breach in the top fuselage made by the cannon shell on exit. Once he was half in, half out – chest down on the aircraft's back –

he told me that it seemed that his lungs collapsed in a sudden vacuum as the slipstream hit; and the sensations that normally signify the concrete presence of things evaporated in the tearing sucking roar. Mouth open like a vacuum cleaner drawing in whatever scraps of oxygen were around, only the pull of gravity around waist and pelvis provided by Ellis' line provided any sense of weight and position. Thus he waited, head down, trying to get the feel of the situation. Apparently he concentrated on sensing exactly where his arms and belly pressed against solid metal locations in order to gain a sense of security in terms of what was solid and secure and what was not; where the void was and where it wasn't. The thick cloud turned out to a blessing. It streamed from the trailing edge of the mainplane giving the illusion of a continuation of surface, transforming hundreds of feet of space into psychologically acceptable *terra firma*. He said that the wind remained the major shock to the senses: screaming, grabbing at every slit and crack between body and clothing, helmet and head, freezing, blinding, deafening, numbing.

Face contorted, he forced his head up a fraction to assess his position with regard to Guterman and the turret; saw that he needed to pull clear of the hole another two feet. By turning slightly on his right side he was able to move his left arm forward – stretched it as far as he could without losing his hold, felt the tips of his fingers slide up the slope of the turret fairing. Already his hands were cold, tactile sensitivity considerably diminished.

"Right: ease your body up a fraction," he told himself, "Ellis has the line tight. Now grab hold of the fairing rim. Good." The instructions came coolly and precisely, his own voice sounding internally, an undercover intelligence weighing up the situation. He became less aware of the wind – used to it almost – as if the only world he'd ever known was the aircraft's back. "Now turn a touch on the left side and bring the right arm forward . . . slowly . . . very slowly: right – grip the rim. Right: now you're stretched out – two good handholds – but still half of you inside. To get the blanket in position you're going to have to raise up and let go one hand. Best way to do it is turn more on the left side – pull forward on the rim, lever upwards with the right knee against the top of the hole until you can bring your balls outside – just on the rim – plonk 'em dead on the edge. Grip with the pelvis. Pressure both thighs inside to jack-knife them hard beneath the turret fairing. Then you're hinged and anchored at the same time. Thigh pressure against the intact fuselage roof between you and the fairing is the trick. The thigh vice. Concentrate on the thigh vice. And you feel the rope. Good. Now you can let go on top; grip . . . grip like hell below – work the blanket with both free hands. Don't pull your head up suddenly . . . or too far. Wind'll whip you off . . ."

This was the point, said Duncan later, when he knew he was going to succeed.

The turret was beneath him. Guterman's head almost in his lap.

Half an inch at a time Duncan eased his chest off the fuselage until the blanket was free of his weight. Keeping head well down he let go of the fairing rim with his right hand. Immediately he felt the line taut at his back as Ellis adjusted the length to his movements. Imperceptibly he loosened the left hand's hold. With every fractional release he intensified the vice-like thrust of pelvis and thighs.

The gale plucked at him as if he were straw, but he felt a brief surge of optimism as he realised how well he was anchored – hinged, with the rim of the hole as his fulcrum. "Don't get carried away, old chap . . . Christ, what a stupid pun. Remember – keep the blanket and yourself as flush with the fuselage as you can. Present as little surface as possible to the wind . . ."

Suddenly the aircraft dropped. Straight down. Several feet. Luckily the wing remained level – no falling off to port or starboard. Duncan told me he stopped breathing at this juncture.

Just lay flat as a wafer, head down, both hands gripping the fairing with the intensity of *rigor mortis*, pain gnawing the abdomen as he forced thighs and stomach into a superhuman hold.

"Brief turbulence. Forget it. Don't look beyond the aircraft. Look in the turret." Duncan was finding it difficult to co-ordinate movement – to identify the different parts of his body and ascertain their position on the fuselage. Not much time. The excoriating slipstream and intense cold were beginning to dull the mind – induce a touch of dreaminess.

"Look in the turret."

Duncan dragged his eyes from the pull of the wind and saw he was perfectly placed to fix the blanket in position. It was now or never. "Don't let it get away in the slipstream. Pull it out of your jacket a bit at a time – keep it tight between your chest and Dick's head. Right: hands off . . . one at a time – grip like hell with the vice – keep as flat as you can. Now the blanket – slowly . . . slowly . . . chest down, don't let it get away from your flying jacket . . . "

Duncan's face was now brushed by Dick Guterman's streaming hair, and for one brief second the scene in the turret etched itself permanently on his mind: the frost-sealed eyes and twisted red-smeared mouth; the dark crimson rips in the leather jacket where the guns held him.

The sight caused Duncan to forget the danger of his own exposed position and the seemingly impossible physical nature of the task he had set himself. He became oblivious to everything save getting the blanket in position.

Lying out almost completely flush with the fuselage – just raised sufficiently at the shoulders – he was able to finally ease the thickly folded end of the protective pad clear of his jacket, push it into the space between Guterman's head and the turret fairing, and jam it temporarily in place. From there he could pull out the front end with its strings, bring it forward over Dick's head and tie it down to the gun barrels. All that remained was to secure the pad more firmly behind the air-gunner whose body, pushed forward by the slipstream, was providing insufficient weight to keep the blanket in place. Only one way to do it: take a last second to wedge it between the sharp shards of fractured-turret metal at the air-gunner's back. Guters was finally cocooned by the blanket; enclosed, at least in part; sheltered from the cold and utter hopelessness of infinite space. Duncan was very moved when he came to this point in the story – needed a little time before continuing.

He went on to describe the overall numbness that was setting in; how the combination of horrendous engine noise, force of wind and biting cold, was insidiously sapping all reserves of mental and physical control; how he knew there was no time left for finesse or caution. No instructions were coming from anywhere at this point. He raised head and shoulders just to the point when he felt the slipstream begin to take him, eased the hold of thigh and crotch and, controlling himself like a sail spilling before the wind, pushed backwards the required couple of feet to the edge of the hole. The whole venture was nothing less than a superhuman feat of will in which the normal laws of gravity and human physical endurance were transcended.

Even so, had it not been for Ellis, Duncan would have been lost. After finally securing Guterman's cover the bomb-aimer had no reserves left. As he fought the slipstream on the aircraft's spine, traversing those crucial two or three feet to safety, Ellis had moved in beneath him, pulling in the lifeline to keep it taut. He saw Duncan's legs drop fractionally as the thigh-grip was eased, saw his backside slide closer to the rim, saw a last urgent jack-knifing as Duncan momentarily had to regain balance, saw the rough edge of the hole cut deeply through the flesh at the top of the thigh and the blood begin to flow.

At that moment we came out of the cloud, and through the wispy remnants of moonlit vapour Ellis observed Duncan – now almost upright on the aircraft's back – preparing to fall back into the aircraft. But it was already too late. The last conscious thing Flying-Officer Jimmy Duncan did was to hunch-up and make a ball of himself against the wind. His helmet had gone, his arms were loose at his sides, and only the fierce bloodletting-vice maintained by pelvis and thigh bone somehow held him aloft.

Later, Ellis made light of the fact that without his split-second action Duncan would never have made it into the aeroplane. For only by forcing himself up into the space beneath and behind his colleague, ramming through the broken metal higher in the turret and stretching his right leg out at almost ninety degrees onto an intact fuselage stringer below, was he able to raise himself and grab Duncan by the hips and yank as hard as he could. The manoeuvre worked. The jack-knife hold that had kept Duncan aloft for the last four minutes collapsed and he fell limply into Ellis' arms, tearing only a great rip in the right sleeve of his flying jacket as his arm snagged on the edge of the hole.

Arms around the fallen man's waist, Ellis lowered the two of them down and half carried, half dragged, Duncan up the fuselage to the restbed where he lay shivering uncontrollably, eyes closed, breathing in short and shallow gasps. The skin on his face was blue and mottled; a slight nosebleed had left his chin streaked as if with red spittle. But it was the sight of his hands that caused Ellis to whistle softly; wonder how best to treat them. Both of them had been severely flayed by wind and cold: large areas of skin were hanging loosely away like the membranous and diaphanous fins of some unusual tropical fish, exposing the red meat of flesh, damp and slightly glazed. In addition the fingers were deeply cut about – every joint on the underside bearing witness to the fact that Duncan had in fact been more or less hanging on by his fingernails.

Both trouser legs were soaked in blood. As was the inside fleece lining of both flying boots. For a moment when Ellis saw this he thought that Duncan had severed an artery, but then realised that the flow was drying; the thigh wounds could wait.

Gently, he bound Duncan's hands with a wide sterilised bandage from the first-aid kit; then, turning his attention to the legs, poured iodine liberally onto two large surgical pads which he placed over the shredded rents in the trousers, saturating both fabric and flesh. Better, he thought, to sterilise the wounds in this fashion rather than attempt to cut the material away. There was no sign that the patient was aware of any of this – but his breathing became deeper, more measured. In the absence of blankets the flight-engineer covered him with the silk from his own damaged parachute. Then he returned to the mid-upper: no sky was to be seen through the turret – the blanket was taut; the slipstream washing over.

We were out of the cloudbank just in time so far as I was concerned – altogether too long lost to the ground. I asked Ellis about Duncan and Guters. He reported briefly on Duncan's heroic achievement; said the details must wait for later – and that there was no way to tell anything about Dick until we landed.

We continued our very shallow descent to fifteen hundred feet, advancing the throttles gradually for minimum strain on the mid-upper's blanket. One hundred and seventy airspeed indicated. Ellis went back for a second check: reported the covering holding firm; he returned to the cockpit and checked the starboard-inner: it was behaving itself – exhaust flame visible enough but traps still partially effective.

Noakes reported our position as north-west of Celle, about seventy miles from Diepholz: a dangerous region – Hanover with its airfields lay only some forty miles to the south-east. But we felt reasonably secure flying so low: over the last few months we'd seen first hand that German night-fighter pilots did not relish low-level attack from beneath, fighting our slipstream with the ground so near. Yet I can tell you that flying long distances at low altitude has its own problems and dangers. Depth perception plays tricks: altimeters are not reliable to within one hundred feet; and in relying on visual contact with the ground for long distances – especially over flat terrain and water – the eye can deceive, convince one that a constant height is being maintained when all the time the aeroplane is getting closer and closer to zero altitude. It's a dangerous optical illusion. And it goes without saying that any pilot indulging in such tactics must be aware of this tendency to "fly in" – have other eyes watching for him. He must also know the topography of the land beneath, be able to maintain reasonable visual contact, keep instruments frequently calibrated, and always fly higher than the highest point around.

Within the last few weeks the Luftwaffe had started to concentrate night-fighters at key points on our return journey. For once a target city was attacked, and thus identified, it was not difficult for them to calculate when and where homeward-bound raiders could be found. There were Junkers and Messerchmitts lying in wait all the way to the coast. I was worried that because of the damaged fuselage and tail-drag Titty B-O was not able to attain her cruising speed of two hundred plus miles per hour. And the starboard-inner rev counter was beginning to do some strange things. Ellis left the co-pilot's seat and went back to check on Duncan. He called up with a brief report: "He's unfreezing; I've given him a shot of morphine – he'll need it when circulation comes back properly. Going to strap him down here: there's no way he can hold on if we run into trouble. Be back up in a minute."

The sky had become a vast moonlit desert of brittle space. A sky to worry about. Anyone up there would see us miles away. Low altitude was our only security. Intercom silence was broken by Sergeant Smith calling from his station in the rear-turret. "Messerschmitt about a mile to the right – flying parallel course – about six thousand. Doesn't seem to have seen us."

He was right. Looking out through the far canopy window the silhouette was clearly recognisable: a twin-engined 110. I wondered why the hell the so-and-so would be flying a parallel course. He might have been there with us in the cloud cover all the time. Anyway . . . bound to see us now whatever we did.

"Tubby" – to Entwhistle in the front turret – "see him? Turn the turret full right while Smithy goes full left; then you can both get him with crossfire if he decides to come in amidships. We're taking as little evasive action as possible now we're down here. He might not like the idea of joining us this close to the deck."

The flight-engineer was back in his seat. I always felt somewhat vulnerable when he wasn't there, checking, anticipating; I sometimes thought Ellis knew a damn sight more about flying than I did.

"He's coming down" – from Smithy. Mindful of Guters and the blanket, and Duncan on the restbed, I gently advanced the throttles a notch. The Lanc didn't like it. Tail shimmying. General vibration. Trimmed nose down. Smoothed herself out. But the control column continued to buck and the rudder pedals demanded constant correction. A quick glance out and I saw the German diving in, lined up to attack dead-centre. For the second time that night the thudding of cannon shells sounded above the beat of the engines.

The whole aeroplane must have heard my sigh of relief. The Luftwaffe pilot had to be new at the game. He was coming in at a very steep angle and had opened fire much too soon – from about four thousand feet, I'd say – and his shells were dropping out of the sky beneath us. The German would have to pull out very soon unless he wanted to fly straight into the ground not far below. Thank God he carried no radar aerial – had no observer watching a screen.

In the rear-turret Smithy was waiting – waiting for that moment when the fighter's belly would be exposed as he pulled his nose up. Then both the Lancaster's turrets opened fire simultaneously – four guns from the rear, two from the front. The gunners must have had the German dead in their sights, for the hammerblow result of six machine-guns catching a Messerschmitt engine was – for any flyer – an extraordinary spectacle: sobering in the extreme. Oil-bathed bits and pieces whirred madly before the moon: fire, explosion, disintegration – wings, tail, cockpit – the fluttering to earth of cardboard remnants. No parachute. Impossible to get out when an aeroplane breaks up like that.

Relief that it was him rather than us. But none of the usual jubilation on the intercom – just sober congratulations all round. We were tired; had seen too much death and destruction for one night. Images of Matthews, Dent, Chalky White, returned . . . interspersed with those of a shrouded turret. Suddenly I wanted to go to sleep. Eyes were straining desperately to close and shut everything out; arms and legs wanted to fold themselves up and lie down.

Tail a-flutter – as if it was loose – as if the whole back end was loose. I was searching for the trim wheel again. Throttles back a notch. Rudder-pedals kicking with a life of their own. Two and a half to three hours left to go . . . with a bit of luck.

I was jerked rudely back to the world of cockpit and sky by the abrupt appearance of long tongues of flame streaking from the exhausts of the starboard-inner engine. Ellis quickly throttled back but the rev counter was flickering wildly, power coming and going erratically. The needle on the oil-pressure gauge was sinking steadily back to zero.

"It's gone" – from the flight-engineer – "main bearings from the sound of the clatter. Shutting it down and feathering. Now." He was about to shut off ignition and fuel supply to the stricken engine, press the fire extinguisher button as a precaution, and set the propeller blades to give minimum resistance to the airflow and prevent windmilling, when the engine blew up with a hell of a bang. A dense but quickly dispersing cloud of black smoke momentarily obscured the wing, and was followed by the gasping hiss of coolant escaping under pressure. Ellis had immediately gone through the emergency drill the moment the engine blew.

So there was no fire. I compensated quickly for the loss of starboard power by adjusting the throttles of both port engines – action that must be taken quickly with multi-engined aircraft when one power-plant is lost.

"Also broken a connecting rod or two," continued Ellis – "that last supercharger boost over the target probably did it . . . we were nursing it most of the way out. Oil pressure was fluctuating even then. Lucky we had the flame-trap problem and had to cut back on revs. Helped the engine stay with us this far. Well, one less mouth to feed. May get home with juice to spare. What's our position? How far to the coast?" – as he leaned back to Noakes. Ellis' voice was laconic, matter-of-fact. He knew as well as I did that the Lancaster could fly perfectly well on three engines, all other things being equal – which, of course, they were not.

At this juncture I did not feel very sanguine about our prospects. Almost ever since the damage sustained in the first attack I'd been fighting the controls; constantly trimming to keep the aircraft balanced and airworthy; now the unequal prop pull added to the struggle – and at a height which allowed no room for manoeuvre. Even trying to gain altitude would be a slow and laborious process.

I was aware that Ellis was watching me with some concern. I pulled myself upright in the seat and gave the flight-engineer a grin. Tried to put on the "keen-eyed commander" kind of look.

Noakes came on the intercom with a response to Ellis' query about distances: "Diepholz is behind on our left. The Ems'll be coming up in seven or eight minutes . . . then we've got one hundred and sixty to one hundred and seventy miles to Alkmaar and the sea. We have two choices: south-west to the East Anglian coast the most direct course – about one hundred and fifty miles of water – but gives us a lot of choice if we have to put down early – Lakenheath, Feltwell, Woodbridge, Mildenhall . . . all the East Anglian 'dromes. Or we could swing south-west now, head south of Rotterdam and then go due west to the Suffolk coast. That would cut the sea crossing by almost half, but we'd have twice as much enemy territory to cover – and be about sixty miles longer overall, give or take for drift."

"Alkmaar," I said. "There really isn't a choice, even though we're limping along a bit. Alkmaar's the longer sea stretch, but if mechanical problems get worse I'd rather ditch in the sea than face German problems on land. Better for Guterman, too. A less destructive landing if the sea's calm, less chance of fire, and we might be able to get him out of the turret from the top. What do you say, Frank? What's the petrol situation?"

Ellis was making calculations on a pad. He didn't reply immediately. "Alkmaar – got to be – given the fuel situation. It's going to be tight. Also – and I don't want to add any unnecessary notes of alarm – the port-outer's swallowing petrol. Don't like the way the revs are surging. Either fuel-pump or carburettor trouble. I'll try and nurse it along. But if it packs up and we can't keep airborne I'd rather take my chances ditching in the North Sea – with Air Sea Rescue looking for us – than coming down somewhere in Holland with the Jerries."

"Right: Alkmaar it is, Noakes . . . " I heard my own voice somewhere in the distance and I knew I was beginning to function at a purely mechanical level – opting out as a controlling factor: seeing myself as simply the tool of fate. Once Ellis announced the problems with the port-outer – which I hadn't picked up on the instruments, I suppose I subconsciously decided that it was simply a matter of going through the motions until the end. At the back of my mind I knew it was an attitude that had to be shaken off – I was the one in control, damn it – and already the power surges of the newly troubled engine were causing me to work the rudder bars and the trim-wheel simultaneously to maintain our heading. Neither could I put the picture of the blanket-covered turret out of mind – nor stop the continuous running of the question as to why I'd decided to proceed on the bombing-run before turning around for home. It seemed to me at that moment that some other person had made that decision, on some other operation, in some other aeroplane.

"What the hell . . . " I exclaimed. Duncan was standing quietly behind the flight-engineer's seat looking out aimlessly at the dead starboard-inner. His left hand, bereft of bandage, was purple raw, resting incongruously on the seat's cold metal back. It was the kind of shock I needed. Pulling aside my mouthpiece I yelled across the cockpit: "Dunc, what the hell are you doing up here? How did you get out of those straps with hands like that? Get back to the restbed. Now!" The bomb-aimer didn't reply. Just gave a half-grin and shambled down the fuselage, steadying himself with his elbows. Ellis waited for me to clip the mouthpiece back. "I'll go down in a minute. Just watch this engine a sec."

The incident was a godsend, a revitalisation. "Noakes, check our course directly to Alkmaar. Visibility's good enough for Tubby and I to follow all the landmarks. After Alkmaar, a direct course for Lowestoft. From there we'll go on to Woodbridge – I know the approaches and it's equipped for emergencies. Safest bet for us in our condition. And Tubby" – to Entwhistle in the front turret – "keep checking ground features below – you've got the pad of one-inch maps Noakes put together. We'll sight the River Hase anytime now. Flowing due north. We'll meet it where it swings west to join the Ems at Meppen. Shout out when you spot the confluence. Then watch for the Vechte – it'll come up very quickly after about twenty miles flowing west. We follow it all the way to Zwolle in Holland. Confirm when you sight it. Heading a touch north-west after this – want to cross the Zuider Zee at the narrowest part. Pass over Hoorn on the other side of the Zee, then straight to Alkmaar – eight miles left to the sea. You know the route – we've been this way before."

"Once we clear land get back to the wireless table. You'll have to get cracking on the R.D.F., start preparing to get fixes for homing once we're clear of the Dutch coast. And transmit emergency signals to base."

"O.K., Noakes . . . did you hear that? In Duncan's absence Tubby'll be using the hand maps for ground checks; help you confirm our position more or less exactly.

"And Tubby – better be ready with the guns too. Just in case we run into any ground batteries down here firing low-level shell repeater stuff. You and Smithy can put them off their aim."

Ellis glanced at his watch; held it out for me to see. Nearly quarter to one in the morning. I made a quick calculation: allowing for the loss of an engine and our reduced speed we should be touching down somewhere in England in about two hours and a bit.

Port-outer rev-counter needle was jumping around wildly again. Always the chance it was a faulty instrument. I pulled the port-outer throttle lever back until the needle settled hesitantly at 2500. Watched the boost gauge as I did so: it flickered from plus four to zero. No doubt the engine was in trouble. The left-outboard petrol tank showed almost empty. I tapped the gauge. No change. Ellis, back in his seat, nodded and fiddled with the elaborate cross-feed system which allowed the engine to draw from the port-inboard tank. Made no difference to the rough running port-outer. "What do you think?" – looking across to Ellis.

"Most likely the fuel-pumps – petrol's there but the engine's starved," responded the flight-engineer. "Don't think it's the electrics – mags or distributor: the engine's still running, after all, and surges when it does get the juice. Unless it's just pissing petrol out from the carburettors somewhere, but then . . . " His voice broke off as he advanced the throttles of the starboard-outer and port-inner engines to compensate, watching their gauges intently as he did so.

A heavy bank of cloud was running across the northern sky, dimming moon and stars without obscuring their light. Ground details seen from twelve hundred feet were still easily discernible to the practised eye. Even with no moon at all and minimum cloud, there was often enough lucency in the sky to allow one to distinguish rivers and major changes in the terrain. And no unpleasant surprises lay ahead in the form of high ground – the highest elevation anywhere around was no more than three hundred feet; and once into Holland the countryside lay at sea-level or below. Nothing to obstruct a ground-hugging escape.

A few wisps of misty vapour floated past the cockpit windows and then the moon cleared the lower edge of the cloudbank and a lighter sky took over. I pulled forward in the seat, peered out over the front-turret, searched the ground ahead. About five miles away was an important landmark which fixed both latitude and longitude – the north-flowing river which made a leisurely but dramatic ninety degree swing to the west: the Hase. At that moment Entwhistle announced he'd spotted it. Course change – two degrees north to bring us directly over the river; then due west to follow it closely to where it met the Ems at Meppen about thirty miles away.

"Going to check on Duncan" – again Ellis disappeared down the fuselage.

Smithy called up from the tail, formal as always. "How's Guters, Sir?" Isolated in his turret he was less in touch than anybody with what was going on in the aeroplane.

"Don't really know, Smithy. Can't get in there to give medical help. Tubby says he responded when he touched him. Duncan managed to get out there – God knows how – and rig some protection from the slipstream over him. And now our airspeed's down . . . reduce the exposure factor a bit. Can't do much more except get home."

It was almost half-past twelve. The hours after midnight are never on anyone's side. Life's on the ebb that early in the morning. Metabolism slows down . . . cortex and respiratory system expect their nightly snooze; the so-called "vital juices" slow to a trickle. A time of let-down for the bomber-crew. Have to fight powerful natural rhythms in order to stay in charge and not fly like a zombie. At this stage of a long flight I found it was always necessary to combat a strong mood of pessimism. For, hopefully, having overcome the worst of the night's dangers, I felt we'd earned the right to get home free and clear. Yet knowing that the Gods were never happy with such displays of hubris – were only waiting contemptuously to put a few more spokes in our wheel – had me in the fingernail biting category until we were way over the sea. Guters always said he had the same reaction when about halfway home – the "Hero and Leander" syndrome he called it.

I'd found the only way to tackle it was to deliberately and wilfully go to the other extreme: indulge in a hell of a dose of bravado; nonchalantly challenge fate to do its worst. Christ, we were a tough and independent bunch well able to take care of ourselves – responsible for our own destiny. Needed no help. No snivelling about bad luck. None of that kind of thing. The truth is, of course, that the psychological boost of a belief in self-determination is one thing; the physical realities with which one is having to deal, another. Nevertheless, the psychic capital gained more than balances the books when morale is at a low ebb. For there's no surer time to discover the fragility of one's hold on existence than when keeping a few tons of aeroplane aloft at one o'clock in the morning, flying home over enemy territory.

The Ems lay gleaming ahead. Beneath us the Hase wriggled in a series of hairpin turns as if trying to escape joining with its grander colleague and being forced to run northwards to the sea. The town of Meppen was a blacked-out smudge a couple of miles away to the right. I made the course correction – two degrees south-west to pick up the Vechte. Four minutes and it came into view: a slim, snaky river after the broad flow of the Ems. Hamlets, copses, fields, sauntered by below, looking dangerously close in the now unclouded moonlight. One eye on the altimeter – visual check downwards to judge the perceived depth of space and relate the sense of distance to the instrument reading; glance back to the altimeter needle – down to the ground – back to the instrument. I had to constantly double-check in this way in order to reconcile any slight shift in the altimeter reading with changes in the appearance of the ground relative to the last check. It was hard work to keep the eyes at it. But it was the only way not to be deceived by the instrument, or by one's own visual shortcomings in situations where optical illusions are known to be the rule rather than the exception.

Just off to the right, running east to west and close to the river, the main road swinging down from Meppen came into view; if the map was accurate we were some twenty miles from Zwolle. At least everything on the ground was where it should be.

The terrain some miles ahead seemed to be in deep shadow – a darkened region that gradually burgeoned into trees, became a small forest on both sides of the highway and river: row after rigid row of even-pointed young German firs, sharp tips spiking the air – a floating carpet of steel tacks.

Until the mosaic of points broke up at about five hundred yards and each tree point seemed to explode in recurring flicks of flame, a series of staccato flashes cracked through the low heavy beat of our three remaining engines. I brought the nose of the aircraft up, manhandled Titty B-O into as steep a climbing turn as I dared while Ellis took up the remaining reserves of power. The altimeter registered a mere nine hundred feet. I cursed silently: despite all my efforts we had been gradually descending. And I'd missed it on the instrument.

The poor old aeroplane shuddered uncertainly, obeying controls hesitantly. As the forest wheeled down and away I saw a long convoy of trucks and armoured-cars hidden in the trees, the latter with mounted machine-guns elevated, and flame from the muzzles indicating they were still firing. And then we were high over the centre of the wood, the armoured column left behind.

The encounter had been too sudden to return the German fire from the front turret, but Smithy was perfectly placed to retaliate and raked the area from the rear, his four thumping Brownings going hell for leather. We levelled out at thirteen hundred feet. The incident had lasted barely five seconds.

When the rear-turret guns stopped firing everything seemed strangely quiet: just a muffled "Jeeze . . . " from somebody over the intercom. But now we were really lumbering along – the aeroplane hesitating from time to time as if there was insufficient airflow to buoy her up. Airspeed was a mere one hundred and sixty miles per hour: way above our stalling speed – around ninety-five miles per hour depending on nose up or down altitude and wind speed – yet, given both engine loss and shellburst damage, the kind of sudden manoeuvre just demanded of the old kite was obviously putting her under great strain.

It was at this point that I felt my right leg stiffening up: a strange sensation of heat, particularly around the ankle where it was beginning to glow red-hot and pulse with sharp jabs of pain every time I put pressure on the rudder-pedal. I caught Ellis' eye, bent forward and jabbed a finger at my right flying boot. The flight-engineer bent low beneath the instrument-panel, intercom line fully extended; flashed the small pocket torch he always carried.

"There's a lot of blood around the ankle . . . something's gone through the boot. Did you feel anything hit back there?" I said I'd felt nothing. Ellis straightened up, nudged port-inner and starboard-outer throttles, and bent round to Noakes at the navigator's table. "Noakes, grab the First Aid kit from the restbed – check on Duncan while you're there – and bring the box up here. And see if they've peppered us along the fuselage as you go."

A minute or so and the navigator returned with the small medicine chest, unclipped his mouthpiece and shouted above the noise of the engines: "Dunc's alright. He's holding on with his elbows. Couldn't see any bullet holes anywhere. Think they were too surprised to shoot straight."

But then Ellis was leaning across in front of me, staring out of the left window. When he pulled back he made a grimace. "Well, they had a couple of lucky hits. Looks as if one got the skipper in the leg; and I reckon they got the rad on the port-outer and it's dripping coolant. Not exactly pissing out, but bad enough.

"Johnny . . . Noakes should put a dressing on that leg. Noakes, look, see the hole in the suede where something's gone through? We can't take his boot off, so bandage right round the ankle over the boot. Soak a dressing in iodine and strap it directly over the hole to soak up the bleeding. Plenty of iodine now – use the whole bloody bottle if you have to: it's got to soak and penetrate the fleece lining."

"And no bloody finesse, Noakes," I added; "none of the fancy bandaging technique you picked up on that First Aid course. Just bandage the pad on as if you were tying the boot up with string."

The navigator complied; had the job done in a couple of minutes. "Marvellous," I said. Then, "Christ . . . " biting my tongue as the iodine soaked through. But after the first shock the pain worked to bring the leg back to life and I could feel the pressure of the rudder-pedal beneath my foot for the first time in several minutes.

"How long do you give that engine?" I'd been putting off asking the question until Noakes retired to the navigation table. "Will it get us to the coast?"

"It might: it's leaking about a couple of ounces a minute, I'd say that's a pint every eight. Zwolle is coming up ahead, and then it's about another sixty miles to Alkmaar and the sea. At our present rate of knots that's about twenty-two minutes' flying time. There'll be some glycol left, but not enough to be circulating much – that's the problem: every pint we lose diminishes coolant distribution and efficiency. On top of that the engine's been losing power for the last half-hour and oil-pressure's on the blink. Anything we get out of it now's a bonus. I'll just watch it; won't feather the airscrew until the last minute. We'll have to try and gain a little height over the sea. Prevailing wind's behind us – that'll help. Then if we start a very gradual descent – assuming we have altitude – we might make it to East Anglia on two engines alone. But we'll have to hit the runway right first time. No chance to go around again."

Ellis was giving me some searching glances. He told me later that I looked terrible: forehead glistening with perspiration; eyes narrowed; mouth pulled tight. He had strong doubts at that stage about my physical ability to hold our old battered aircraft up much longer. And I'd probably have agreed with him had he voiced his fears. The hole blasted in the rear fuselage diminished elevator control, requiring that I counter a constant tendency for the nose to fall by keeping the control-column close in to the midriff. Aileron movement was sluggish, and rudder-bars were just anarchic, jigging up and down to their own tune. Any further power loss would simply compound these aerodynamic problems.

The cockpit was now a cocoon of dull pewter-gray light cast by a waning moon. We constituted a remote microcosm of a world, intercom mute, Ellis and I wrapped in our own background concerns and fears; yet somehow managing to live every crisis-ridden moment objectively, utilising all the intelligence and skill we could muster. For me there would be no question of abandoning the aircraft: Ellis had no 'chute and Guterman was trapped and helpless. When and if the time came I'd see that the others got away. But I'd continue to fly Titty B-O in the direction of home as long as there was a foot of airspace left.

Zwolle lay behind and to the south. I'd moved a degree or so north before the attack from the woods in order to bring us onto a straight westerly approach to the narrow crossing of the Zee: a course we could continue directly to the town of Alkmaar on the coast – thirty-five minutes ahead at our present rate of knots: one hundred and forty, "freewheeling" at times to one hundred and fifty. Altimeter holding steady at thirteen hundred feet.

I decided to try and gain some extra height whilst we at least had two and a bit engines. The chance of any further attack from the sky was now pretty low, and there was nothing much in the way of ground defences between our present position and the sea. And as Ellis remarked, quite rightly, the higher we were when the port-outer finally gave up the ghost, the better the chance of reaching the English coast – enlisting the extra speed and airworthiness provided by a slight angle of descent. We need three thousand feet minimum, I thought to myself.

It was 02:25. Fifteen minutes since the surprise attack from the trees. I tried to sit up straight in the seat and find the extra space required to bring the stick back, and waited for the nose to lift. Nothing for several seconds then gradually, and very grudgingly, she agreed to the slightly elevated line of flight. The altimeter-needle began to wind up. Ellis looked across in surprise: despite acknowledging the need for freight, this wasn't the way to nurse an engine. Obviously he thought better about saying anything and looked out across my front again to check on the leaking coolant as it frothed away in the slipstream. When he pulled back to scrutinise the instrument panel it was as he feared – the port-outer's temperature gauge showed a slow rise as the engine began to further overheat. He pointed to the gauge. I nodded: "Radiator shutters full open," I commanded, going on the off-chance that an increased intake of cold outside air might help the engine in the short run. A couple of minutes later the needle of the temperature gauge had moved no further into the red – was holding steady. Ellis smiled grimly and put up a thumb.

Fourteen hundred feet on the altimeter. The old girl was literally rising to the occasion. (As I write – so many years later – I remember with gratitude what a heart that aeroplane had.) We levelled off with some difficulty at fifteen hundred: elevators were lethargic – not bringing the tail up very enthusiastically. But at least we were halfway there so far as altitude was concerned. I'd now definitely decided that we should try to make an emergency landing at Woodbridge, an aerodrome with a long runway and fog disposal facilities. I knew the airfield layout fairly well. Had flown a Wellington in and out several times in 1941. Yet there was a hazard in returning to land in the fen country: it could be blanketed by ground mist in the hours after midnight, especially in the autumn. We might have clear sky at one hundred feet, yet runway and buildings would be invisible, obscured by clinging, low-lying fog that only gave way when burned off by early morning sun. Yet we had no choice. Our own base lay too far north – extra mileage we'd most likely not be able to make. So be it – one thing at a time, I reasoned – deal with the weather situation when and if it becomes necessary.

"Zuider Zee coming up, skipper." Tubby Entwhistle had spotted the water ahead. I checked the ground on the left side. There it was – the small town of Kampen, just where it should be at the tip of the eastern arm of the dike-enclosed inland sea the Dutch call *"Ijsselmeer"*. The grassy banks of the Zee, now beneath our wings provided anchorage for barges sleeping out the night – unarmed merchantmen offering no opposition, their sleepers cowering beneath their blankets as we roared anxiously overhead on our precarious way to cover the remaining twenty miles of land that stood between us and the open sea.

Ellis' eye roamed the instruments. The two good engines were holding up well, operating temperatures normal at boost plus three. Yet even as he scanned the port-outer's gauge the needle began to creep more deeply into the danger zone. He tapped the glass of the gauge in frustration. The precious coolant must have been trickling away faster than ever over the last few miles. The flight-engineer knew the engine must ultimately seize-up but was determined to keep the prop turning as long as possible. Five more minutes flying on all three engines could mean the difference between reaching the end of a runway at home, or falling short in open country.

The fire caught us both off guard. An eruption of flame from the stricken power-plant that flared across the mainplane blotting out the wing-tip. The propeller windmilled aimlessly amid the clatter of rammed metal, turning floppily as if attached by a toy's rubber-band.

I rammed the control-column forward as the plane dropped, fighting the pull of the tail for a stall; I had to push my body against the column to get the nose down and maintain flying speed in a shallow dive. One way to get the fire out – let the rush of air do it. At the same time Ellis went professionally and calmly through the emergency drill: fuel-switches OFF – fire extinguisher button pushed – throttle back to end of gate – feather airscrew.

Three hundred feet lost and the flames were gone; gyrating prop feathered and stationary, offering minimum resistance to the air. But I could not bring her back up to resume straight and level flight. She was not responding to the elevators. Rivulets of sweat ran down my face as I pulled back on the control-column, squeezing the last, vital gut-pulling inches necessary to arrest our descent. The altimeter-needle wound downwards. At nine hundred feet Ellis pushed the throttles of the two working engines through the supercharger gate. Momentarily. He was taking a real chance with our last two sources of power. But the surge of speed increased airflow over control surfaces, buoyed up the mainplane, gave the elevators purchase, and with the column at its last inch of pull . . . the tail dropped. Nose came level. Ellis immediately brought the throttles back: boost plus three again – temperatures normal – airspeed one hundred and twenty.

My right instep was throbbing painfully; every push of the rudder pedal sent a sharp stab into the lower shin; the ankle joint connecting foot and leg didn't seem to be part of the anatomical situation anymore. But the altimeter was registering between eight and nine hundred feet, pressure on the rudder-pedals had eased, and ailerons and elevators were functioning – if protestingly. By now my face felt as if it was formed of damp wax: I had to clear a film of perspiration from my eyes to see the instruments clearly. Whatever had happened to the ankle seemed to have transferred its effect to the kneecap which had become a throbbing pulse, sending jabs of pain high into the thigh.

"Right" – I was the first to speak since the engine fire – "how do the other engines look?" Ellis responded with unusual formality. "They're O.K., Sir – temperature, pressure. O.K. at plus three."

Desperate situations called for desperate measures. I decided to see if Titty B-O could once again be nudged into the shallowest of shallow climb angles. But I felt her tail dragging, sensed there was insufficient power to maintain enough forward momentum to provide the necessary lift – a classic stall situation – and quickly brought the nose back down to the horizon. Ellis shook his head. "Better stay down here. It's a matter of fuel as well as engines."

The last stretch of German-occupied territory lay beneath us, dark against the pale reflective surface of the Zee. The lush, watery land lay quiet and still – almost inviting. Not a bad place to come down if one had to, I thought.

"Alkmaar ahead, skipper" – from Tubby Entwhistle spotting in the front-turret.

Minutes later and the roofs of the town lay directly before us. After the lowlands of the last hundred miles the high mediaeval gables came up like a range of mountain peaks, the taller chimneys reaching as pinnacles to grab the Lancaster from the sky. Straight across town we flew at what seemed roof-top height, causing panic in many a bedroom where it must have seemed that the lumbering monster above was about to land on the tiles.

Seven miles left to the open sea.

Just clear of the town the prevailing coastal wind caught us – a sea wind out of the east/north-east – as the Meteorological Officer had forecast. It pushed us strongly from behind on the starboard side, three-quarters on, boosting airspeed a good thirty knots, easing the workload of the two remaining engines, but forcing me to make constant rudder corrections in order to maintain a true westerly course. Amazing how everything's connected: the knife-like twinges in the leg were no longer localised but flickering through the pelvis to irk the shoulder. We were almost away – no challenge to our passage across the last strip of Nazi-occupied territory as we headed for the sand dunes and the North Sea. It was the same ten days ago coming home from a raid on Dortmund – no enemy opposition: the strong coastal defences lay west and east of Alkmaar. I made a mental note to let Intelligence know that we had found what seemed to be a safe little corridor. Then decided against it. We should keep the information to ourselves. Might have to let the low-level cat out of the bag in interrogation.

"Marked our exact position on the chart, Noakes?"

"Yes – dead on the dot. We maintain present course three minutes' more flying time over the sea. Then I'll give you a correction – no more than a degree, a fraction south-west. Have some fixes soon on the Woodbridge beacon when Tubby's down from the turret. Should bring us directly north-east of the Woodbridge runway. Wind might have caused a bit of a problem – it's about thirty-five miles per hour right now. Have to work out drift. But say two hundred miles to go, and allowing one hundred and forty knots with a tail wind, Tubby should be able to get cracking with the R.D.F. for beacon fixes in about twenty minutes."

"Hear that, Tubby? Stay up there another ten minutes – just in case any sea-patrolling Jerries are around."

I'd no sooner finished speaking than we were hit by a sudden down-drafting squall – a rush of wind that must have briefly gusted to fifty or sixty miles an hour and which, almost literally, pushed us downwards and out of the sky. Titty B-O just dropped, as if into a gigantic hole. There was nothing any of us could do except sit there. A muffled, "Christ . . . " from Ellis as he saw a wild sea about half a mile away sending high showers of spray into the air as it broke against the dunes. And, "Hell's bells – how about taking her up a bit – we're going to get wet," from Entwhistle in the front turret.

I was quite helpless. Miraculously the Lancaster stayed absolutely straight and level. No need to work the ailerons to keep port and starboard wing-tips parallel to the ground. And then we were below the squall line and the vortex let us go. I could feel pressure lift and release control surfaces, feel the aircraft move forward again, begin to fly again. . . propellers once more taking command. For what seemed a long drawn-out moment of time I was aware of the land's dune-humped edge seemingly almost at eye-level – cutting across a heaving and spray-rising ocean, a barrier between us and home. And nothing to be done about it because the next second we were into it, into a wall of spluttering white foam soaring directly in our path as strong swell hit high dune, obliterating land, sea, and sky.

Sea water streamed the cockpit windows, flushed the aeroplane from nose to tail. In the brief watery darkness I had a picture of a windblown blanket flapping loosely over the shattered mid-upper, soaked in salt, dripping brine silently down through a dank turret.

Titty B-O lurched from the spray like a sperm-driven salmon reaching for upper pools. For several seconds neither Ellis nor myself could see anything through the front windows until the film of salt gradually dissipated in the wind. All I could do was watch the artificial-horizon gauge and try to keep both wings level. The altimeter showed zero altitude.

"Right wing's low. Bring her up . . . she'll be in the drink in a minute." Ellis was at the relatively clear right window; his voice was calm enough, but sharp and staccato, demanding instant response. I automatically worked the ailerons – left up, right down. It was tricky: too much one way or the other and we'd be in the sea. I was flying more or less blind, a few feet above the surface, going through the motions mechanically. Any other bomber in service would very likely have gone down. But the Lancaster has a large wing and a long nose, so was well balanced fore and aft of centre, and we were pretty well trimmed before the squall hit us. So once free of the downdraft, and elevators functioning, the fuselage found longitudinal stability naturally and quickly. That was the beauty of the Lanc. She found aerodynamic posture almost without need of a pilot. We owe our lives many times over to that excellent, built-in characteristic.

Yet for what seemed an eternity after Ellis' warning the old kite hesitated – still a fraction right wing low – before the wing-tip sluggishly heaved itself up completely horizontal and the sea fell away. "Must get some height," I muttered quietly to myself, voice barely audible over the intercom. Taking control of the starboard-outer and port-inner throttle levers I increased power on both engines. Rev counters moved obediently upwards; boost gauges up a plus and steady. Ellis told me afterwards that at this juncture I abandoned reason and acted like some bloody test pilot who had to know what an airframe could and couldn't do – what sheer flying limits he was dealing with in terms of general performance, given engine losses and fuselage damage. So a slow, almost imperceptible, pull-back on the column. The sea began to recede. Angle of climb about ten degrees. At four hundred feet I levelled off and eased the throttles. Airspeed – with tailwind – around one hundred and thirty-five knots. "What a plane" – talking quietly to myself – "a bloody great hole dragging her down in the rear, a couple of engines gone, and she's still doing her best to fly."

"One degree sou'west," Noakes came on the intercom with a reminder. I carefully caressed the rudder bars; a slight slither of the wheel for the ailerons, and she came round – a little uncertainly and with a bit of a lurch – but round she came. The turn brought the wind directly astern, eliminating the need to keep plying the rudders to counteract its previous slanting push leftward. Altogether, an increase in airspeed of twenty-five knots.

A shower of rain fell softly over the canopy; streamed away the last clinging remnants of salt. The sea still looked uncomfortably close. Yet I was abundantly thankful for small mercies. To have been forced to try the crossing flying just above sea-level – given our mechanical condition and tiredness of the crew – might well have proved impossible.

My wristwatch showed just after two-thirty. The sky was dark gray, stained with that slightly reflective silver lustre which hangs between night and day when the moon has passed through. It was a hostile sea that raced with us towards the English coast – a six to eight foot swell with crests of white foam stretching to the horizon in lace-like threads. No prospect of ditching in those wind and tide-driven troughs. The plane would break up with the first remorseless, pile-driving slap. Noakes passed a note over from the navigator's table. It gave our position: latitude fifty-two and a half degrees north, longitude four and a half degrees east. Something over one hundred miles to go.

"How're you feeling?" Ellis leaned forward, looked first at the bandaged flying-boot, then gave me a scan.

The first intimation I had that things were not right came when the flight-engineer's face began to move in and out of focus; then floated bereft of neck and shoulders, a ghost-head bizarrely wrapped in a flying-helmet, a myriad of moisture-beads gathered high on the forehead ready to run. Strange that he should be sweating, I thought – it's been getting increasingly colder in here . . . An involuntary fit of shivering seized me at that point, and I fought desperately to overcome it before my grip on the controls was affected. "It's getting damn cold in here," I said into the mouthpiece. "Noakes, would you get back and see what things are like down there. Check on Duncan. And . . . well, there's not much we can do about the turret . . . but take a look inside – see if he's still protected by the blanket. And see if the skin around the holes is pulling away – opening things up – could account for the increased cold; or explain why the tab trim isn't helping as much to keep the rear from getting restless. And Tubby" – calling the wireless-operator who was now back in his radio niche – "it might be a little early . . . but worth trying R.D.F. and beacons. And send an S.O.S. to Base: give them a fix; tell them we're shot up and need to divert to Woodbridge."

The navigator found Duncan lying flat on his back, holding on with elbows jammed hard against the side of the restbed, both hands now bereft of bandages held vertical, congealed and ugly. His face was the pallor of old cheese and his eyes were closed, mouth tightly set. Noakes leaned over to speak but then thought better of it, realising that even a whisper might break the hold of those clutching elbows. The large surgical pads taped over the leg wounds were stained red. But drying out. The bleeding had stopped. Lower down the fuselage, beneath the mid-upper, damp and colder air struck, smelling strangely of salt and hydraulic oil. When he returned to the cockpit after playing his torch on the ragged wound in the fuselage floor, Noakes reported that thin strips of loose metal skin were buckling; looked likely to pull away where the lines of holding rivets were beginning to pop under the stress. The continued fraying of the skin was occurring where the fuselage sides curved round and under to form the belly of the aircraft. It was only a matter of time before the stressed duraluminium areas peeled away, extending the damage up and around the whole fuselage tube and causing top and bottom holes to join up. Should this happen, only a skeletal framework of formers and stringers would be left to hold the tail section in position. And even the power of four engines, never mind two, would be unlikely to overcome the horrendous drag this would create.

So far as the turret was concerned, Noakes grasped the lower rim with one hand, and swung his right foot to rest on the one intact floor stringer to the right of the hole. Anchored in this position he was able to twist himself beneath the mid-upper and scan the jumbled interior. The damp wind funnelling through caught at his flying-helmet, forced his eyes to squint. The turret was open to the silvered cloud-running sky. No sign of the blanket which Duncan had tied in place. He told me that Sergeant Guterman had slumped beneath the level of the rear-fairing; that he was no longer held by the butts of the two Brownings – no longer propped up to catch the brunt of the slipstream.

As Noakes returned to the navigator's table, I briefly lost control. Ellis saw my eyes close and hands slip from the half-wheel of the control-column. Immediately he reached forward and grabbed the stick in time to bring it quickly back to a central position. His quick movement brought me back in charge. "It's alright," I heard myself say, "I've got her. Just went dizzy for a moment." Which was something of an understatement as I'd almost passed out completely, weak as a kitten, arms and legs mere rubbery extensions flopping around out of wack.

Uncertain, Ellis let go of the controls.

But then he abruptly bent low to peer beneath the instrument panel, using his small pocket torch to search where the rudder-pedals were lost in shadow. What he saw made him call Noakes back into the cockpit. The brown suede flying boot on my right leg was apparently blood-soaked and black, but not as a result of damage to the ankle. Ellis tracked the flow with the torch beam to a neat puncture high on the leg, just above the flying-suit thigh pocket.

"Get a tight bandage above that, Noakes. Not a tourniquet now – just tight enough to discourage the bleeding. He's got to have sensation in that leg and be able to use it. Right. How's it feel, Johnny? Not too tight?"

"No: it's fine – a bit numb above the knee, but the foot seems alright. I can feel the pedal pressure perfectly well. It's just the whole leg that's difficult to move. Damn stupid thing to happen."

"You don't feel any pain in the thigh?" I shook my head. "Well, whatever's caused it seems to have made only a flesh wound. Missed the bone and muscle, otherwise I doubt you'd be able to push a rudder pedal. I didn't notice it bleeding before. You're sure Tubby hasn't done it up too tight? I want to cut down the bleeding without stopping the circulation. What do you think?"

I put pressure on the right rudder-bar – couldn't prevent a grimace of pain – but the leg knew what it was doing: was sensitive to touch and the aeroplane's response.

"It's alright." I checked the altimeter and looked down at the sea. I reckoned we were holding our own so far as altitude was concerned. Bad tail shimmying as we encountered a patch of turbulence. Sergeant Smith came on the intercom: "Things not good back here – vibrations are pretty grim. The whole tail-end's quivering like a jellyfish."

"Smithy," I responded, "get out of the turret and move back to the restbed. On the way tell me if any of the control rods are exposed in the fuselage. And keep Duncan in his place." It took the rear gunner a couple of minutes to extricate himself from his turret before he could report that the control rods seemed untouched.

"What about Duncan?"

"Pretty much out of it, I think. But he's holding on with his elbows. Hands look a real mess. Must be giving him trouble."

"Right: stay there then, Smithy; stay on the intercom."

Headphones now silent, I went off the air in more ways than one. Without the voices to confirm the actual happening of things, I found myself losing touch with the reality of what was going on for long seconds at a time. I can best describe it now –

writing so many years after the event – as a sort of "cottonwooling" of the senses: the kind of dream-like "going through the motions" – without actually being part of them – that effectively disengaged one from the real world of aeroplane and sky. As if the whole operation belonged to the phantasmagoric realm of the magic-lantern show at which I was but a spectator. I was flying mechanically, airborne in a soundless vacuum, the two last propellers whirling away devoid of engine noise, and the aeroplane floating like a gas-filled dirigible, lighter than air, in complete harmony with the elements. I clearly recall the dim light from the navigation table imparting a dull spectral sheen to the metal surfaces – an unreal science-fiction atmosphere, turning the cockpit into the front innards of some Jules Verne invention sliding through the sky. Everything was going so well, so benignly, that I wondered if I shouldn't wander down the fuselage myself to view this great hole everyone was talking about – grab some of that cold air at the back. Might be a good thing to do. Eyes were pressing to close – take "forty winks": the stepfather's way of announcing his regular nap after Sunday lunch. Right knee was beginning to stiffen; could feel the tightness reaching its way along the sinews . . . click, click, click.

"About ten minutes to the coast." Noakes' voice splintered the illusory calm; restored the clamour of engines and motion of Titty B-O's shuddering progress through the bumpy, storm-fringed air.

My own voice sounded from somewhere: "Tubby . . . send our new position to Base; say our petrol situation is dicey; hope to have enough to reach Woodbridge but doubt we can go round for a second approach."

"Right, Sir," responded the wireless operator who was already hunched up over the Marconi, manipulating knobs and dials.

The familiar, homeward-bound routine at last. With a bit of luck we could be on the ground in half-an-hour.

The low-lying coast of East Anglia was a bluish, pencil-thin line in the distance. Ellis was worried about the fuel situation; he always hoped the gauges were not registering accurately when petrol levels were low. Automatically I was checking wing-tips and nose posture against the artificial-horizon, an instrument which showed how straight and level we were flying. I also double-checked all the gauges on the instrument panel. And it was then that I felt the terrible emptying of will and loss of physiological function that accompanies real fear.

The needle of the starboard-outer's rev counter was flicking around, dropping back two hundred revs, trying to regain its setting, dropping back three hundred . . . a slow but steady loss of power.

Ellis nodded across. He'd already seen it; was watching the instrument and the boost gauge with a resigned concentration, mentally preparing to pursue ditching procedures. I decided to ignore the whole thing; proceed on the assumption that the instrument itself was at fault. Even so, at the back of my mind I was thinking ahead – how to get as close to home as possible with one good, and one failing, engine. It would have to be almost a matter of gliding – adopting the slightest necessary descent-angle to keep the nose down and avoid the stall, maintaining just sufficient airspeed to keep the kite airworthy, and hope to come to ground in a convenient place: the end of the runway at Woodbridge, preferably.

Calculation: with about fifty miles still to go, starting from a height of four hundred feet (give or take a bit) and to sustain a minimum flying speed of one hundred and ten knots, we would have to descend approximately ten feet every fifty seconds. A pretty shallow rate of descent. Could the aeroplane now be flown within such demanding parameters? More to the point, was I capable of handling her? If it could be done, we would be at zero altitude somewhere in the vicinity of Woodbridge. The unknown factor in this bleak prospect was, of course, the failing engine.

Every extra minute or so those twenty-four pistons kept the prop turning increased our chances of reaching the 'drome with sufficient height to make a once only, relatively controlled, approach to the runway.

"Well, there it is . . . " Ellis spoke softly, reflectively, like a man already resigned to the worst. About five miles ahead the English coast was vaguely defined by a line of white-breaking waves.

"Got our position, Noakes?"

"Just a sec," – from the navigator. "Right: we'll be crossing the coast about ten miles further south than I anticipated, due to drift. Means we'll be better placed for Woodbridge. Course correction to two-six-o right to the beacon. I'd say about fifteen to twenty minutes' flying time – allowing for circling and making the approach."

I was about to add that old Titty B-O's condition might not allow us the luxury of a circling, conventional approach, but thought better of it.

Ellis was nursing the tired engine: watching each new downward swing on the rev counter and assessing the overall loss of power evident over the course of several minutes. He would then compensate by demanding less from the engine – throttling back a fraction to keep demand commensurate with diminishing performance.

"She doesn't like this at all," I said to nobody in particular. "Airspeed's really too low to guarantee safe level flight with the tail drag we've got. Going to move her slightly nose down – give her a bit of help from gravity – can't afford the risk of a stall at this point."

"Start our descent now, you mean," said Ellis.

"No alternative. We might have enough height to hold a straight course to the runway. But when the height gives out, that's when we come down, wherever we are. How's the petrol situation?"

"Touch and go – if the gauges are their usual thirty or forty gallons optimistic, that is. There'll be none left to jettison anyway. Bit of a bonus there."

The first streaks of mist bled eerily across the wings as Ellis was speaking. Up ahead the fog was now clearly visible, hugging the ground up to about fifty feet, hanging back from the sea. Upper air was clear apart from a few high-flying strands of cirrus. Below us the coastal flats of East Anglia presented a dark and featureless profile against the invading white surf.

But it was land. It was home. We had at least got back. All we had to concentrate on now was getting down – in one piece if possible. No thoughts of German reception committees and prisoner-of-war camps; no worries about ditching in the sea and getting Guterman out of the mid-upper in the minute or so we would have – if we were lucky – before the aircraft sank.

I could not disguise my disappointment at the state of the weather. "Damn ground-mist like the Met man said. For God's sake you'd think he might have been wrong tonight. He usually bloody well is. But, Jesus Christ, can you believe it: we have to choose a night to get shot-up when the bastard happens to be on form! Can you see any breaks north or south?"

Ellis stretched in his seat and peered through port and starboard windows. "Not really: it's thicker towards the north and over the Wash; about the same to the south as it is here. It's got to be covering the whole of Norfolk and Suffolk. You know what it's like when it socks-in down this way. Anyway, we don't have a choice of going north or south – we haven't got the capability to start looking around. We'll have to hope for some gaps at lower levels. These East Coast mists can be patchy nearer the ground."

For the first time during the whole operation Ellis sounded tired and discouraged. Like myself, I suppose, he felt that the appearance of the ground-mist was the last straw – that some good luck was due us at this stage of the game. Reaching the coast even twenty minutes earlier – which we could have done on three engines – might have made all the difference: these ground-mists tend to thicken up as the early morning hours wear on. Yet even under the best visual conditions – given the state of the plane – our chances of making a halfway-normal approach and landing would be slim enough. I was really no fatalist, but the thought did cross my mind that the fog hazard seemed to be Fate's way of delivering the *coup de grace*. I shrugged my shoulders involuntarily and continued to coax Titty B-O along.

Given our height and angle of descent I estimated we'd avoid slipping into the pea-soup below until on the last few miles of our approach. Then we would at least have VHF radio communication with Woodbridge to let us know the local conditions, tell us our position vis-a-vis the aerodrome and its long runway. In the meantime I prayed for frequent gaps in the mist to let us see where the hell we were – give us some idea of our height and position in relation to ground and airfield. We were now about forty-five miles from our emergency destination. Some good news from the wireless operator: Tubby reported that Lincoln had alerted Woodridge. And good beacon transmissions had enabled Noakes to plot our exact position and confirm our heading on our present trajectory.

I made another survey of the instruments: the weak engine was just about holding its own, delivering about seventy percent of normal power output. The altimeter registered a height somewhere between two and three hundred feet. And the nose-down attitude was providing enough forward momentum to keep Titty B-O airborne; I still had the feel of the aircraft, allowing me to fly her rather than the other way round. "Pray for the starboard-outer," I said loudly, intercom or no intercom.

The tail wind was gone. Airspeed now only about one hundred and ten. Message from the navigator: "If we maintain present speed and heading we'll be in the vicinity of Woodbridge in about twenty minutes plus. And skipper, they're lighting F.I.D.O. on the main runway."

"Good: that'll give us a chance to see them." (F.I.D.O. – Fog Intensive Dispersal Operation – was a system of petrol pipelines laid along both sides of the runway. When lit, the burning fuel took about fifteen minutes to disperse the fog. Precious fuel; but it saved over two thousand aircraft by the end of the war.)

Not much more to do. Just try and maintain straight and level flight on the present heading at the present approach angle. There would be no question of going round for a second try. It would be a one-shot attempt. The aeroplane would have to be flown in. No chance of holding off and flaring-out for a gentle touch-down.

I turned to Ellis for confirmation – detached my mouthpiece to shout above the cockpit noise without benefit of intercom. "What do you think: suppose our approach is really lousy – we might not be able to see much – would we have enough power to pull up and go round again if we used both supercharger boosts?"

"No, not a chance. The port-inner couldn't do it on its own, and we'd just blow the starboard-outer up."

There were places in the mist beneath us where the vapour thinned, opening up illusory avenues which invited exploratory descent: seductive approaches which, if explored, would rob us of our one asset – height. Looking back, I can recognise other less obvious dangers such a blanket of fog presented during the final stages of our night's journey. Rather like flying high above thick cumulus cloud when one develops a false sense of security with a ready-made, distinguishable "floor" beneath one: a surface against which a pilot can visually assess the aircraft's posture, feel comfortably "cushioned" so to speak – an appealing psychic bonus in that it relieves the sometimes disturbing sense of absolute isolation produced by vast unarticulated reaches of sky-space. The difference and danger being, in our case, that we really had no space at all – only the illusion of it.

"Ellis, watch the instruments a sec." I didn't tell the flight-engineer that I was suddenly seeing everything double – that when I looked at the instrument-panel nothing came sharply into focus; and that I was having difficulty co-ordinating movements of arms and legs. And there was this incredible temptation to call the whole thing off; give in to the overwhelming desire to close the eyes; sleep. Thank God that the beaten-up old aeroplane was flying so roughly, vibrating and bucking the controls, that the mere act of hanging on kept the eyes open, had me functioning involuntarily like a puppet.

Open and close; open and close . . . I kept jamming my eyes bruisingly through the exercise routine . . . Instruments suddenly sharp-edged and unmoving again. I pulled off the heavy gauntlet flying gloves: grip and release, grip and release . . . Naked touch with the cold hardness of the "steering-wheel" restored the feel of handling twenty-three tons – *sans* bombs – of flying metal. Ellis had noticed nothing. He was methodically scanning the "dashboard" – looking for the slightest clue that might allow him to take remedial action – left hand ready on the failing engine's throttle-lever. I offered a short prayer of thanks to the Gods, or whatever, for having such a man in the next seat.

"Eighteen miles . . . " from the navigator.

Ten minutes and we should be sighting the petrol-lit runway. But the starboard-outer was losing ground. Both boost-gauge and rev-counter registered falling power. And as the pull of the props diminished, the more the tail began to drag. I had to drop the nose a fraction. The cushion of fog moved closer.

The Lancaster was starting to lurch from one wing to the other like a punch-drunk boxer. Corrections administered by rudders and ailerons were having diminishing effect. At that point I knew we hadn't a cat in hell's chance of making a normal landing: she'd never be able to handle the drag of wheels and undercarriage. Yet

God only knows what possessed me to try and find out. "Select undercarriage down."

Ellis looked up in surprise: "Now?"

"Now – got to see what happens when the undercart drops."

The oleo-legs carrying the giant wheels started on their usual rumbling protest from behind the inboard engine-nacelles. Immediately the whole airframe began to vibrate madly, shaking equipment loose and jerking everyone about like so many sacks travelling in a square-wheeled truck. The nose pulled up dangerously. Three seconds into the drop and the wheels stuck – obstructed by damage done to the retracting nacelle doors, obviously hit in the attack from the wood. And, as it turned out, both tyres were hopelessly collapsed, riddled with bullets.

"UP . . ."

But Ellis had anticipated the command, at the same time giving a short boost of power to the one good engine. Neither he nor I knew whether or not the wheels would retract fully – what damage by German rifle fire might have been suffered by the whole undercarriage gear. Yet back they went, leaving the twisted doors dangling. The extreme vibrations petered out; the power-boost allowed old Titty B-O to respond to the forward movement of the column; the tail stopped its sabotage.

Well, I thought – at least we know: it would have to be a crash-landing. Wheels-up. It would have been in any case – we could never have made a controlled approach with wheels and flaps down. Only way down is to fly her in as fast as we can on the belly.

"R/T with Woodbridge, Sir: just coming through." The wireless-operator's voice was strained after the last fifteen seconds of lurching confusion. "Woodridge . . . Woodridge control: this is Lancaster F Freddie, 218 Squadron . . . over."

"We have you, Freddie. Got a good reception committee for you. North-west/south-east runway's cleared – fog dispersal burning now for ten minutes. Fire-tenders and crash crews standing by at the end of runway. Please inform of aircraft condition. You are right on the line of the beacon. Over."

"Woodbridge . . . about ten miles out. Height between one hundred and one hundred and fifty feet. Aircraft state is poor: two engines out and a third pretty ropy. Major cannon-shell damage aft of the mid-upper turret reducing elevator and rudder control. Very little manoeuvrability. Undercarriage jammed – but we couldn't use the wheels anyway. Little fuel left – nothing to jettison. Will try and maintain present approach and follow standard crash-landing procedures – present airspeed around one hundred and ten. If we overshoot, no chance of going round again just have to finish in the fields. Over."

"Very good. Keep your R/T on 'receive' – will have a better idea of your position in a couple of minutes to help on the approach. Over."

"Right: wireless and navigation seem to be spot-on. Should sight you soon. Tell your medical people to get to the mid-upper first. Our gunner's trapped in the turret. May have to cut him clear. Can you give me the ceiling of the ground-mist and the extent of forward visibility . . . over."

"Fog's very patchy here – drifting a great deal – dense in some places, but one hundred and fifty plus feet clear above runway due to F.I.D.O. Forward ground visibility on runway a good twelve hundred feet. Over."

"Good: we'll try and get home in as much of one piece as possible. Over."

Noakes' voice cut in on the headset. "Slight course correction, Sir – on the beacon: two-five-zero degree heading."

I glanced down to where the magnetic compass was slung beneath the instrument-panel and gently nudged Titty B-O round the slight angle required. She wallowed uncertainly, demanding a hell of a lot of rudder and aileron.

The first flecks of upward drifting mist brushed the nose and bomb-bay as she settled into the turn. My leg was numbing up again. I tried to flex the foot. Impossible. Ankle rigid. All congealed from toe to thigh.

We were now immersed in mist. Committed to the ground.

"Smithy's at the restbed?" I asked the question absently: the rear-turret now seemed so far away on the other side of that no-man's land represented by the continuously expanding void around the mid-upper, that I'd forgotten what had happened to the tail-gunner.

"Yes, Sir" – from Smithy himself – "been with Duncan at the restbed for the last few minutes. I'll see him out when we land."

"Good lad. Listen everybody, in four or five minutes we'll be on the ground – somewhere – hopefully on the Woodbridge runway. It's a belly-landing so, as they say in the train manuals, 'get your backs to the engine,' down behind the main spar and close to the restbed – grab onto the bulkhead former. I'll try and set her down as gently as possible. As soon as we came to a stop, out through the hatches and the door. Smithy, have the axe handy. You'll be first at the door. Fire shouldn't be a problem. We've hardly any petrol left. Just enough to get down."

When I'd finished the cabin seemed strangely quiet. Ellis had the mannered look of a waxwork figure. He surprised me when he came to life and read off speed and estimated altitude. "Guess we're about one hundred feet, Johnny. Airspeed about one hundred and five. Will she level out a bit?"

Back a little on the stick. The nose came up a touch. Now at the slightest of glide-angles. She shuddered but kept the posture. I reckoned that five knots an hour less and she'd stall. Gray opaque fog shrouded us – denser now than the vapour above. Wing-tips completely lost.

I looked back to see Noakes twisting in his chair, leaning round the corner of his table and waiting anxiously. Entwhistle gave him a nod and continued to delicately manipulate the fine-tuning of the R.1115 Receiver and transcribe figures to a signals-pad. It was a difficult job in the unsteady aeroplane and a fine sweat ringed the wireless-operator's forehead as he worked, beading where the flying helmet gripped. He pushed the pad over. No way I could see his figures. Heard from Noakes:

"Final position, Sir. A little further out than we thought. Six miles north-west of main runway. Should be showing up any minute."

I spoke to Woodbridge: "We're six miles out on final heading. No sign of you yet. The weather's very thick up here. We're in the middle of it at something under one hundred feet."

"Very good, Sir. You're doing well. Fog's lifting a little here. Have some clear patches. Ceiling above runway improving by the minute. You should be in clearer air and spot us any second. Good luck. Over."

The Woodridge controller went off the air. The remaining moments were our own. Gently, very gently, I held the control-column steady. I wondered if I should follow the book and put on twenty degrees of flap. Absurd thought. We were only making a few knots above landing speed as it was – already in a landing posture without need of any air brakes. She'd fall out of the sky with any increased drag – as we saw a few minutes before when the wheels were partially down. I remembered Matthews once saying, "Better go in fast and straight on the glide if the power's gone. Might avoid falling short, for God's sake – which you'll most likely do if you try to make a conventional, calculated piss-arse approach. At least if you overshoot going like hell on your belly you're on the deck when you go off the end of the runway – with luck into the fields."

The port-inner was holding up at maximum revs; the starboard-outer was surging from one to three thousand.

Dead ahead, a patch of clear sky revealed one fugitive star. But it was as Titty B-O heaved herself gratefully into the open space that I saw the flaring runway about a quarter mile off to the right. Before Ellis could move a hand I thrust the throttle levers of both engines through the red of the supercharger gate and kicked left rudder. The Lanc shivered over every inch of her worn body as she dragged herself hoveringly and terribly slowly into the turn. It was a supremely dangerous moment – a tremendous risk to take at that height with a large, crippled aircraft – and if both engines had not responded to the sudden demand for ultimate power, we would have stalled and that would have been that. How the ailing starboard-outer managed to come through at full boost is one of those inexplicable mechanical marvels.

Yet I had no choice but to try and pull round once I'd spotted the flare path. For if we'd continued on course – irrevocably committed to a crash-landing – I knew from my knowledge of the airfield that directly ahead, roughly at the point of touch-down, lay the messes and living quarters of many aerodrome personnel.

During those long seconds as Titty B-O wallowed into the last turn ever demanded of her – avoiding a certain stall, I am convinced, only because flaps were level – I decided it really was all over. For although now pointed in the right direction, and with the runway almost directly beneath us, we were not well positioned to make the best use of it. It had taken us by surprise, so to speak. The successful belly-landing demands a long and low ground-skimming approach; yet ironically, in finally attaining this distant pinpoint of land we had tried so hard to reach, we found ourselves hovering like a moth, unable to make proper use of it.

A split-second decision. Forget about how much runway one's got. Drop her right now. Nose down – whatever maximum power's left – fly her in – level out – drive her forward – let her find her own moment of touch-down dead straight and level –

doesn't matter where she stops – enough forward momentum to minimise the inertia of impact – like sledging – a flying toboggan . . .

I estimated we were about seventy feet up. Slammed both engine throttles through the gate again. Pushed the stick forward. Twenty degree angle nose down. Wings waggling uncontrollably. A few scant patches of ground-mist deflecting and diffusing the flames. Visual contact one second – none the next. But we were straight. We were travelling with the flames coming up to meet us on either side.

"NOW. . . NOW. . . " Ellis yelled.

I cut both engines, pulled hard back on the column – no final trimming, putting airscrews into fine pitch: she wouldn't know the difference – fighting to keep the nose up, wings straight, to avoid ploughing in, and bring the whole length of the fuselage to touch down as one piece. I saw nothing of the ground itself – just the endless blur of orange fire rushing past. Ellis waited for the split-second of impact to shut off the fuel-lines; to activate engine fire-extinguishers.

There couldn't be much runway left. I'd desperately hoped we'd get the last thousand feet. We needed the hard surface to stabilise the aircraft on a straight-line skid, an even keel, before meeting whatever obstacles lay beyond the runway in the Suffolk countryside.

When the belly of the aeroplane finally touched down it was as if the familiar element of air had suddenly solidified. The control-column sheared; the instrument-panel broke away in dozens of small pieces – gauges, bits of glass, coils of wire, falling eerily in apparent slow-motion into the depths of the bomb-aimer's position. The thudding shock of first impact lashed the spine, jerked head backwards as if trying to push teeth high in the skull and shiver the skeleton that held you together – physical sensations that were then all but anaesthetised by the deluge of retching, screeching sound, awesome and mind-piercing, as twenty plus tons of violated and resisting metal abraded concrete at about ninety-five miles an hour. Bones screamed like exposed teeth; the mind tried to hold on; the spirit cringed. In the depths of both ears a thin-bladed knife turned at high revolutions, metal screaming at high-pitch against metal, a personal playback of the outside mayhem invading every part until one was surely dismembered, surviving only as a pair of eyes that could do nothing but hold on, recording only, incapable of providing intelligence that consciousness could use, a sense castrated, without reason for being. And the caustic smell of smoking rubber, spilled hydraulic oil and duraluminium being finely ground up, harsh in the nostrils.

And then we ran out of aerodrome. I caught a glimpse of the last few fog-dispersal flares on either side as our aeroplane went straight as a projectile, veering neither right nor left in her death run.

She ripped off the end of the runway like a comet, a great plume of sparks and smoke breaking from the nose, flaring down both sides of the cockpit. Nothing to do except put the head down and hold onto the sides of the seat, the only solid support left.

The scream of shredding metal ceased as she gouged into soft earth through a black haze of pulverised soil, speed seemingly undiminished, suffering a violent bombardment over the length and breadth of fuselage from sod, stones, rocks – everything that was ploughed up as she tore along: hedges, walls, ditches, a stretch of road . . . penetrated, flattened or bounced over . . . in the mad cacophonic disintegrating pile-up of ourselves and our machine.

We came to rest in the half-light of early morning hard up against a copse of tall trees. There was no fire. No-one spoke or moved. For several seconds an abrupt silence held us in limbo.

Smithy and Tubby Entwhistle were the first to break from their crash stations and reach the door. They struggled vainly to wrench it free but were impeded by the tangle of metal that had become the rear fuselage. The crashes of Smith wielding the axe sounded like explosions in the brittle silence of the cockpit. The air was thick, difficult to breathe, filled with lingering smoke fumes and fine particles of soil. I couldn't move my right leg; neither did I particularly care whether I left the wreckage or not. Finally, after crawling beneath the collapsed instrument-panel and freeing one leg at a time from the tangle of rudder-pedals and general debris, Ellis was able to help me out into the aisle. Once upright and out of the parachute-harness, applying weight gingerly to the bad leg, I was able to wobble off down the fuselage under my own steam. But as I lowered myself off the main-spar I suddenly felt sad to my stomach. Even though we had done it – against all the odds we had done it . . . I knew in my heart of hearts we were too late for Dick Guterman. And I also knew it could have been otherwise.

I got to my feet and slithered down the fuselage. It was impossible to get near the turret. The fuselage floor aft of the bomb-bay already weakened by the penetration of the cannon shell had split wide open on impact with the runway, causing the tail-end to partially separate and angle high in the air at forty degrees. Jumbled bulkheads and floor-stringers completely blocked any approach to the base of the mid-upper, and until Smith had smashed a way through, even exiting by the rear door was impossible. Thank God there had been no fire.

Damp early morning air drifted in, sweet to breathe, a poignant reminder that – save for one of us – we had indeed returned to a world beyond the aeroplane.

"Come on," said Ellis, taking some of my weight and steering me through the open door, "they'll be getting to him from the outside: quicker and safer for him."

Faint wisps of persisting mist hung here and there over the land, trailing like white pennants from the twin rudders now angled crazily together with the rear-turret between them – some eight feet off the ground. Duncan, who'd held on to the restbed all the way by sheer elbow-power, was sitting blankly on the grass facing what was left of the aircraft. He held up one unbandaged hand in greeting; said nothing. From the ground I could see very little of what was left of the mid-upper turret – just a few jagged shards of the dome remained in situ on the upper rim – and of Duncan's blanket there was no sign at all. I wondered how long it had afforded Guters some protection; if the heroic and supremely dangerous act by which it was placed in position could be judged in terms of results, in terms of any real benefit and succour it had provided for Dick. Neither was there any indication that the turret was occupied. As Noakes had reported just after we had almost been blown into the sea off Alkmaar, Guters, no longer supported by the barrels of the two Brownings, had slumped forward in the turret; could not be seen now from down below. Noakes came alongside, stemming a slow trickle of blood seeping into his left eye from a gash on the forehead. Smithy and Tubby Entwhistle were standing by the broken high-angled tail, seemingly mesmerised by the airborne rear-turret.

A faint residue of smoke and dust still rose from the deep trough of ploughed-up earth. As far back as I could see the land was rent and scarred as if a meteorite had torn across its surface. Parts of the aeroplane lay scattered all along the route. The two outboard engines – propellers twisted in knots – had severed first, taking both wing-tips with them. Smaller debris was strewn like confetti – engine radiators and cowlings, large sections of mainplane skin, pieces of the bomb-doors, wing-tanks . . . all the depressing paraphernalia of a twisted, utterly broken, gallant aeroplane.

Surveying the scene under a gradually lightening sky it hardly seemed possible that the main part of the fuselage – carrying us all with it – could have survived intact. The two heavy landing-wheels and their once gleaming oleo-legs, wrenched like sticks from their housings, provided a grim reminder of the forces old Titty B-O had encountered and which we, her crew, had survived. The undercarriage had come to rest on the far side of the stone wall which we had breached as effectively as any tank. Both wheels were up in the air, still slowly turning, tyre rubber burning and sending up a stream of smoke, blacker than a funeral pyre.

Bumping along, masked headlights swinging crazily, a small convoy of vans, fire-tenders, ambulances – plus a mobile crane – were coming across the field, heading for the gap in the wall, avoiding bits and pieces of Lancaster as if competing over a slalom course. Weaving their way round the debris they pulled in to surround the airborne tail of the bomber. In a matter of seconds the fire-tender crews doused the centre-section wing-tanks and two remaining inboard engines in foam. Two ladders were quickly placed on either side of the mid-upper.

The driver of the first Hillman van on the scene – a burly Squadron Leader who could hardly contain his obvious delight that we had come through – shook all our hands, took a look at Duncan and patted him on the back, and kept repeating, "Christ, bloody marvellous, bloody good show; Christ . . . " Then, "Station Engineer Officer Bawdsley's the name. My Flight Sergeant's up there now" – nodding towards the mid-upper – "with the Station Medical Officer. I'm going to go and survey the whole thing inside. We'll get him out, don't worry. God, you had me worried when I saw two engines feathered. Came in at a hell of an angle – never thought you'd be able to line her up and flatten out like that. But you pancaked it beautifully. Bloody marvellous . . . " He grabbed a flashlight from the car and ran over to the fuselage door that Smithy had broken out with the axe. He had no need of the usual ladder – the earth was level with the sill.

We just stood there. Nothing to say. Each still living his own experiences of the last few hours. The large Bedfords had disgorged a sergeant, a group of orderlies, and a very young-looking second Medical Officer. Curious, I thought, as the Engineer Officer disappeared into the fuselage, how good the Wombat looked; how bright the colours were in the reflected glare from all the headlights, and how ironic that the metal skin around old Guters' emblem had survived intact.

Medical people wandering around – hauling stretchers – God knows what else. "We're alright," I said to the young M.O. – "walking wounded only. I'd like you to go and see if you can help the S.M.O. at the mid-upper turret. Our friend in there needs more help than we do."

"But I think . . . look at your leg, Sir – it's bleeding through everything you've got on there. You shouldn't even be walking on it."

"I really would be very grateful, Doctor, if you'd go and help look after our air-gunner. Your sergeant can see to us for the moment." I suppose it was more an order than a request; fortunately the M.O. took it that way.

"Yes, Sir. Sergeant, see about a little first-aid here before . . . "

"I would suggest" – I went on – "that we get Flying Officer Duncan to the Sick Bay immediately. His hands are raw and he has deep cuts in his thighs from trying to help Sergeant Guterman in the turret. The rest of us would like to stay here for the moment. I can lean on Flight Lieutenant Ellis indefinitely."

Up on Titty B-O's broken spine the two men working over the shell of the mid-upper were now joined by the young M.O. and the Station Engineer who'd just completed his interior survey. It was getting lighter. I looked back the way we had come and saw that the patchy ground-mist over the runway was settling in again now that F.I.D.O. was out. A forlorn damp morning which bore no connection to the real world of yesterday. Again I found myself wondering about Duncan's blanket. How long it had survived. If it had helped.

Nothing yet from the men clustered around the mid-upper. I riled bitterly against myself. What I'd done was inexplicable. I knew I had not acted out of any fervent, gung-ho, militaristic attitude – the "get to Berlin at all costs", kind of thing. None of us thought about our job in such idealistic "glory boy" terms. We valued, above all, effectiveness: based on survival, preparedness, skill, caution, and a modicum of straightforward luck and cunning. So either I had just lost my marbles – had not grasped the full nature of what had happened, or I honestly thought that to make a return circle over Tempelhof – and go through a bombing run – was as good a way home as any other. I tried to re-live the moment after the Junkers attack when Tubby Entwhistle had reported the damage to the mid-upper turret. What was in my mind; what was my thinking about it; how did I come to make the decision I did? But at this point I could clarify nothing. The details of the night's operation simply dissolved into a series of kaleidoscopic general impressions.

The Station Medical Officer, who was bending awkwardly over the turret, straightened up; waved to an orderly on the ground who then climbed the ladder carrying a large box. Voices in the fuselage were shouting urgently, causing the Engineer Officer to slide down from the turret and disappear inside. The ambulance carrying Duncan whined away in low gear, bouncing awkwardly as it headed for the rift in the wall.

The remaining five of us stood together without speaking, loathe to leave, waiting for word on Sergeant Richard Guterman, D.F.M.

I felt an immediate need to get to the turret – pulled away from Ellis and walked stiffly towards the ladder. But the way was blocked by the Engineer Officer who unexpectedly emerged from the aircraft door, still shouting instructions to members of the crash-crew working inside. When he spoke his breath frosted faintly in the rapidly chilling pre-dawn air.

"Well . . . it's a mystery to me, Squadron Leader Graham, how the heck you kept her in the air . . . never mind got her down. Control rods to rudders and elevators are just about split through . . . barely hanging together. How they gave you any control-surface capability, God only knows. And flying her on two engines – if you can call it that – one and a half more like." His voice tailed off. When he continued his tone was softer. "The turret's a mess. Can't cut through to him with snippers. Have to get him clear with torches. But we've got to give the wing tanks another dousing of foam first – they're bust wide open in the centre-section and there's a strong smell of fumes in there. Can't risk 'em going up when we light the oxyacetylene. We'll start in a minute. Sorry we can't do more at the moment."

I found myself staring at the Wombat; momentarily recalled Dick on the trestle painting it. Bits of our conversation floated by. I looked up at the turret. A thin wisp of whitish vapour hovered the length of the Lancaster's broken back. The S.M.O. climbed down as I watched, came round from the other side and spoke quietly. "Well, we've got him clear of the gun-barrels: didn't seem to penetrate – basically heavy contusions, skin broken here and there allowed some bleeding. It looked nasty, but you know it might have been a good thing: those Brownings pinned him in there – he couldn't move, couldn't be bounced around. Don't know about the rest of it until we get him out. There's been some internal bleeding – concussive damage from the shellburst, I'd say, or splinters. Can't determine properly until he's released – it's the lower torso that's taken the brunt of it. There's a jumble of twisted stringers and lengths of broken turret-frame holding him around the pelvis and legs. Again, can't ascertain the damage until they're cut away. Anyway, we've got an oxygen-bottle connected up and I've given him morphine and a heart stimulant . . . "

"You mean he's alive . . . "

"Just. I didn't think so when I got up there. Respiration was barely a whisper. But it's stronger since I put the mask on him. I mean, it's really a marvel he hasn't died of exposure, never mind everything else."

"There's nothing I can do? He wouldn't know me if I got up there?"

"Afraid not. He's in a coma of sorts. Been so since the attack, I'd say. Besides, look at that leg of yours . . . that's fresh blood on the pad – it's wet; you're bleeding at the ankle as well. Sergeant," – shouting to the senior medical orderly – "take the Squadron Leader to the Sick Bay, please. Get the trousers off him and see what the damage is – ankle and thigh. I'll stay on here with the ambulance. We'll have the gunner out in five or six minutes; tell Corporal Jamieson to have oxygen ready in the Emergency Room when we arrive – everything set up for life support."

The M.O. turned back to me: "Are the others alright? We'll want to have a look at them, of course."

"Yes, they're O.K. But Flying Officer Duncan – he's gone already – is going to need some expert attention. His hands are badly flayed, wind-burned, and he got some ugly leg wounds when he . . . well, I'll tell you about it later." I paused for a moment. "You can't, I suppose, say what you think of old Guters' chances?"

"Guters? Ah . . . no: impossible. Once we know the extent of the injuries we'll have a better idea. We'll try and stabilise things, and, if he can be moved, get him into the local hospital. After that, Cambridge or Cranwell, depending on what he needs. The Station Commander's on his way out here, but nobody's talking to you yet so far as I'm concerned. First we get you cleaned up and then you get some sleep. You're as white as a sheet – some fever too, I'd say. I'll keep you informed, don't worry.

"And by the way, Sir: that was an incredible feat – just getting back; never mind setting her down."

I nodded – I remember saying something like, "It was all of us – we all did it together, and that includes the old kite – all of us." And then I limped off to where the medical sergeant was waiting. I hardly dared hope for Guters, but if there was a chance . . . God, I prayed it might be so.

Chapter Six
Aftermath

Our stay at Woodbridge on that Saturday was short-lived. Noakes was quickly patched up – the cut on his forehead was superficial and required no stitching. Both Duncan's hands were going to require plastic surgery in the form of skin-grafting. The cutting-edge of the metal, against which he had pushed with that scissor-like grip of the thighs, had come very close to severing an artery. Dirt and oil in the wounds hadn't helped, and he had already been despatched to the Royal Air Force hospital at Cranwell. As for myself, the leg had been hit in two places by half-inch fragments from Titty B-O herself – pieces of engine-cowling from the port-outer which had penetrated the fuselage when the ground-fire from the woods had knocked out the radiator. After they were removed I was up and about, incapable of sleep, dealing with Intelligence de-briefing, and arranging on the telephone for a Lancaster from the squadron to come and pick the five of us up after lunch.

Guterman had not recovered consciousness. They had freed him from the turret very quickly once the oxyacetylene-torches had gone to work, and the combination of oxygen and masses of blankets providing warmth was working to keep vital functions stable, and his breathing shallow but regular. Apart from the bruises and abrasions caused by the grip and chafing of the turret wreckage, the major injury had been caused by a massive blow to the chest. Several ribs were cracked and three were broken. The sternum was caved-in and a huge purple-blue bruise extended across the whole thoracic region. But there was no sign that shrapnel or metal fragments of any sort – even from the tangled fuselage and turret hardware which entwined him – had penetrated the body. The Medical Officer thought that internal bleeding had stopped. He decided that Dick's best chance lay in being transferred immediately to the excellent hospital facilities at Cranwell.

We all saw him off. Not much of him to be seen: sheeted to the chin, breathing through an oxygen mask, strapped to a stretcher; he was loaded into an Avro Anson with the junior medical officer in attendance.

The Anson took off for Cranwell in Lincolnshire at eleven-fifteen that Saturday morning. And Lancaster V Victor, flown by Flight Lieutenant Philip Groves and a skeleton crew from the Squadron, took the rest of us back to Lincoln and home at two-thirty the same afternoon.

Sunday evening. Curious, I thought, how all that acute tiredness experienced during the last hours of the flight had completely dissipated. Even though I'd not been to bed for practically forty-eight hours and felt no desire to do so. Neither did I want to appear in the Mess and talk about the night's operation – respond to inquiries about Dick Guterman; to all the "flying" questions about how and why we did this, that, or the other. I'd given a full account to Group Captain Hawksworth the Station Commander, and to Wing Commander Nettlestone commanding the Squadron. And that, as far as I was concerned, was all the talking I wanted to do about it.

The mood of the place was sombre. The Squadron had lost three aeroplanes and crews: L7513 with old Matthews, and two others seen to go down over Germany, fate unknown. Twenty-one of us.

I was alone. Flight Lieutenant Ellis had taken a week's leave and left after lunch. Likewise Sergeants Smith, Noakes and Entwhistle. I could also have taken myself off for seven days, but felt better staying on so that I could visit Duncan and Guters at Cranwell. The hospital was only a short distance from the aerodrome. First thing Monday morning I'd drive over to see them. Late that Sunday afternoon I'd had the leg dressed at the Sick Bay. Hobbling out after treatment, I'd dismissed the driver of the Flight's small Bedford van, put myself gingerly behind the wheel and started the thing off in second gear – which is where I left it, driving slowly around the airfield perimeter track, engine acting as a brake to ensure that the groggy right foot need only exert minimum pressure in order to slow down and stop. I passed the empty spaces once occupied by the lost Lancasters and saw clearly in my mind the faces of the aircrew I knew. It would only be a few days before new aircraft stood there. To be flown by new faces. Friday's operation and the losses entailed were standard. It was said somewhere – although to talk about it was tacitly regarded as both insensitive and stupid – that every six weeks fifty percent of the aircrew members of both Sergeants' and Officers' Messes were newcomers. Such a turnover numbed finer sensibilities. But it did not allow us to forget the missing flyers. Neither did we mourn them in a conventional way – that would have made our own position untenable. We shrugged our shoulders; then lived privately with the images and memories of one or the other of them as they came freely to mind – anywhere – whatever we happened to be doing.

When I came to Titty B-O's old dispersal point I drove the van onto the circle, going round and round, checking the familiar trestles, starter-trolleys, oil-drums. I would have liked to talk to the ground crew, tell them about their magnificent aeroplane, about Guters whose eccentricities they greatly appreciated, and about Duncan's heroic venture on his behalf. But it was a stand-down weekend – no operations planned – and most of them were away on forty-eight hour passes.

I left the Bedford in the forecourt and limped in to the Mess ante-room, taking up my familiar leather chair and pulling in a second in order to put my leg up. I was hoping that Joe would turn up but it was an unfamiliar waiter – a new posting – who arrived and took my order for tea: the usual plate of whatever sandwiches were going; with the bread thickly cut. Meat paste on margarine – same as Friday.

Friday?

Friday – exactly forty-eight hours ago, sitting here in this same chair, reading Guterman's Journal, reading about Lena – the girl Lena who was expecting to meet Dick tonight. There was nothing I could do about it at the moment. No idea how to contact her. The Robin Hood? Nothing really to go on there. Too tenuous. I decided to wait until Monday. Dick might have regained consciousness. Then I'd find out how to contact her. A visit from Lena could work wonders.

The Mess was deserted. Those not on weekend leave would be living it up in Lincoln. I gathered myself together and shuffled into the entrance hall where the telephones were and called Cranwell. Duncan was doing well; wanted to see me tomorrow. Guters: no change.

For the first time since our return the leg was making itself felt: both punctured regions throbbing and emitting short stabs of pain moving out in all directions; I told the orderly on duty to wake me in the event of any telephone call from Cranwell, then clumped along to my room. I wished I'd taken the walking stick offered by the M.O. Pretty stupid to wish not to look incapacitated.

I lay on the bed and tried to read a Sunday newspaper to keep the thoughts at bay. When sleep finally arrived it came at me like a brick wall – a sudden blow to consciousness, out like a light.

I knew somewhere at the back of my mind that it shouldn't be this way – Dick Guterman no longer captive in the turret but standing alongside the flight-engineer's position, chatting away conversationally despite the lurching uncertainty of Titty B-O's landing approach. Mist was everywhere, as much inside the cockpit as outside. In fact it was difficult to tell where inside stopped and outside began, where Guters was standing and where he wasn't.

Ellis was not in his seat – no need for him anyway as none of the gauges seemed to be working: all the needles were at rest. And the engines were so quiet one would easily get the impression they were in a glider, bouncing up and sliding down the other side of thermals. The old girl was flying herself. I took my hands off the stick as if there was nothing more for me to do and turned to look at Guterman. He was leaning forward in front of Ellis' vacant seat, the old twisted smile playing over his face.

"With the advantage of hindsight," he said, "we should be able to get the old kite down pretty well. After all, we've done it once before – it was a good show, Johnny – and I want you to tell Dunc that the blanket made all the difference. It was unbelievably cold before he went out there and risked his neck. I might even be able to tell him myself yet. I'll have to see once we're down. Although, of course, we can't change the outcome: just see through the glass a little less darkly, as some good book says somewhere. My legacy, old son. You'd do the same for me."

I searched hard for signs of injury but could see none. No splitting of the flying-jacket where the guns had pinned him; no trail of blood from the mouth indicating internal bleeding. Nothing. He stood his full height easily, gesticulated freely with his hands as always. He seemed to be in no pain.

"How the heck did you get up here?" – I realised I was shouting, that in the whispering silence of this dead-engine descent I need only talk normally – "I mean, how did you get out . . . out of the turret? Ellis and Entwhistle couldn't get anywhere near you in there."

"Ah, that was on the last trip, Johnny. This is a different kettle of fish altogether. As you'll see when we get down." His voice was resonant, speech clipped and clear as always – no muffled old movie sound effects echoing hollowly through the theatre, kind of thing.

"We'll be out of the mist in a minute, skipper. Then you'll see a sight for sore eyes. Nothing you have to do about it. Don't bother with the stick. She'll get down herself. The old girl's bringing me home, after all. Why do you think I painted the Woombat on her . . ."

Heavy ground-mist obscured the runway, even creeping up to shroud the struggling wings. The only sound was a gentle swishing as if we were running through water. Dick was peering ahead through the windshield. "Won't be long," he said softly, "I can begin to see the sun already."

He was right. The menacing grayness of the fog was giving way to the sparkling brightness of millions of individual vapour particles which bounced off the aircraft, separating and falling away from Titty B-O like a shower of diamonds. It was like flying through the fringes of an ice-storm with the sun getting brighter by the minute. And then we were clear, gliding down through a copper-silver field of space, intense in luminosity, a pulsating sea of flashing light-particles. But there was no runway beneath us; no aerodrome buildings. Just miles of flat hard sand flanked by a brilliant cerulean sea on the left and green-topped, terracotta cliffs on the right.

Christ, she was taking her time to get down. I took hold of the control-column. "No need, Johnny. We're not quite there. When we're beyond this bluff you'll see the place, the whitest, purest sand in creation. She'll make it very gently on her own; no help required. Even from old R.A.F. aces like us."

Dead silence now in the aeroplane. No more comforting swish against the sides of the fuselage. Like being in a sealed capsule dropping through a vacuum. Then we were beyond the headland and everything speeded up. I caught a glimpse of a stretch of incandescently white sand before my eyes involuntarily slammed shut to escape the ferocity of light. The nose of the aircraft went down steeply – too steeply – and I braced for the impact. But she levelled out beautifully, swooping and defying gravity in the way low-flying swallows do. I forced my eyes open to squint through the blue electric glitter that arced across the cockpit and out over the top astrodome, and witnessed our sand-cushioned glide-landing; hardly a grain displaced as we came to a sudden stop like a plane catching the trip-wire on the deck of an aircraft carrier.

"Come on, we have to walk. What I want you to see is not here." Guters spoke cheerfully, yet his voice possessed the sort of authority that would not welcome questions. We were sitting on a rock some distance from the aeroplane – but an aeroplane the likes of which I had not seen before: a long and sleek silver dolphin possessing the twin-fluked tail of a giant whale and extended wing-like fins. The sand beneath her was undisturbed, and there was just the faintest of movements from the throat, beneath the high-domed head which looked for all the world like Titty B-O's canopied cockpit.

"Not much time, Johnny. Come on. I have to leave soon. Don't worry, your eyes are not ready for this light. Just squint. You'll soon adjust. We have to go to the headland above the cliffs, beyond the town and port you see over on our right. The great trireme is still there. I remember it coming in . . . "

We set off up the track to the headland, an easy enough walk demanding only careful navigation of the many viciously spiked thorn bushes which littered the way. My eyes were now open to the light; skin tingling in the electrically-charged atmosphere. I felt light-headed and expectant, like a schoolboy released to explore wilderness country with his best friend. We emerged high above the harbour on to bright green turf, thick and springy. I wondered what the hell I was doing with flying boots on in such an idyllic situation. But as I bent down to take them off Guters cautioned against it: "Keep them on, Johnny. You'll still need them."

The light was more diffused at this height above the sand – a cooler, more lustrous and silvery glow, altogether kinder to the eye than the excoriating glitter of the beach air. I noticed that the trireme was leaving harbour, heading for the open sea – or the open sky – no way to determine where one finished and the other started in this place. The echo of the rowmaster's gavel beating out the stroke for the oarsmen came faintly across the water. Ahead lay a plain of yellow gorse-blossoms, undulating to the far cliffs on the other side of the headland, and above the flowers millions of bees – each one a tiny spark of light – rising and falling, creating a rhythmic up-and-down droning, sensuous and hypnotic.

"What's the rush, Guters? Look at that gorse! My God, what a view – why don't we rest here a bit? Don't think I'd mind staying here the rest of my life."

"Sorry, Johnny: we have to get on. You have more time to spare than I do. And I want you to come with me to the Guardians – the spot where you can see me off, so to speak. Important you should do that. For both of us. Now we've to get through the gorse. The path is narrow, but just follow me closely."

For the first time I noticed the dark traces of a large abrasion on Dick's forehead. "Is that still painful?" I asked. "Just noticed the bruise on your head. Everything else seems to have healed up."

"Don't feel a thing, Johnny. It'll disappear soon. In this climate everything heals very quickly. Come on. Now for the Guardians."

He set off at a run. I jogged behind, surprised at the ease with which my companion wended his way through such a tangle of brush, pushing aside the thorny branches which gave way unresistingly. Above our heads the bees rose and fell, the droning of their squadrons a familiar and welcome sound in this foreign place. The fragrance of blossoms was heady, intoxicating. On and on we went, tirelessly and with a relaxed and pleasurable rhythm, until I was aware that the ground was falling away rapidly, the bees were no longer with us, and I could hear the sound of the sea.

The gorse thinned out and we emerged onto a ridge of sand dunes, could see the water breaking on the beach. And beyond, two huge conical rocks rising fully one thousand feet. They were not free-standing rock islands jutting from the seabed as at first appeared, but vertical buttresses forming the seaward end of two sweeping promontories or arms, enclosing what I took to be a lagoon – and, by their size and position, almost completely obscuring the topography of the bay within.

"There they are," said Guters evenly, showing – in marked contrast to my own heavy breathing – no signs of breathlessness: "The Guardians."

Now we were once more in the coppery zone of heat. "Let's have a swim," I suggested. "For me, yes, when we get to the Guardians. But for you, no: it's dangerous water and your journey demands you continue overland for a while."

He then gave me a searching look; went on, continuing to hold my eye like the Ancient Mariner: "The main thing is that you remember this place, and what went on here between us." The brief moment of seriousness quickly gave way to the crinkly Guterman grin: "I had a date for Sunday, remember? Well, I'm a bit late in keeping it – Monday morning already – but that's what I'm here to do. Keep the assignation. After all, I promised you a meeting, didn't I? Crucial for both our futures that you should be in on this. You've read the Journal . . . so it won't come as any surprise to know that she's seen me through this far. Had already prepared me, in fact. It was all in the cards, as they say. What happened could not have been prevented. Was nobody's fault. The important thing is that we all got out. All of us together. Do you understand what I'm saying, Johnny? After all, here we are, you and I."

As he spoke a strong wind came off the water, causing waves to break strongly over the rocks piled along the base of the promontory to our right. And the coppery hue had deepened, merged with the sea, until sky and water were one. A new look of urgency narrowed Dick Guterman's eyes. His face became set – not exactly suggesting fear or panic, but certainly anxiety. He set off at a run along the beach towards the low spit of land giving access to the nearest Guardian. "Quickly," he shouted over his shoulder, "come on."

Scrambling over boulders close to the water and up the shallow-sloping scree we gained the top of the low headland; headed for the first of the Guardian pitons. Once up there it was difficult going – the ground was treacherous, quick-sandy shallow pools which had to be jumped, and at times the sea-spray shot high enough to hamper vision. This narrow land-bridge brought us hard up against the leeward, vertical side of the giant monolith to stand on a wide ledge which ran its entire girth. "Now round to the sea," said Dick quietly. "Then you will see where I am to go."

The surface of the ledge was smooth, almost polished in appearance, and sloped away slightly to the outer edge. I followed Guters carefully, keeping close in to the wall of rock on the left which rose to what seemed an incredible height. Everything about this Guardian outcrop was larger than it had appeared from the sand dunes.

It seemed we had been circumnavigating the great piton for ages before the scrub and scree of land below gave way to the sea and we faced the second Guardian rock. Frighteningly close. Separated from us by only a narrow channel – no more than thirty or so feet – through which the sea raced to form a deep pool-like lagoon edging the narrow beach.

Neither of us spoke. From our vantage point high above the water we could now look directly inland and appreciate the crescent-like symmetry of the bay; I also become aware how quickly the in-rushing swell spent itself to join calm, emerald-clear water that allowed sight of a jet-black sand bottom. And the roses – roses everywhere: red, white, floating on the water and covering the countless bushes which spread upwards from the curving sand-line of the lagoon proper to take over dune and cliff-fringed hinterland. The scent! It floated off the water, pervaded the air . . . an exotic, honeyed, yet wine-tart fragrance that almost eliminated every other sensation; acted like a tonic, stimulating well-being, optimism, expectancy. The backdrop to this half-moon panorama of lagoon and beach was a dramatic and high caldera, all that was left of a volcanic crater now invaded by the sea. Beyond the roses the twisted and ridged slopes of massive lava flows ascended to the rim.

A change in the light. An amber haze settled high atop the caldera edge, turning the bleak lava cliffs into soft golden uplands, and illuminating a singular feature previously lost in the shadowed bluffs.

"Time to go, Johnny." The sea air around the ledge was now damp and cold; the light gradually fading, while the water in the channel between the Guardians ran more strongly, swept by frequent white-capped surges.

Dick Guterman came forward and put his arms around me in a strong bear-hug, then pulled away and held both my hands, crinkly smile in place, eyes excited, mischievous – like those of the Guters expounding on the theory of the relationship of heavy breast to clavicle to an aged art teacher.

"Keep the Journal and the water-colours. And don't forget the bike. Ride it around to keep the cylinder lubricated. Now you can see where I'm off to. Look . . . "

Above and beyond the beach, completely revealed in a play of electric-blue light, a great mushroom-topped rock projected from a high lava column. On it stood the figure of a girl whose hair appeared to be a coppery conductor for the energy surrounding her; and whose face when she turned to look out towards the Guardians reflected the radiant energy and could be seen – as if in close-up – to be ceremonially silvered and masked.

When I brought my eyes back to the ledge, Guters had gone. His flying jacket and uniform lay scattered at my feet. The jacket was blackened by heat across the front; ripped and frayed beneath both shoulders.

I watched him emerge from the water at the centre of the black-sand beach, and experienced a wave of deep depression: a sense of total isolation, an emptiness that tightened throat and knotted viscera. But not for long. It was overwhelmed, washed away by the beauty of the phenomenon that followed.

As Guters walked naked up the beach, a broad avenue of red and white roses became strangely agitated. From the first bushes by the dunes, up to those at the edge of the lava flow beneath the mushroom rock, I witnessed a trembling and swaying of flowers, a serpentine dance of colour and mist with each bloom throwing off an ever thickening shower of pollen, a golden cloud hanging low over the bushes . . . marking an airborne path up through the widely spread tangle of briars below.

The air was utterly still, the hovering snake of pollen motionless. Then gradually, part by part, starting at the head, violent undulations spread the entire length of the snake's body until with one final heave the contrail-like form broke free and started to glide sinuously down the hillside. Coils rose and fell as the serpent – head now clearly defined – moved towards the beach, swaying from side to side like some casually swimming sea-snake, clearing the rocks to drift over the sand and coil itself around Richard Guterman.

After that he was not to be seen. There was just a spinning cloud of pollen that drifted back into the forest of roses and slowly dissipated. With Dick's disappearance the light over the Guardian rocks began to dim and, for the first time, I felt afraid in what I suddenly felt to be a terrible place. I had to overcome a certain paralysis – a hesitancy in putting one foot before the other in order to start on my way back round the ledge. I turned to take a last upward look at the high rock beneath the caldera. The aura of amber light was sinking beneath the rim, but in its failing glow I saw two figures up there, not one. Two figures: the long, finely-spun copper hair of one falling loosely around the shoulders of the other.

A Stygian darkness descended abruptly. I could neither see the ledge nor feel the vertical wall of the piton at my back. Impossible to know in which direction to move. I edged fumblingly to the right where the rock face should be and fell. Down and down and down . . .

I awoke wet with perspiration, mouth open wide, throat dry from the scream. My right leg had stiffened during the night and when I turned to switch on the light and pull myself up in bed the pain was intense.

The clock on the bedside table showed it to be six-fifteen in the morning. The first gray light of a damp Lincolnshire day was breaking through the gaps left between hastily pulled curtains.

I lay back on the pillows, heart still racing from the terror of the fall, mind and senses still in the dream, replaying vignettes which projected themselves at random, every visual detail sharp, all the sounds clear as a bell. Then I found I could recall any particular aspect at will, and dwell on it as if looking at a photograph. The odd thing was that, despite the horror of the last annihilating seconds, I desperately wanted to stay in the landscape of the crater rather than accept the dreary reality of the familiar bedroom; face the approach of the day. Unaware of time I forced the dream-memory to take me through the whole experience again – chronologically – so that I could etch every detail into day-time consciousness; that way, I felt, the images of the journey would never slip back into the realm of the subliminal.

It was seven-thirty before I put on a dressing gown and hobbled into the front hall of the Mess to find a cup of tea. I thought I should wait until eight o'clock before calling Cranwell. Let them know I'd be on the way by nine. I wandered into the ante-room and looked out at the rose beds in the garden – weak and pale autumnal specimens after the voluptuous pollen-ejaculating roses of the lagoon. That memory sent the tummy into an involuntary fluttering, tremors which translated themselves into the easily perturbed right leg. I took to my familiar chair and put the leg up. Ordered tea and toast.

At five to eight I shuffled to the telephone booth and called the R.A.F. hospital at Cranwell and was put through to the ward. The staff-nurse there asked me to hold on. Several difficult minutes went by. I can remember – even now – pushing hard against the back wall of the booth to take some weight off the bad leg.

"Squadron Leader Graham?"

"Yes."

"Flight Lieutenant Morris here, Sir. I'm the Medical Officer on duty at the moment. I was going to call you a little later on this morning in case you were sleeping. You had a pretty grim time from all accounts."

"Well . . . "

"It's bad news I'm afraid, Sir. Sergeant Guterman died this morning at six-fifteen. We did the best we could to make him as comfortable as possible – but there were major internal injuries we could do nothing about. I'm terribly sorry. He went very quickly. There was no warning – we couldn't have called you in time. He never regained consciousness."

"Were you with him when he died?"

"Yes, I was. He was very peaceful. There was a moment at the end when I saw him smile, I know I didn't imagine it. He was not in any pain: of that I can assure you."

I went on talking automatically, seeing nothing around me, hearing my voice coming from somewhere in the distance. "Well . . . I'll be coming over this morning to see Flying Officer Duncan who was also on my crew. He went out of the aircraft to fix a cover over the turret for Sergeant Guterman."

"Yes, I've heard about that. And the amazing thing is that the sergeant showed no signs of hypothermia – body temperature normal: no exposure effects at all."

"Could that have been because of Duncan's blanket?"

"Quite likely, if it stayed in position long enough; especially flying at low altitudes like you were."

I thanked the doctor; told him I'd like a few words with him when I got over to Cranwell. I replaced the receiver very deliberately on its hook. Limped back to the bedroom to dress. I'd felt tempted to tell the M.O. that there'd really been no need to call me to Dick's bedside . . . but that knowledge was mine alone. Not for talking about even to Duncan.

Monday morning. "Mundane, bloody Monday," as Matthews was fond of saying. But, thank goodness, a lot to be done. Keep busy. Get the leg dressed, go visit Duncan, on to see Farmer Jones at Eastgate Farm and collect Guter's bike, Hercules II. And then I thought I'd like to go to the Cathedral for Evensong – a practice in which Guters and I had indulged from time to time. And go on the bike: the leg would have to be up to it. Guters would appreciate the gesture.

I suppose I'd always thought of myself as a practical and efficient kind of chap, but there was nothing systematic about the way I organised myself to face the outside world that morning. The desire to keep busy, tick things off as done, one by one, had evaporated. Now I was loathe to leave, lingering here and there reflectively, finding that the once neutral bedroom secreted a numinous atmosphere conducive to the evocation of the night's sensations and images: the strong scent of roses, Guters leading the way to the Guardians, the face of the girl, then the two figures on the rock . . . And despite the overall sadness and disorientation that took over after the telephone call, I felt consoled by the fact that unlike normal dreams which fade – never to be reclaimed – I could bring back at will the events of that last journey with Dick Guterman. Here, in my own room, I was aware of a tangible and persisting link with him. In contrast, the world outside seemed less than real. In fact – and I suppose I should say it at this point – the conventional goings on of life in the world of time and place have never since represented the "be all and end all" of things for me; never satisfied as fully as those forms generated from the unconscious depths of the mind.

Good news from the medics: the leg wounds were healing well. Of course I knew as much by driving myself to Cranwell in the Flight van. It was a pale, watery sun, kind of day. The trees were shedding. A pity the leaves had to go so soon; yet perhaps the trees themselves welcomed autumn – were relieved by the abdication of their finery, ego mercifully done with in the final colourful exit from the world, the near naked limbs whispering "to hell with it" and withdrawing to the other life of the deep roots.

"That's the way to do it," I said to myself: "retreat into the soil, into humus . . . in our case, as lost souls, into the humus of faith." And then I realised those weren't my words at all. That was how Guters had put it last week when the copses around the aerodrome dispersal points were aglow with leaf-light.

I got to Cranwell just before noon. But it was a wasted journey. The S.M.O. had sent Duncan off to a plastic surgery unit somewhere in the south. Apparently it had been a quick decision due to the extensive flaying suffered by his left hand. They had flown him out in the hospital Anson only twenty minutes prior to my arrival; said that "the office" had telephoned the Mess to save me a journey, but that by then I had already left.

The doctor on duty also said that on the orders of the S.M.O., Flying Officer Duncan had not been told about Sergeant Guterman. Further, that if I was free tomorrow, Tuesday, the

Senior Medical Officer would like to have me as his guest for lunch in the Cranwell Mess.

Mundane, bloody Monday. I'd been looking forward to seeing Duncan. Disappointed, left high and dry, my head was suddenly filled with memories of old Matthews and his zany eccentricities, of the fourteen men lost in the other two Lancasters, and a bleak emotional current of deep sadness at the pain and waste of such tragedies caught me off balance. I desperately wanted to get back to my room and hide out – forget Farmer Jones and the bike, forego the Cathedral . . . Tomorrow was going to be a hell of a day – reports, interviews, further de-briefings. With no certain future in sight. Dunc and Guters gone; no aeroplane any more; tour of operations probably considered by Group to be finished; Ellis and I posted to some ground job; Smithy put to another crew to complete his last three missions. The inevitable break-up.

I moved awkwardly back to the van, functioning mechanically, feeling no joy in the fact that this was most likely IT: operational flying days over. I had survived. Now if Dunc and Guters were around we'd all be heading for The Saracen's Head – and beer and sandwiches all round. Maybe the whole bloody crowd of us in Dent's M.G.

I drove slowly back to the aerodrome. I felt in no need of any lunch and went straight to the Motor Transport section and requested a driver. We would go out to Eastgate Farm, see Farmer Jones, pick up Hercules II, and I would ride the motorbike into Lincoln. The M.T. driver could then take the Bedford back.

The track leading to Eastgate farm came up on the right about a mile down the lane we had taken off the Fosseway. I had a clear picture of the farm in my mind – a ground-plan seen from about six hundred feet when taking off to the south east. Heath Lane it was called – a sandy road running between privet hedges. Half a mile along, through an open gate, and we were enclosed by large barns on both left and right – separate buildings which, from the air, always gave the impression of being one. Another fifty yards and the van entered the farmyard – an open arena of slippery cobblestones. Cows everywhere, milling around uncertainly, and at the centre, ankle-deep in mire and beaming happily on this circus, the portly ringmaster, Farmer Jones. Mr Alfonso Jones – gentleman-farmer, to be exact – turned out neatly in huge black gumboots, leather-patched tweed jacket and shapeless deer-stalker hat.

The noise of the Bedford's engine was lost in the throaty protests emanating from fifty or sixty animal jaws, and Mr Jones did not immediately notice our arrival. Finally, some kind of order gradually evolved in the yard as the call of the pasture began to get through, and the animals started a meandering exit, a procession of nodding heads and swinging tails. As I watched, I imagined Guters riding in and out of here, feet dragging through mud and cowpat as he slithered along dodging the cows. I wondered if Mr Jones would remember that I was the one who'd driven Dick here on a couple of occasions to pick up the bike.

When the last cow had cleared the gate the farmer sloshed forward, shook hands warmly, asked after "the Sergeant." He turned away when told the news; silently watched the last of his cows amble into the field. Then he said he had a son in the Fleet Air Arm – a navigator – and how Mrs Jones and he always looked forward to the afternoons when the Sergeant came to ride around and tinker with his bike.

"Well: it's bad news alright. Can't say we haven't thought about it, Mrs Jones and me – both for our own lad and him. Mrs Jones is going to be very upset. She thought a lot of Sergeant Dick – that's what we called him, you know. Nay . . . we'll both miss him."

"He had a wonderful quietness to him, that lad. And some of it rubbed off. You forgot your own worries because he seemed a bit beyond the usual trivial stuff we worry about – you know what I mean? Mrs Jones used to say that when he came into the room everything seemed to change – you felt right, and the place felt right: as if things were meant to be just the way they were at that very moment. 'Because it was goodness itself that came in,' she said to me once.

"I always had the feeling that if I'd asked him one of those bloody silly questions like, 'what the 'ell are we doing here' kind of thing, he'd have had a good answer. I remember one afternoon when he was having a cup of tea, and the missus was going on about Hitler and what an evil man he was, and Sergeant Dick said, 'Yes, he must be very lonely.' 'And what's loneliness got to do with being evil?' she said. And he said that when you get that bad the soul can't stand to stay with you, and leaves, and that's the worst loneliness of all. 'It's one of the reasons for trying to live a fairly decent life' – he told her – 'because if the soul gets discouraged and quits, then you'll really know what a living hell is all about.'

"Took me a bit of time to digest this" – Mr Jones went on – "and while I was sipping the tea he looked up with that big lopsided grin of his. 'Of course,' he said, 'the trick is to know how far you can go. The old spirit doesn't mind you having a bit of a fling so long as you stay within earshot when it finds it's time to speak out. Best of both worlds, you see. The great gift of being human'."

Mr Jones fell silent, obviously moved. I had to smile to myself, imagining the scene in the kitchen as Guters leaned back from the kitchen table, no doubt striking a gesticulating pose like the sitter in a Frans Hals portrait, just as he did at the bar in The Saracen's Head.

I accepted the offer of a cup of tea in the farm kitchen, asked the driver to join us, and sat for half an hour to await the return of Mrs Jones from Lincoln where she was visiting a sister. But when she had not arrived by two-fifteen I apologised to Farmer Jones; said I'd have to get on if I was to be at the Cathedral in time for Evensong. The driver departed with the van, and Mr Jones and I took the back door from the kitchen to the shed where Guters kept Hercules II.

"You know he painted it up last week – British racing green - lettered the name on the side of the tank. Looks a real treat. What are you going to do with it? Send it back to the family?"

"No: he said he wanted me to have the bike. So I'll look after it for him . . . take it out from time to time. Perhaps pop in on it to see you and Mrs Jones sometime, if that'd be alright."

"You'd be very welcome. Now see you do. It'd mean something to us. And I can speak for the wife."

The motorbike gleamed in the pale autumnal light. The enamel had been applied faultlessly; the lettering was elegant – gold on green. It was a pre-war 350cc A.J.S. side-valve, carefully rebuilt and restored by "the Sergeant" in Mr Jones' garden shed. I polished the tank up with a handkerchief, switched on, adjusted the mixture and primed the carburettor; stood alongside and kicked the starter with the good leg. Hercules II started with that slow pop, pop, pop of all side-valves and then, as I weakened the mixture and twisted the throttle, settled into a throaty and healthy hum. I swung myself into the saddle, engaged the gear on the side of the tank, let out the clutch, and taking the weight of the machine on the left leg eased it from the grass to the gravel of Heath Lane. A final wave to Farmer Jones – causing an almost disastrous front-wheel wobble – and I was on my way to Lincoln.

I left the bike in the backyard of The Saracen's Head in the safe-keeping of Bert, the odd-job man, and walked painfully up the steep hill to the west-front of the Cathedral – leg finally protesting the prolonged use to which it had been subjected that day. There was a surprising number of people around, and all making for the south transept door. But inside the great church they were easily lost as they sought their own solitude.

Five minutes to go before the choir was due. The organ should be opening up any minute. I wandered over to the west side of the north transept where the light filtering through the stained-glass windows was intimate and subdued. On several occasions Dick, Duncan and myself had spent the late afternoon wandering the aisles towards the end of Evensong, waiting for opening time at The Saracen's down the hill. Not irreverent wanderings: we were thirsty in more ways than one.

The first few minutes of the organ voluntary were not particularly inspiring; gave no hint that the organist might surprise one and turn in a virtuoso performance. Initially he produced none of the acoustic clarity demanded by each individual note of a Bach Toccata and Fugue. I remember thinking how curious it was to hear Bach sounding like Debussy. But once I got off the high-horse of connoisseurship – which it is usually best to do as soon as possible – I realised how well this even modulation of sound reinforced the mood of quiet, even peaceful, acceptance that had been steadily growing since I woke from the dream. So it came as a shock when, without warning, the temper of the playing changed – when the first subject of the fugue sounded in the pipes with the notes sharply articulated, each hanging solitarily in the air for a fraction of a second at a measured and staccato point of sound which pierced the ear and ended up at the back of the head, striking as if on an anvil. This dynamic reversal of accoustical impact left me transfixed, hard up against the back of my chair, almost having to remind myself to breathe.

I can't say exactly how long it was that I sat so thoroughly immersed in this rendering of the fugue – perhaps only a few moments at most – before the hold of the music was broken by the unexpected arrival of a more powerful sensation: the honeyed, wine-tart scent of roses drifting through the transept – a euphoric cloud of fragrance. A couple of deep breaths and my body relaxed; the Bach floated in, carried on the perfume. The columns and arches of the transept faded, and I was back at the Guardians looking out over a sea of roses.

"Remember that night at The Saracen's" – Guters' voice in my ear – "when I said no more bothering with the books after the war – just music? Well now you know what I was getting at. This chap's good, Johnny. Get ready for when he opens the great diapason. He's going to rattle the building . . . God, what a sound! Music's the only way, old lad. The only way to . . . "

Off to the side, slightly distorted as if seen through a pane of whorled glass, I was aware of others in the audience, of the flickering of candles in their long holders illuminating the chancel. But it was the rim of the caldera and the golden-lit mushroom rock that occupied the centre-stage of perception as the last mesmeric notes of diapason sound died away.

And then – it seemed as if there was no pause in the performance – an extraordinary cry pierced the high vault of the Angel Choir just off to my left. A boy's voice holding a long, ethereal vocal line, sustained like the plaintive wail of some high-wheeling, solitary, pelagic bird. On and on it flowed, breaks for breath not apparent, a cadence formed of two words which, repeated, formed the lament, "Pie Jesu . . . Pie Jesu . . ."

I brought my head up to lean back over the rail of the chair and closed my eyes, washed through by the beauty of it. And filtering through the Cathedral stone came the misted, flat fields of Lincolnshire: those expansive, almost horizonless vistas wheeling giddily on the approach at five thousand, flare path bled white in the moist early morning air of the hours just beyond midnight. I let Titty B-O drift in, body numb and cold, pushing aileron and rudder to line us up, mind struggling to exercise judgement for touchdown.

Came down to earth with the sound of the audience singing a closing hymn. And Guters slipped away, gently brushing me across the shoulders – a touch that brought with it a breath of frigid air, and the whispered words, "Nice landing, Johnny."

Chapter Seven
The Visitations

I must go beyond the war years if I am to give you more than just an inkling of how my life continued to be affected long after that disastrous night in 1942. But before rounding off this saga I should tell you that the writing itself has brought with it a certain serenity – expiation is, I think, too strong a word – more a calming of the mind . . . for the first time in years. The lurking sense of guilt has been exorcised: the constant feeling that my poor judgement alone was responsible for Dick Guterman's death and the loss of the aircraft has gone away. Enough is enough.

It is said that only with the passage of time does one gain a degree of objectivity about events: a statement with which I must agree – but not without noting that in my own case it took a long, long time. In fact, it was only when I began to ruthlessly and conscientiously re-live such long-gone happenings, that I began to appreciate the role played by all the impersonal forces that work together and influence the shape of one's destiny – as well as coming to the realisation that we seldom act, if ever, as creatures of pure reason. As a result I reached the conclusion that sanity depends on becoming a fatalist. Only then was it possible for me to be kinder to myself and to those around me. Late in the day, I'm afraid.

When I talk of "visitations" I refer of course to the psychic phenomenon known as "haunting". And, if I understand correctly, the controversy surrounding such happenings is whether or not the thing doing the haunting has an independent, autonomous existence . . . or is simply an entity projected by one's own mind. Despite being subjected to a great deal of haunting I cannot resolve this question with any certainty. Yet I can say that never once – neither during nor after a particular manifestation – did it seem possible that I was imagining what was going on. But that issue I must leave you to decide.

Dick Guterman's activities did not commence until after the war. I am not talking now about experiencing a sense of the lingering presence of one who has died – that was constantly there – but, if I may borrow a current term, of "hard-core" haunting: physical, concrete manifestations accompanied by the transference of thought, mind to mind, without benefit of speech; and lesser but more frequent interruptions in the form of brief appearances and vanishings in the manner of the Cheshire Cat in *Alice in Wonderland*. All on the most unlikely occasions, in the most unlikely of places: cocktail parties, soccer matches, symphony concerts, intimate moments in the bedroom . . . I never knew what was coming – positive on-stage performances, intense in the state of mind they generated; or simply short, mischievous, theatrical entrances and exits.

For what reason? Well, his casual arrivals had a sort of simple *joie de vivre* about them, ironically enough; make what you will of that. But if I am to find some overall rationale for the others, I can only suggest that he was seeking to impress upon me two beliefs which he had always passionately held and about which we had constantly argued: first, that death is not the end but a form of metamorphosis; second, that transcendence – in terms of reaching the spirit – is always available to us through loving, and through the adventure of aesthetic emotion. He desperately desired me not just to have faith, but to know. He frequently urged me to write about the war: what it was like to be aloft over enemy territory – alone at one's battle station in the small hours of the morning in an ailing bomber. He was fanatical in his passion that the "Matthews" and the "Dents" – the fifty and more thousand of us who were lost – should never be forgotten. When I told him I doubted my ability to be an effective author he suggested that he dictate the words; that with practise, under his tuition, I could function as a medium and perform what I believe is called "automatic writing". My refusal to put pen to paper earlier was a great disappointment to him.

The last time he appeared was towards the end of October 1983. It was a disturbing manifestation, unlike any previous appearances: almost malevolent, not a word said, very pyrotechnic. Just before midnight, forcing the bedroom door so as to split the catch from the door-jamb, exploding all the electric light bulbs save one, to stand glaring alongside the bed. I cannot account for this performance from a ghost who had always been calm and benign. He disappeared when my wife of but a few weeks shouted angrily at him to go. And I had the strong feeling that, finally, old Guters had moved on. His anger and frustration must have abated now that I have at last told the story and resurrected us from some musty vault of Air Ministry files.

Perhaps the motive behind his last explosive and threatening appearance was to force me to act. For the timing was perfect. He no doubt knew full well I was beginning a new life with my wife and would not want to be dragging all the old baggage from the past along with me. A wily bird, old Guters.

You will be curious about the girl, Lena. I tried to find her the week following the crash. One bartender thought she might have seen them that night – just the once – but couldn't swear to it. There was no other information in the Journal to provide even the slightest clue.

All I can tell you is that I knew in my dream, the morning he died, that the girl he joined on the mushroom rock after being transported by that wonderful snake of pollen, was the Lena of his Journal.

The initial visitation came without warning on a September Saturday in 1946. Sipping tea in a suburban sitting-room, the coals of a dying fire dispelling the chill of an autumn dusk which already masked the garden, we sat, this great slab of a woman and myself, shadowed in opposite corners of the fireplace.

For some minutes the woman had been slowly and rhythmically stroking my old leather wallet, pale blue-white hand gliding back and forth in the chair's dark space like some tank-trapped phosphorescent fish. Wrapped from ankle to chin in dull black satin it was difficult to make out the rest of her. But the sound of her heavy breathing and the rustle of material stretching tightly across stomach and breasts were clearly audible. And then, abruptly, respiration stopped – or so it seemed – as her hand hovered aimlessly in mid-air and only the faint hiss of breath escaping through clenched teeth broke the silence. The wallet fell soundlessly to the carpet.

It was then that I felt the first cold draught sweep across the face, hair at the nape of the neck stir uneasily. An odd kind of disembodiment followed – senses playing tricks – a feeling of weightlessness in the chair; the walls of my stepfather's study dissolving, fading away in the dull gray light of a rising ground mist; the fire's glowing embers retreating to become a pinpoint of red in the distance. A moan of wind sounded from the now obviously distant garden, bringing with it the uneven splutterings and surgings of failing aircraft engines. I listened sadly, awash in memory, anticipating the shock wave of sound which was to come. A final roar of last minute power and then somewhere to my right, the screeching, numbing jar and appalling scream of high-speed disintegrating metal scouring concrete, skidding through space. Choking in the acrid smell of burning rubber and spilled hydraulic oil, I heard my voice shouting for them to get Guterman out of the turret as soon as we came to a stop; before the chance of fire. Instinctively I jammed both feet firmly to the floor, met no resistance, yet winced as pain shot through the right leg.

Now a breathless silence. No light at all to see what was going on. An infusion of damp cold air completely overspread us. Mrs

Iles, my mother's friend, began to cough violently – a harsh and constricted gasping in the throat through which words escaped painfully. "God . . . they're coming to pieces: flames, sparks, trailing from the belly, great red scars – and smoke, thick black smoke all the way behind them." She paused and then went on softly as someone awed by the events they witnessed. "They can't stop it; soil and metal everywhere; hedges ripped out across the road. Through the wall . . . " The words ended in a long sigh. When she spoke again I had to strain to catch the last whispers. "Look at the wheels turning, blue smoke from the tyres, there on top of the ditch. The aeroplane's all broken – in two parts – engines are back on the road . . . and bits of wing. And lights now, coming across the field. Do you see the lights . . ?"

I saw nothing. But in the distance I heard the clanging of the fire-tender bell; picked up the sharp bite of smouldering rubber; suddenly realised that both my feet were newly still, that the rudder pedals had stopped their frantic juddering, control rods finally separated.

"Now we are going to have some tea!" The unbelievable irrelevance and inanity of this interruption brought my head up sharply. My mother was wheeling the tea-trolley through the door; had just switched on the lights. The fire was burning brightly. Mrs Iles retrieved my wallet from the floor and placed it in that tightly satin-stretched lap. She started to pour the tea as if we'd just been talking about the vagaries of the English weather.

Such was the nature of my introduction to the medium, Mrs Iles. That Saturday was my first time back at the house in three years. I'd never taken my leaves at home – too many negative memories of domestic strife.

Sipping tea, still somewhat befuddled by such a phenomenal immersion in the past, and wondering how to account for it, I studied the woman sitting over by the fire. Short and massively square, shoulder line seeming almost to equal her height, wearing a plain black dress which, I noticed when we were introduced, hung vertically to the floor without sign of waist. When she moved, feet hidden, the impression was that she travelled on a cushion of air. During the course of the afternoon I had become increasingly curious about those lost feet, hoping to glimpse the means by which such bulk moved so effortlessly over the polished floor like the most svelte of mannequins. And just once, as she stood to replace the teapot, I caught a glimpse of taut sinewy ankles streamlined down from heavy yet nicely curved calves, and small high-arched feet enclosed in shiny black shoes. I tried to visualise her without clothes but the imagination was not up to it.

The face atop this physiological phenomenon was small and oval, smooth and doll-like without a bone suspected. Yet the eyes appeared monstrous, curving back and round to the ears like those of some exotic oriental courtesan. Two brightly rouged circles substituted for cheek-bones – a couple of maculae glowing feverishly like a second pair of eyes in that small white orb of a head. The crowning effect came from a single, jet-black braid of hair which curled round and round atop itself to form a bizarre vertical accent to the squat figure beneath. Goya would have gone out of his mind.

The ritual of afternoon tea over, I sat lost in the capacious privacy of the large wing chair which had been my favourite retreat since childhood, listening idly while my mother talked away. As usual I was bemused by her talent for hyperbole; by the unintelligible fantasies she wove in stringing together a series of totally disassociated thoughts, most of which were invented. Mrs Iles seemed unperturbed. No doubt she had become familiar with my mother's remarkable ability to create her own world – a child's world really: all genteel goodness and light.

From time to time I noticed Mrs Iles watching me closely as I retreated ever more deeply into the great wrap-around wings of my chair. Then I must have opted out completely; closed my eyes and drifted off.

"What will you do when you get out?" The voice was husky and deep, emanating from the fireplace corner. Sitting up quickly, fighting the sleep which was well set in, I tried to collect my thoughts. I realised I must have been off the air for at least half an hour – it was completely dark outside. No sign of my mother.

"Your mother's had to go into town . . . something your father wanted."

"Stepfather," I interjected automatically.

"Well . . . yes. Anyway, she'll be back in under the hour."

Damn it, I thought: I should do better than this – first time home in years and falling asleep with a guest in the house.

"Don't worry about it," she said, reading my thoughts. "I had a good talk with Annie while you nodded off. A remarkable woman, your mother. A great healer. We met in the Spiritualist Church, you know."

Ah, so that was it: that accounted for Mrs Iles – my mother's interest in faith-healing or, as the stepfather called it, "spirit raising". It had brought some odd characters to the house even in my day.

"So what will you do when you get out? Will it be long?"

"Perhaps six months. Not sure what I'll be doing yet: history, drawing, painting . . . something in what they loosely call 'the arts'."

"Yes, I knew it would involve your interest in drawing and things." The white, toy-soldier head in the corner bobbed up and down, nodding rhythmically in affirmation.

"Mother told you about that?"

"No, I didn't need to ask her. I've been getting things from you all evening. That's why I asked at the beginning if you had something very personal – something you'd had a long time – so that I could absorb its secrets. You must have thought it an odd request. But you humoured me very graciously . . . handing over your wallet."

The wallet: the handsome crocodile-skin present given to me by Guters on behalf of the crew during the beery celebration of my twenty-first birthday. In The Saracen's Head. Since that day it had always occupied the inside pocket of whatever jacket I wore: a reassuring shield and talisman. Now only a few die-hard threads held it together. But I went nowhere without it. Too good a run of luck. And it kept the past alive and part of the present: everything relative.

More or less for something to do I grabbed the long poker and began to stir the coals of the dying fire.

"Sssh . . . no flame, please!" Her voice was hushed, almost a whisper. But I had disturbed the red ash enough to release a brief haze of light – sufficient to see that the old tattered wallet was held tightly in both hands again, deep in her lap. Curiously enough she seemed smaller – crumpled, as it were, deep in the chair – eyes closed, head to one side supported by the corner wing. Her breathing sounded shallow and forced and the rouged cheekbones appeared inflamed as if she was running a fever. I wondered if she'd fainted; if I should try and revive her. But as I started up she gave a long fluttering sigh. I stopped, half in and half out of the chair.

"Wait: the fog's just beginning to lift . . . " The voice was unfamiliar, no longer London-suburbs-Cockney but sibilant and monotone. The flush of light from the fire was short-lived and as I sat back in my own chair her face was all but lost. Just visible, deep in shadow, her right hand moved rhythmically back and forth as she stroked the wallet. Absolute silence now in her corner – breath and movement both suspended.

"Now what about a little more coal on the fire: it's getting quite chilly." There she was, eyes smiling, back to normal, just like that. I nodded and removed the last few lumps from the scuttle. She sat up and pulled her chair nearer the fire, then pulled forward, holding out both hands to the warmth. Knees apart, stretching the black material to breaking point, she was a cartoonist's dream: a black wedge of body surmounted by the white face of a doll ballerina. The dishevelled old wallet lay abandoned in the wasteland of her lap.

"It's not going to last much longer, is it?" She was a move ahead of me again, reading my mind. "You must put it safely away somewhere before it comes to bits. In a special place – after all, it's not any old wallet, is it? Why not put it where you keep his paint box?"

At this I was sure I must be hearing things. "Er . . . excuse me, what did you say?"

"I said why not put it with the old paint box he gave you." She was watching me unblinkingly, eyes wide like some black night owl on the hunt.

We talk casually of time standing still, but when it actually happens it's both mentally and physically threatening. Body functions become partially arrested: breathing, heartbeat, temperature control, on the blink; and the mind seems to shut down, mainspring snapped somewhere at the base of the skull. Because how the hell could she refer to the paint box? Duncan had been the only one I'd ever told about that – nobody else: not on the crew or in the Squadron; certainly not my mother.

There was a gravid stillness in the room at this point, relieved only by the hiss of new-burning coal. I was casting around for something to say, to quiz her without appearing really interested, when I noticed that her gaze had shifted – that her head was inclined towards the far corner of the study which lay in heavy shadow. Without looking in my direction she began to speak softly in her own natural tone of voice.

"He told me about the water-colours – about the night in Lincoln when you went to the figure-drawing class at the art school and he give you the paint box afterwards. Wait a minute . . . " She paused for several seconds before going on, head and body rigid in concentration. "He says you'll remember his demonstration with the model . . . "

Now I was absolutely petrified. I mean, how on earth could she have picked that up? Of course the story had gone the Squadron rounds properly embellished with every telling – but that was four years earlier and the chances that she, Mrs Iles, might have heard it were extremely remote. And nobody here at the house knew of it.

I played for time, smoothing pocket flaps down, tightening the knot on my tie, stroking my chin contemplatively – all the while trying to straighten my face out into something approaching a natural look; iron out the incredulous open-mouthed grimace which I could feel pulling like an overly tight mask.

"How do you mean he told you about it?" was all I could lamely manage.

She turned away again and stared off into the far corner. "He's been here since your mother brought the tea in – since we came back from the crash."

I followed her gaze and looked hard into the shadows. There was nothing to be seen. But I suddenly felt compelled to turn my head slightly to the left where heavy crimson curtains covered the door into the garden. No sooner had I done so than both scalp and back of the neck began to prick as if in response to dozens of lightly applied needles; palms became ice-cold and clammy at the same time; underarm sweat gathered quickly.

"He tells me you must listen to the Etudes – Chopin 25 in particular – your favourite . . . the one he used to play if you paid for the beer. And . . . " she leaned out over the arm of the chair as if to hear more clearly, "he says . . . I can't get the word . . . " Her voice tailed off but she continued as if listening, head on one side. Creases played across that polished forehead, and worry lines nicked the skin at the outer corners of her eyes. "It's a funny word – woombats? That's what it sounds like. Yes, that's it. He says that's it – and to tell you that the old Woombat really helped him do his stuff."

At this I was deeply moved. Whether Dick Guterman was in the room or not he was suddenly vividly present in my mind – grinning in the wry, turned-up-corner-of-the-mouth way he adopted when he won an argument or felt particularly pleased with himself. I struggled to keep some kind of composure as the wartime days came trembling back.

"Come on," he seemed to be saying, "you remember the old Woombat – capitalised, don't forget – not a bad bit of painting, was it?"

Mrs Iles had shrunk into the depths of the chair, flowing to fill every crevice as if it were some giant mould. No longer tense and rigid, her body had become limp and amorphous, face marble smooth without a line or wrinkle to be seen. "It's a pity you can't see him. The aura is very bright now: vivid clear blue like all the young ones. He says it's difficult to make contact like this – to re-enter time at will but that he must 'leave some relic in the ruins' – those are his words."

This was the moment when the whole affair became even more of a challenge to credulity, forcing reason – in sheer self-defence – to step forward and assert a healthy scepticism before the rot set in. For at this point Mrs Iles went off the air and Dick Guterman came on. It was as if she relapsed into a coma, eyes closed, no apparent respiration, merely a faint pulse fluttering in the neck. And I found myself hearing Dick's voice – not coming from anywhere outside myself, but apparently originating from somewhere deep within my own inner ear: a long-distance telephone call kind of sound, muzzled somewhat, yet undeniably his slightly rasping bass and authoritative delivery

"Some unfinished business, Johnny. Can't get clean away until the frustration and anger are exorcised. Anger for all of us of the untimely deaths: Matthews, Dent, Chalkey White . . . Snipe, Broadhead . . . and the others. Has anything changed in the world after such a squandering of souls . . . a greater wisdom . . . more caring for mankind . . . humility and respect in the face of life's mysteries? Have our deaths contributed anything to the future? No, my boyo. Nothing's changed; no lessons learned. It was all a waste. We won no lasting victories for faith, hope and charity."

I had to strain to catch the last few words. His voice was fading, thickening, becoming almost guttural. "True compassion for everything that lives and dies: that's the way to approach the Infinite, Johnny. Be patient with me – I may only be able to do some good by showing up from time to time; giving the lie to death that way; provoking you to tell about us – keep our memory alive, inspire the living and the dead. And by the way" – voice almost gone – "getting home earlier would have made no difference . . . "

Mrs Iles stirred in her chair, took a couple of shuddering breaths and opened her eyes. "Well, he's gone," she said cheerfully, scrambling into an upright position. "Time for me to be off too." Standing in front of the fire, blocking all the warmth, she was obviously waiting for me to say something. But although the questions were queuing up I felt some kind of block against airing them: I needed time to come to my own conclusions without being unduly influenced by the professional.

"Well, don't bother now." She was looking at me solicitously, almost maternally. "Phone up if you like, or come down – I'm always in on Sundays." She glided across the floor, feet lost beneath the shroud of satin carrying all that bulk like a pair of roller skates. Hand on the doorknob she turned: "Of course you're likely to be sceptical – but you must be patient: such psychic activity is more for their benefit than ours. But I don't think there's going to be any avoiding him. And I doubt he'll need a medium – any intermediary – next time."

I slipped out and fetched her coat from the hall. Helping her into it was a strongman act.

"Were you with him when he died?" She was looking intently at me over her shoulder, with her huge almond eyes extraordinary, brilliant and piercing. I found it necessary to turn away quickly.

"Yes, in a way I was . . . "

"Mm . . . well, must be off. Glad I could meet you. Call now . . . don't forget. You may need some help. There's nothing predictable about what may take place when a person clings to this earth, has to work something out. You must do all you can to help him get away."

She held out her hand and headed for the front door talking rapidly all the way. "You'll be up north in about six months: York – or near an old house in the country next to a church. That's where your new life will begin to really happen."

With that cryptic statement she left. I listened to her heels clicking on the terrace and then returned to the study to sit for a moment before the dying fire. So what, in fact, was it all about? Was I simply the victim of a clever hypnotist? If so, what possible motive could she have? It was difficult to explain the run of feeling I experienced: a mix of acceptance, melancholy and nostalgia – made more affecting by the worry that I was out of my depth – about to be caught between two worlds. Not comfortable. A vivid flashback of the wrecked Titty B-O came to mind; the space and entwining metal where the mid-upper turret should be. Accompanied by an inexplicable sense of relief that he should have finally turned up – as if I'd been expecting it all along.

I left the house by the French-windows in the study; got away in the car without being seen. Driving back to London there was a moment, somewhere around Burnham, when the colour of the air became so intense, the play of light so scintillating, that I seemed to be driving straight up into the sky. A pity the leaves had to go; yet perhaps the trees themselves welcomed autumn – a shedding of the finery, ego mercifully done with in a final resplendent exit from the world, the near naked limbs whispering . . . Dick Guterman's words in my mind again – etched there from that splendid autumn of 1942 before we left for Berlin.

And so I found myself at the start of a long supernatural marathon. Adjusting to the uncertainty created by his instrusions – never knowing when or where he'd crop up – inevitably turned me into a bit of a recluse. The longer the time between visits – and this could be several months – the more nervously expectant I became, the more I tended to seek my own company. There was no way of knowing what kind of "dropping in" to expect: the Cheshire Cat coming and going – now you see him, now you don't sort of thing; the "telephone in the ear" electronic voice butting in to enlighten, provoke, pass judgement . . . without any accompaning materialisation; and – much less frequently – the physical presence which just showed up, shared in what was happening, but rarely had anything to say on the telepathic wavelength.

While the "Guters Effect" – as I came to call this second life of mine – was trite and meaningless by rational standards it was nevertheless, for me, an occult and mysterious phenomenon: as such it stretched the mind, leaving open the possibility that other dimensions of existence should be seriously considered; and – perhaps more importantly – it cleared the guilt. In return, I gave him the satisfaction of knowing that he'd accomplished something after all – that he'd justified his life – and his death – by successfully beating the evidence of his own continuity.

Consequently his life and death would give hope to all who loved and lost in the war – to all who cherish another human being and must live with the lurking pain that attends the knowledge of inevitable separation. As the years wore on and the events of war retreated from the consciousness of succeeding generations, I finally felt the need to sit down and tell this story. One more chronicle to commemorate the aircrew of Bomber Command – just one branch of one Service; all volunteers who died the most violent and lingering deaths as they dropped from the sky – who accounted for one seventh of all British casualties in the war. An *In Memoriam,* if you like, to keep alive a recognition of their courage, endurance, and mastery of fear, in the face of miserable odds.

I don't know whether I have managed to bring this off: possibly it requires greater literary gifts than I possess to effectively marry two quite distinct realities – the practical aspects of night time flying in war, and the psychological battle that is with the flyers day in, night out.

In any event, as a sort of grand finale, I have decided to end this history with an account of the most memorable of Guters' visitations: the first occasion on which he actually materialised; when he ceased to be merely a disembodied voice and invisible presence. It is one occasion which I can recall again and again to experience not just in the mind, but in the senses themselves – to physically see, smell, and hear.

I spent the spring of 1948 overhauling Hercules II – the motorbike I had collected from Farmer Jones on that Sunday in 1942. It was in a bit of a mess: very little chrome to be seen and much of the original paint lost beneath a scumble of rust. The manufacturer's mark – A.J.S. – was almost gone. I started with a fine-grade sandpaper on the tank, scouring until the bare metal emerged. As the rust stripped off so the intervening years fell away and I remembered how we'd often wondered what Guters really did on those Saturday afternoons when he disappeared to "tinker" with the bike – Dent being firmly of the opinion that if any tinkering went on it was not with Hercules II but with the farmer's daughter, Anyway, I won't bore you with the details – I finally restored the whole machine: engine, frame, wheels, brakes, and lighting system – the *pièce de résistance* being a new monster headlight.

In May I was asked by a London publisher to travel to Ravenna and put together an "illustrated story", as he called it, of the church of St Vitale: an account treating the building as a foremost example of the Byzantine style for an encyclopaedia of religious architecture. I decided immediately to go on the motorbike – a particularly unsuitable mode of transportation when you think of the job in hand. But the idea was fixed; would not yield to reason. I had had two large aluminium panniers built – with padlocked lids – which were then bolted to the frame on either side of the rear wheel: one was to take paper, drawing materials and a couple of reference books; the other would suffice for clothes, toiletries, etc.

We – that is to say Hercules II and myself – left from Dover on 13 May. We took the early morning ferry to Calais, and were well into Alsace by six that evening. I stayed at a small auberge some twenty miles north of Colmar. Resisting the temptation to visit the Grunewald Triptych, I travelled east on secondary roads to Ravensburg and Kempten so as to be well placed for striking south through the Fern Pass to the Dolomites and Italy. Somewhere between Landeck and Nauders – where I was to cut across to Merano – the road became a saddle straddling cliff-sided bowls on either side which, some three thousand feet down, held twin deep green lakes. With nothing but space to left and right and a sharp S bend coming up ahead, I pulled back on the handlebars to gain altitude and slammed on hard left rudder to take the turn. The machine skewed away beneath me at forty-five degrees to the ground, rear-wheel sliding towards the right outer edge. Right heel hard into the gravel countering the slide, I straightened out about a foot from the brink; then, with left heel hard down for the next turn, went corkscrewing through the series of bends at speed, boots alternately digging in to keep levelling and straightening us out until we came to rest at a point where once again the road hugged the side of the mountain. I discovered later that the pinpoint of the lake down in the abyss over which we had been so precariously poised is called Lago Diabolo: being the place, according to local legend, where the devil and his horse returned to the Underworld after a spectacular leap from the adjacent mountain-top. As the earth opened to receive him so the great hole filled with water to become a bottomless lake.

Sitting there, Hercules II between my legs, rock against my back, the sense of being airborne was still strong: the distant mountain peaks were purple-smudged, while far below Lago Diabolo was becoming less and less distinct. Space was the reigning element, inviting lift-off, hinting at the night flight to come. Merano was perhaps sixty miles away, but with the highest terrain behind us, and that damn great headlamp up front, we could do the night journey like old times. Hercules-Woombat – for such I had decided to re-name and re-letter him on our return – performed magnificently on the descent, banking and side-slipping confidently in the turns which came up through the cloudbanks as if illuminated by a great searchlight. We entered Merano triumphantly in just over an hour, cutting a bright swathe between the buildings which turned the street lamps into dim candles.

A short run the next morning to pick up the main road coming down from the Brenner. I took it for fifty miles then cut off south-east through the mountains in the direction of Padua, then to Chioggia on the Adriatic coast before turning north through the flat marsh-like plain to Ravenna. Settled in the hotel by four-thirty. I had been on the road seven hours yet felt no fatigue – the bike drove itself. In fact the opposite was the case: I was possessed by a strong sense of expectancy which kept the adrenaline running, pushed one to keep moving. Realising that the church would still be open I immediately had a strong urge to head for St Vitale – get the feel of the place at once; then sleep on it before starting work the next day. So: a quick wash, change of shirt – the Adriatic air was warm and humid – and on my way.

It was when leaving the concierge's desk after handing in the room key that my eye was taken by a notice on the information board. The lettering was unusual – Gothic capitals of extreme angularity printed a rich antique-brown and announcing an organ recital in the church of St Vitale on May 16 at 8 p.m. A real stroke of luck: that I should arrive on the one night when the building would come alive with light and sound. For Byzantine space transcends itself when host to music . . . becomes an echoing, shimmering mini-cosmos.

Dusk was deeply set – that opaque purple afterglow common to Mediterranean marshlands which sets the seal so satisfyingly on the end of the day – when I left the local *trattoria* after an early dinner.

I found the ancient octagon of St Vitale lit only by candles – hundreds of them – whose soft light flickered uncertainly over the golden mosaic surfaces of wall and dome before drifting to lose themselves in the mobile shadows of remoter vaults. From time to time the encircling higher galleries materialised clearly in the pinpoints of light reflecting from the thousands of *tesserae*, then faded into abstract curvilinear volumes as candle flames flared in new directions. No perceptions remained static: neither the chiaroscuro of light and shadow, the architectural form of column and arch or flat surface of wall and window . . . everything was in motion. One sat bemused, awash in a sea of impressions and fleeting moods.

Initially it was not an exuberant recital – not one of those dashing performances exploiting all the accoustical pyrotechnics of the baroque organ – rather a measured and accademically correct rendering of Faure, Bach, Messiaen and others, which was not without grace and serenity in the sensuous splendour of the night church.

But that all changed after the brief intermission. As soon as the first notes of Saint-Saens' great concerto for organ and orchestra sounded – without, of course, any orchestral accompaniment – I knew we were in for something special. There was a restless growling in the pipes as those wonderful diapason bass chords started their arpeggio-like march to crescendo, rising and falling in varying degrees of progression, taking the heartbeat and emotions with them, sweeping away the fairy tinsel of the church in the pulsing hammerbeats striking the gate of eternity itself. I felt myself slipping, travelling with the sound, when the spell was broken by the strong smell of roses – a drifting, enveloping scent benumbing in its sweet headiness. I say roses because this is the closest I can come by way of analogy. But the comparison hardly does justice to the euphoric lushness of the aroma – musty yet fresh, astringent but nevertheless sweet and cloying, dry as dust but molten as honey: a cosmic rose garden. And, for a moment or two, relegating the music to second place as a mere auditory accompaniment to the fragrance – if that makes any sense.

I glanced curiously around the twenty or so people occupying my cluster of chairs, hoping to discover the origin of this extraordinary perfume, half expecting to set eyes on a Sophia Loren or some similar exotic creature. But there was no such goddess; not even a likely candidate. Neither was anybody displaying the slightest interest in the scent phenomenon – no heads up, turning, noses on the sniff. Perhaps, I thought, they're used to it – local tradition – burn strong incense during evening recitals. Unhurriedly my eye continued to wander, looking for the usual spiral of smoke and the thurible in which the incense would be burning. No luck. But difficult to spot anyway with the competition from so many candles.

Abruptly I was compelled to turn completely round in my back-row chair. The space behind was dark; used for storing odds and ends of church furniture. Yet there it was – a thin wisp of lavender-blue smoke curling slowly upwards into the vault, emanating from a small iron or bronze saucer placed at the foot of a dusty brick column. A solitary, richly carved, black chair stood hard against the side of the pillar, its high back merging into the shadows.

And there sat Dick Guterman, head forward, eyes closed, chin cupped in his left hand – the posture he always adopted when listening to music.

I felt jaw bones lock into place as my mouth involuntarily opened to make some sort of sound; heard the deep rumble of organ music fade and freeze into discontinuous blocks of sound; shivered in damp cold sweat. I turned away in disbelief. Waited. Turned back. He had not moved.

I would still swear today that he was there in the flesh – as convincingly as anyone present. The faded, crumpled uniform was just as I remembered: sergeant's stripes on the left arm sewn on crookedly, air-gunner's half-wing a good inch higher over the left breast-pocket than regulations stipulated. The unruly lock of black hair fell lankly (as usual) over his forehead; moustache was its normal anarchic self, one handlebar pointing up, the other down; and the ring he had fashioned from a scrap of translucent perspex and wore always on the little finger of the right hand, was correctly in place.

The music took over again, an articulated procession of sound, the great diapason stop open and commencing the run of explosive bass chords that concluded the concerto – swelling bursts which sent tremors racing through the delicately columned galleries above the ambulatory. There was an approving nod from Dick at this salvo – he always appreciated the grand fortissimo finales. I don't know what I expected to happen next, other than for him to vanish, fade out, as I suppose all hallucinations do when the mind stops playing games. Yet everything about the whole scene was fixed and concrete – nothing illusory or dream-like about it. Off to the side I was aware of others in the audience, of the flickering candles, and the occasional sideways lurch of the organist. Richard Guterman in his shadowed space was no less three-dimensionally tangible.

Yet how to explain that extraordinary chair – could he have found it in some dark storage corner? Jet-black, arms and legs intricately carved in running tendrils of filigree vine, and backed with a pointed, crocketted Gothic panel: it was a miniature cathedral in itself. The centre panel was cracked – a vertical fracture running from top to bottom which, curiously enough, lent great authority to the piece. Elsewhere, the carving ran riot: berries, leaves, grape-clusters . . . interspersed with a variety of small animal heads. It was only after observing these details that I noticed the heavy ball and claw feet, and the seemingly damp strands of seaweed which clung to them.

By now the scent of roses was growing weaker; the smoke from the saucer thinning out. As the last vibrating echoes of the Saint-Saens were lost, Dick Guterman suddenly pulled himself upright in the chair and stared concentratedly at the ceiling, one hand behind his head, the other gently stroking his moustache. When the audience began to move he stood up hurriedly, smoothed out his uniform, picked up his hat from the seat and straightened to momentarily face me.

He stood absolutely motionless, expression blank. Then a smile, becoming a grin, brought him to life and, like some conspiratorial child urging silence, put a finger to his lips before turning to disappear in the darkness of the ambulatory.

I sat searching the shadows where he vanished, incapable of movement, letting the crowd go first. Must graphically fix everything in the memory if I was to have any hope later of thinking the whole business through. And I needed a little time – a buffer zone – to bring myself completely back to the present. Also, lingering traces of scent remained and I felt it necessary to remain until they were finally dissipated.

"Remember, Johnny . . . " – Dick's voice in my ear – "how many times I said that listening to music is much more a matter of the soul than the ear? Well, now you know what I was talking about. What did you think of those last chords . . . they had the whole of Byzantium rattling! God, what a sound! Remember the choirboy I told you about: the one who wrote that pencilled comment on the organist's copy of Bach's Organ Works – 'So does mine'? Ah well . . . we had some laughs, my boy. The old bike did well, Johnny: a bit skittish in the mountains . . . but bags of power. You did a good job with him. Start work early tomorrow before the crowds get in. Might see you – can't say for certain. Don't forget when you're on the illustrations to break up large expanses of wash with a bit of wax resist . . . "

His voice died away. The air was clear – not a hint of roses. A tap on the shoulder. *"La musica e finita, Signor,"* from the sacristan in his black robe. The church was completely empty and dark. Candles doused. Illuminated now by a single electric-light chandelier reflecting faintly into my small rear space. No high-backed black chair. No incense burner on the floor.

Outside the night had become cool: frosts in May were not unknown in those flat sea-girt regions. Uncontrollable shivering spasms as I walked home. I could not resist the urge to keep looking over my shoulder. Turning the last corner with the hotel in sight I thought I spotted him. I leaned against the wall, waiting. But he did not come on. That night I slept deeply – thoughts, questions, dreams, strangely absent: only a distant stream of organ sound and the faint evocation of roses drifting around the pillow before I nodded off.

I worked for two full days making line and wash drawings – plans, elevations, cross sections, details . . . all explicitly annotated – and what I did not have down on paper I had in my head: mental impressions which remain vivid to this day. While drawing I was attuned to the most subtle of changes in the church environment: temperature fluctuations, the faintest of new air currents and draughts, odd nuances of sound as people moved in and out. And with every shifting sensation I expected him to appear, give me one of those quizzical looks with which my drawings were usually greeted, or, more importantly now that he was able to appear in person, tell me something about existence over there, wherever he was. But there was to be no repeat performance on that occasion.

Before departing I lingered briefly against the dusty brick of the column alongside which his "cathedral" chair had been placed. I could take no quick, casual leave of the place. Yet I was not prepared for the sudden presence of lost friends. Their faces came pressing forward; their names marched through my head – Duncan, Ellis, Matthews, Dent, White . . . and many more I had known. They were there on the sidelines, living vicariously, so to speak, cheering at one's successes, groaning at the failures. I wondered if they approved of my sketches; if they weren't just a bit bored with the conventional nature of my life. Yet there had been moments this last week with Hercules II when we'd all had a bit of a run for our money. Like the old days. I resolved to try and spice things up a bit for them in the future – on the ride home for example, through the mountains. And as I turned to leave I caught the last vestige of rose fragrance trapped in the dust of plaster and brick.